Project Managers: AARON STANG and COLGAN BRYAN
Art Design: KEN REHM
Production Coordinator: YONI LEVIATAN

Contents

Artist Index

ALL I WANNA DO

Words and Music by
SHERYL CROW, WYN COOPER, KEVIN GILBERT,
BILL BOTTRELL and DAVID BAERWALD

end Rhy. Fig. 2
C7
D9
be- fore I die" — says the man — next to me out of no- where It's
hold
hold
w/Rhy. Fig. 2 (Gtr. 1)
E7
a - pro- pos of no - thing. He says his name — is Wil- liam but I'm
hold
C7
D9
sure he's Bill — or Bill - y or Mac or Bud - dy. And he's
hold
w/Rhy. Fig. 2 (Gtr. 1) 3 times sim.
E7
plain ug - ly to me. And I won - der if he's e - ver had a
Gtr. III
hold

C7
D9
E7
day of fun in his whole life.
We are drink - ing beer at
Gtr. II
hold
C7
D9
noon on tues - day in a bar that fac - es a gi - ant car wash.
And the

E7
good peo - ple of the world are wash - ing their cars on their lunch break,
hold
C7
D9
hos - ing and scrub - bing as best they can in skirts and suits.
Bridge:
w/Rhy. Fig. 1 (Gtr. 1)
A13
A♯13
Gtr. II
They drive their shin - y Dat - suns and Bu - icks
A13
A♯13
back to the phone com - pan - y the re - cord store too.
A13
2fr. 4fr. 2fr. 4fr.
B C♯ E F♯
Well, they're noth - ing like Bil - ly and me. 'Cause all I wan - na
Chorus:
Rhy. Fig. 3
E7
C7
D9
(end Rhy. Fig. 3)
Gtr. I
do, is have some fun, I got a feel - ing I'm not the on - ly one. All I wan - na
Gtr. III
Rhy. Fig. 3 A
(end Rhy. Fig. 3A)
hold
hold
hold

w/Rhy. Fig. 3 A (Gtr. 3)
w/Rhy. Fig.3 (Gtr. 1) 11/2 times sim.
E7
C7
D9
To Coda
do is have some fun, I got a feel - ing, I'm not the on - ly one. All I wan-na
C7
B7
do is have some fun, un-til the sun comes up o-ver San-ta Mo-ni-ca Bou-le-vard
Gtr. III
Rhy. Fig. 4
end Rhy. Fig. 4
hold
1.
w/Rhy. Fig. 3 (Gtr. 1) sim.
E7
C7
D9
hold
hold
hold
2.
w/Rhy. Fig.3 (Gtr. 1) 2 times sim.
Gtr. II
E7
C7
D9
E7
C7
D9

Verse 2:
I like a good beer buzz early in the morning,
And Billy likes to peel the labels, from his bottles of Bud.
And shred them on the bar.
Then he lights every match in an oversized pack.
Letting each one burn down to his thick fingers.
Before blowing and cursing them out.
And he's watching the Buds as they spin on the floor.
A happy couple enters the bar dancing dangerously close to one another.
The bartender looks up from his want ads.
(To Chorus:)

ANGELS WOULD FALL

w/Riff A (Acous. Gtr. 1) 3 times, simile
Em C G D/F♯ Em C
Cont. rhy. simile
doubts that have sur-round-ed me are find-ing their way in. I keep it close to me like a
dreamed of the di-vin-i-ty in-side and out of you. I want it more than truth. I can
G D/F♯ Em C G D/F♯
ho-ly man prays. In my des-per-ate hour, it's bet-ter, bet-ter that way.
taste it on my breath. I would give my life just for a lit-tle, a lit-tle death.
Pre-chorus:
Am7 G/B C D(4) Dsus/E* Am7 G/B
Acous. Gtr. 1 tacet
1. So I'll come by and see you a-gain. I'll
2. So I'll come by and see you a-gain. I'll
3. I'll come by and see you a-gain. And I'll
*Elec. Gtr. 1
TAB
*2nd & 3rd times simile.
*Bass only.
C Dsus/E* D(4) Am7 G/B C D(4) Dsus/E*
be such a ver-y good friend. Have mer-cy on my soul. I will
be just a ver-y good friend. I will not look up-on your face. I will not
have to be a ver-y good friend. If I whis-per, they will know. I'll just
TAB

To Coda
Em
D(4)
C
N.C.
nev - er let you know where my mind has been.
touch up - on your grace, your ec - cle - si - as - tic skin.
turn a - round and go. You will
Chorus:
Elec. Gtr. 2
Cont. rhy. simile
An - gels nev - er came down. There's no one here they want to hang a - round.
But if they knew, if they knew you at all, then one by one the an -
- gels, an - gels would fall.
2. I've
Elec. Gtr. 1

2.

Interlude:

Am D Dsus D Em7 A7

- gels, an - gels would___ fall.

Ah.___

An - gels,___

*Elec. Gtr. 3

Elec. Gtr. 1

f hold throughout

*With rotating speaker effect.

Em7 A7

1. 2. D.S. 𝄋 al Coda

an - gels would_

Ah.___

Chorus:
w/Rhy. Fig. 1 (Elec. Gtr. 1) 3rd time only, 2 times, simile

C N.C. Em C

Coda

Elec. Gtr. 2

nev - er know my sin.___ An - gels

Elec. Gtr. 1

†Elec. Gtr. 1

**Vocals ad lib. on repeat.
†2nd (*mp*) and 4th (*f*) times only.

G
D Dsus D
Em
C
Am
D Dsus D
Cont. rhy. simile
nev - er come down._ There's no one here__ they want to hang a - round.____
Em
C
G
D Dsus D
But if they knew, if they knew you at all,________ then
Repeat and fade
Em
C
Am
D Dsus D
one___ by one___ the an - gels, an - gels would_

CANNONBALL

Words and Music by
KIM DEAL

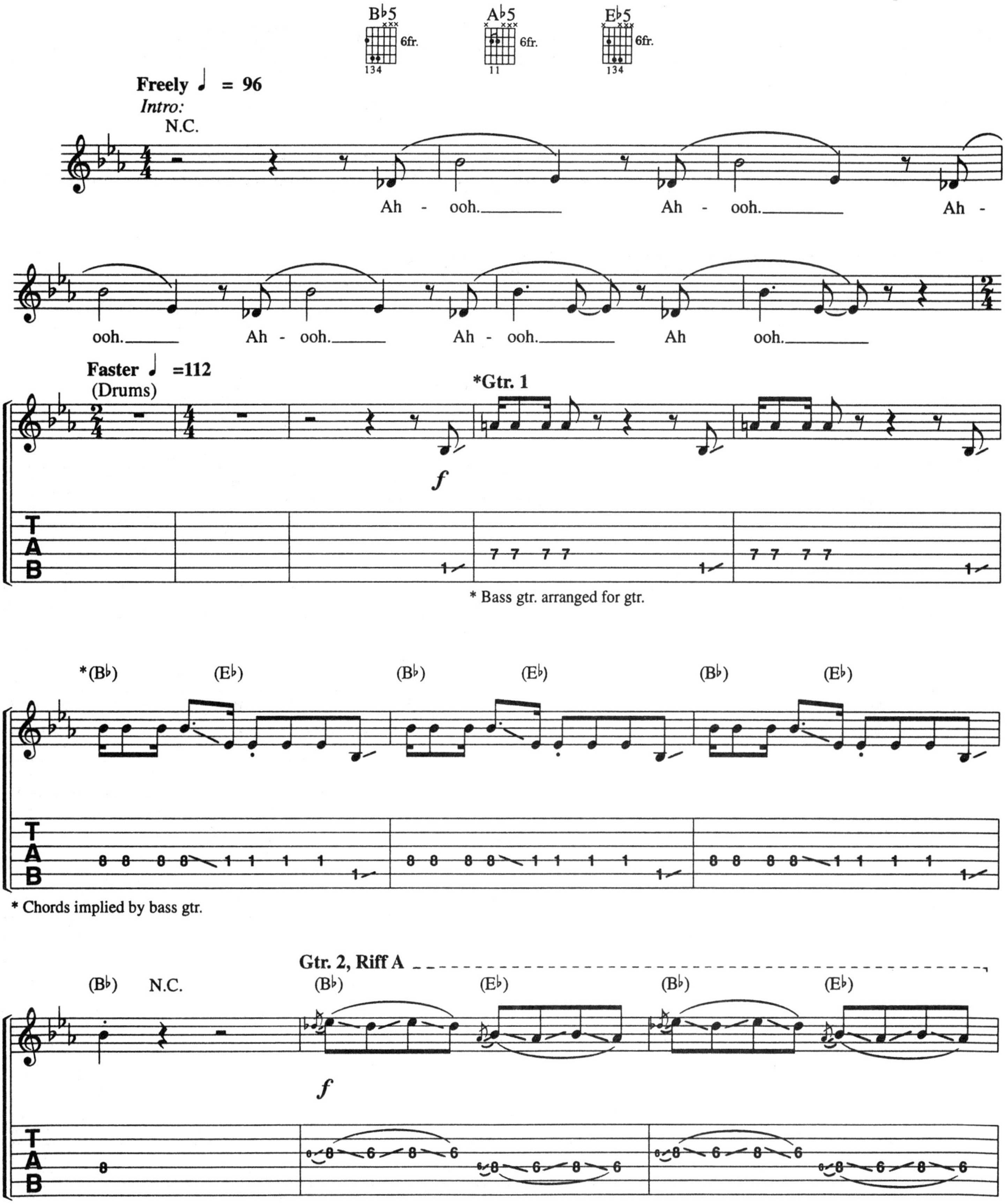

B♭5 6fr. 134 · A♭5 6fr. 11 · E♭5 6fr. 134

Freely ♩ = 96
Intro:
N.C.

Ah - ooh. Ah - ooh. Ah - ooh. Ah - ooh. Ah - ooh. Ah ooh.

Faster ♩ =112
(Drums)
***Gtr. 1**
f

T
A
B

* Bass gtr. arranged for gtr.

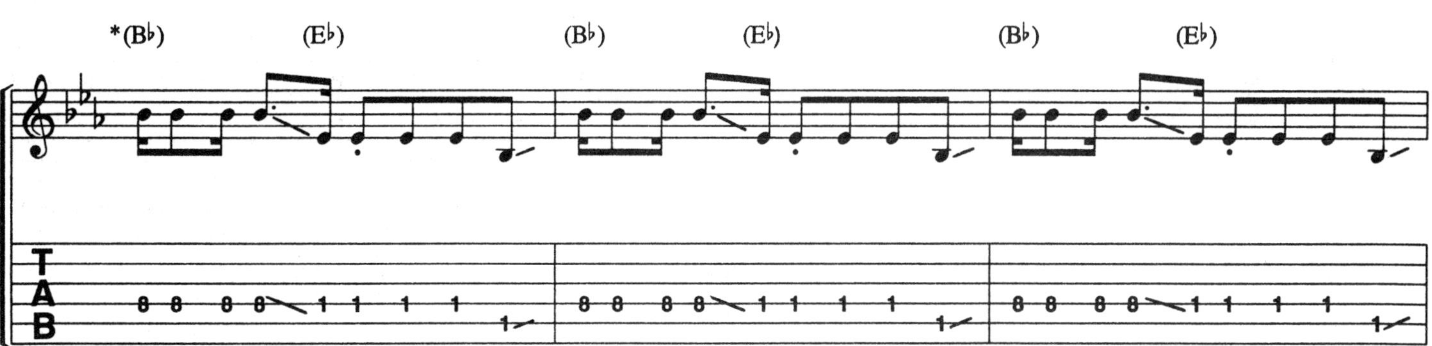

* Chords implied by bass gtr.

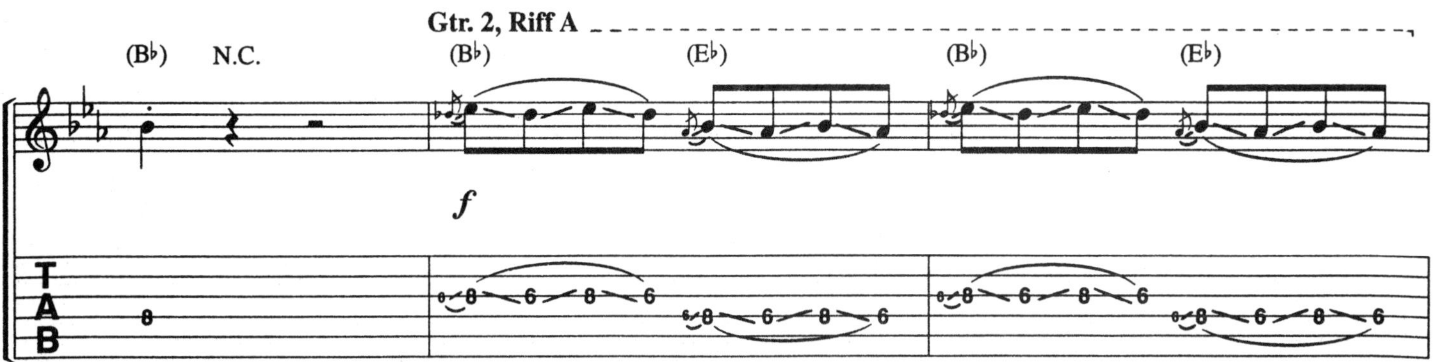

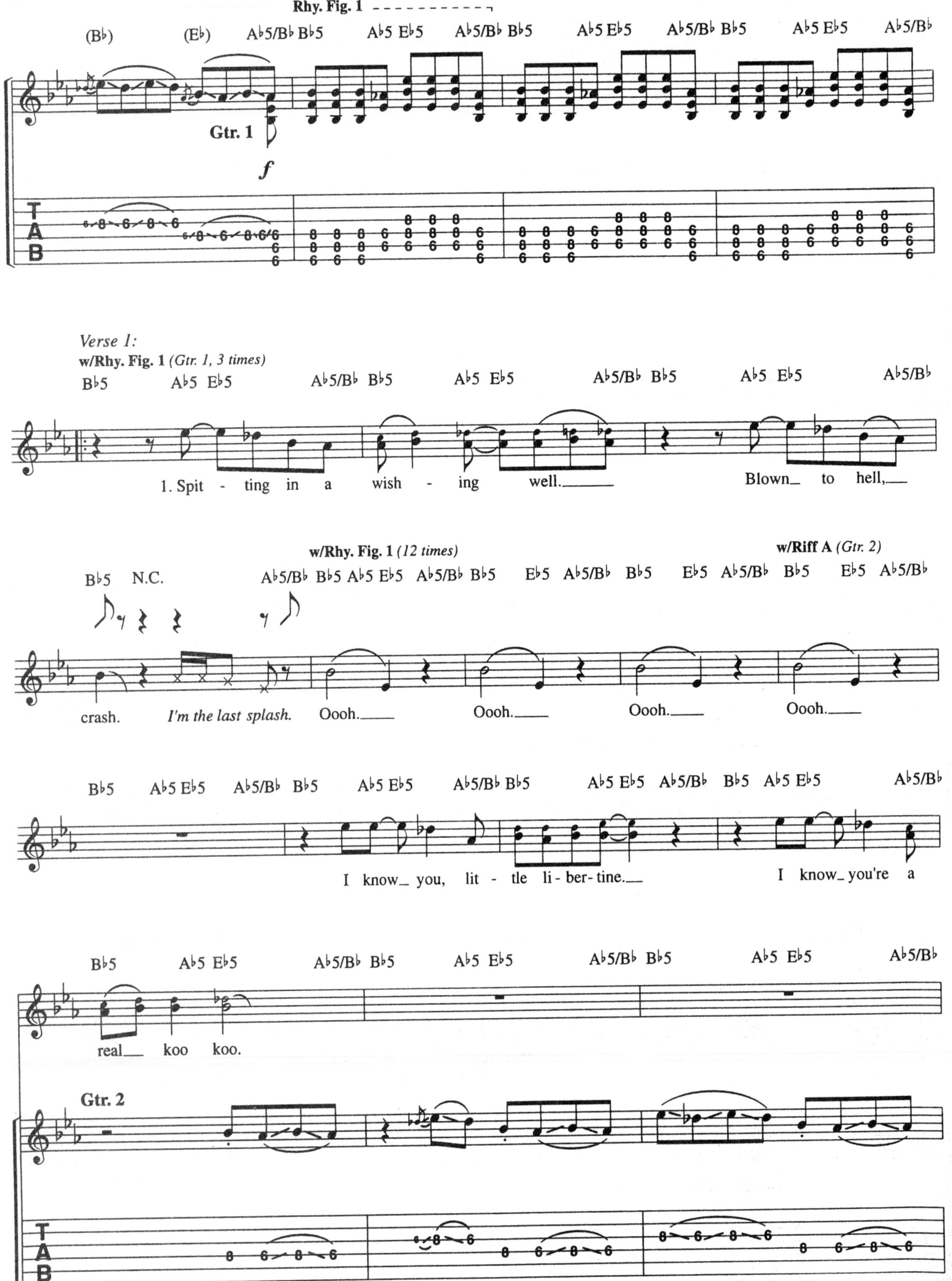

Rhy. Fig. 1
(B♭) (E♭) A♭5/B♭ B♭5 A♭5 E♭5 A♭5/B♭ B♭5 A♭5 E♭5 A♭5/B♭ B♭5 A♭5 E♭5 A♭5/B♭
Gtr. 1
f
Verse 1:
w/Rhy. Fig. 1 (Gtr. 1, 3 times)
B♭5 A♭5 E♭5 A♭5/B♭ B♭5 A♭5 E♭5 A♭5/B♭ B♭5 A♭5 E♭5 A♭5/B♭
1. Spit - ting in a wish - ing well. Blown to hell,
w/Rhy. Fig. 1 (12 times)
w/Riff A (Gtr. 2)
B♭5 N.C. A♭5/B♭ B♭5 A♭5 E♭5 A♭5/B♭ B♭5 E♭5 A♭5/B♭ B♭5 E♭5 A♭5/B♭ B♭5 E♭5 A♭5/B♭
crash. I'm the last splash. Oooh. Oooh. Oooh. Oooh.
B♭5 A♭5 E♭5 A♭5/B♭ B♭5 A♭5 E♭5 A♭5/B♭ B♭5 A♭5 E♭5 A♭5/B♭ B♭5 A♭5 E♭5 A♭5/B♭
I know you, lit - tle li - ber - tine. I know you're a
B♭5 A♭5 E♭5 A♭5/B♭ B♭5 A♭5 E♭5 A♭5/B♭ B♭5 A♭5 E♭5 A♭5/B♭
real koo koo.
Gtr. 2

Chorus 1:
8fr.
B♭5
A♭5 E♭5
A♭5/B♭ B♭5
A♭5 E♭5 N.C.
B♭5
Gtr. 2
B♭ B♭5
E♭5
Want you, koo koo, can -
(To slashes)
Gtr. 1
A♭5
non - ball.
B♭5
E♭5
Want you, koo koo,
A♭5
can- non- ball.
B♭5
E♭5
A♭5
B♭5
In the shade,
in the shade
Hey now.

To Coda ⊕ Interlude:
B♭5
E♭5
A♭5
B♭5
A♭5 E♭5
A♭5/B♭
Hey, now.
In the shade.
in the shade.
Oooh.
Oooh.
Verse 2:
w/Rhy. Fig. 1 (9 times)
I know you, little libertine.
I know you're a
w/Riff B (Gtr. 2)
cannonball.
I'll be your what-
Riff B
Gtr. 2

B♭5
A♭5
E♭5
A♭5/B♭
B♭5
A♭5
E♭5
A♭5/B♭
B♭5
N.C.
ev - er you want.__
The bong__ in this reg - gae song.__
Chorus 2:
④ 8fr.
B♭ B♭5
E♭5
A♭5
Hey now.__
In the shade.
Gtr. 1
w/feedback
B♭5
E♭5
A♭5
B♭5
E♭5
Hey now.__
In the shade.__
Want you, koo koo, can -
A♭5
B♭5
B♭5
E♭5
A♭5
non- ball.__
Want you, koo koo, can - non- ball.__

Verse 3:
B♭5
A♭5 E♭5
A♭5/B♭ B♭5
A♭5/B♭
Spit - ting in a wish - ing well.
Blown to hell,
w/Riff A (Gtr. 2), and Rhy. Fig. 1 (Gtr. 1, 9 times)
N.C.
crash.
I'm the last
splash
I'll be your what - ev - er you want.
The bong in this
reg - gae song.
Gtr. 2
T
A
B

Gtr. 1
D.S. al Coda
B♭5
A♭5
E♭5
A♭5/B♭
Hey!
Hey!
Coda
w/Rhy. Fig. 1 (Gtr. 1, 3 1/2 times)
Ah - ooh.
Ah -
Gtr. 2
ooh.
Ah - ooh.
Ah - ooh.

CAN'T CRY ANYMORE

Words and Music by
SHERYL CROW and BILL BOTTRELL

2.4.5.
G5
D5
G5
D5
Em
But
Gtr. I
cont. w/slashes
hold
Gtr. II (w/tremolo effect)
Chorus:
Am
Em
*Gtr. I
Would - n't it be good if we could hop a flight to an - y - where.
Well, so long to this life.
Gtr. II
* (L) = Lower portion of chord is strummed as in Rhy. Fig. 2
(H) = Upper portion of chord is strummed as in Rhy. Fig. 2
Rhy. Fig. 3
end Rhy. Fig. 3
A
C II
To Coda I
To Coda II
So much for pre - tend - ing,

Rhy. Fig. 4
D5
D.S. 𝄋 al Coda I
end Rhy. Fig. 4
'Cause Bad luck's never end - ing.
And now I know that.
Coda I
w/Rhy. Fig. 4 simile (Gtr. 1)
'Cause Bad luck's nev - er end ing.
It's nev - er end - ing.
Guitar Solo:
w/Rhy. Fig. 1 simile (Gtr. 1)
w/ad lib. vocals
G5
Gtr. II
D5
G5
Em
C
D.S. 𝄋 al Coda II
2nd ending only

Verse 2:
Since I left,
Been feelin' better, cause that's
What you get when you
Stay together too long.
And I can't cry anymore.

Verse 3:
And now I know that,
Money comes in.
But the fact is (there's)
Not enough to pay my taxes.
And I can't cry anymore.

Verse 4:
Well gotta brother.
He's got real problems.
Heroin now,
There's just no stopping him tonight.
And I won't cry anymore.

Verse 5:
Well it could be worse,
I could've missed my calling.
Sometimes it hurts,
But when you read the writing on the wall.
Can't cry anymore.

A CHANGE

Words and Music by
SHERYL CROW, BRIAN MacLEOD and JEFF TROTT

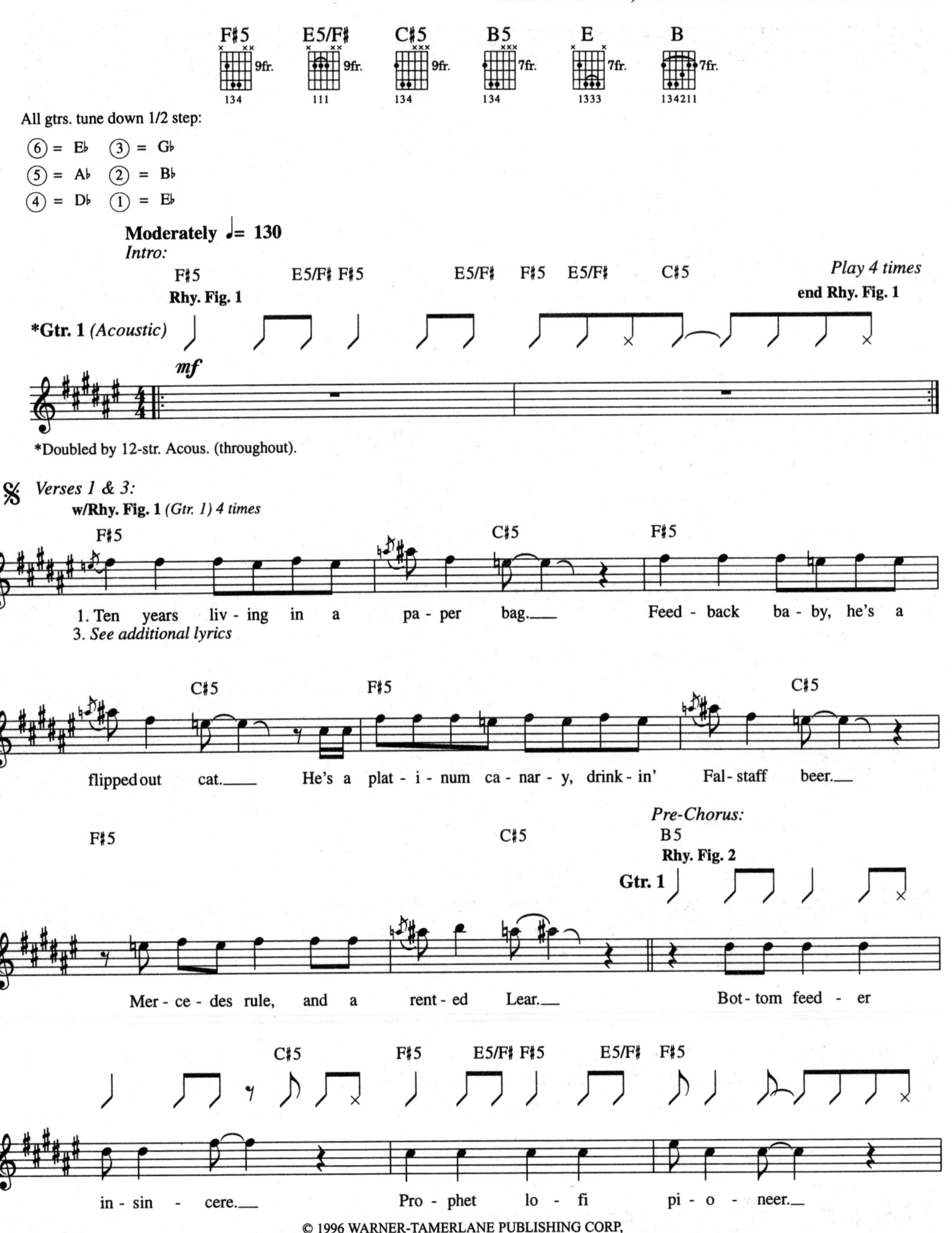

E
B
Sell the house and go to school. Get a young girl - friend,
Chorus:
w/Rhy. Fig. 1 (Gtr. 1) 4 times
A
F♯5
C♯5
end Rhy. Fig. 2
dad - dy's jewel. A change would do you good.
(A change would do you good.
F♯5
To Coda
C♯5
A change would do you good. I think a
F♯5
C♯5
change would do you good.
A change would do you good.
Verse 2:
w/Rhy. Fig. 1 (Gtr. 1) 4 times
F♯5
C♯5
F♯5
A change would do you good.)
2. God's lit - tle gift is
C♯5
F♯5
C♯5
on the rag. Post - er girl pos - ing in a fash - ion mag.
F♯5
C♯5
F♯5
Ca - nine, fe - line, Je - kyll and Hyde? Wear your fake fur on
Pre-Chorus 2:
w/Rhy. Fig. 2 (Gtr. 1)
C♯5
B5
C♯5
the in - side. 1. Queen of South Beach, ag - ing blues.

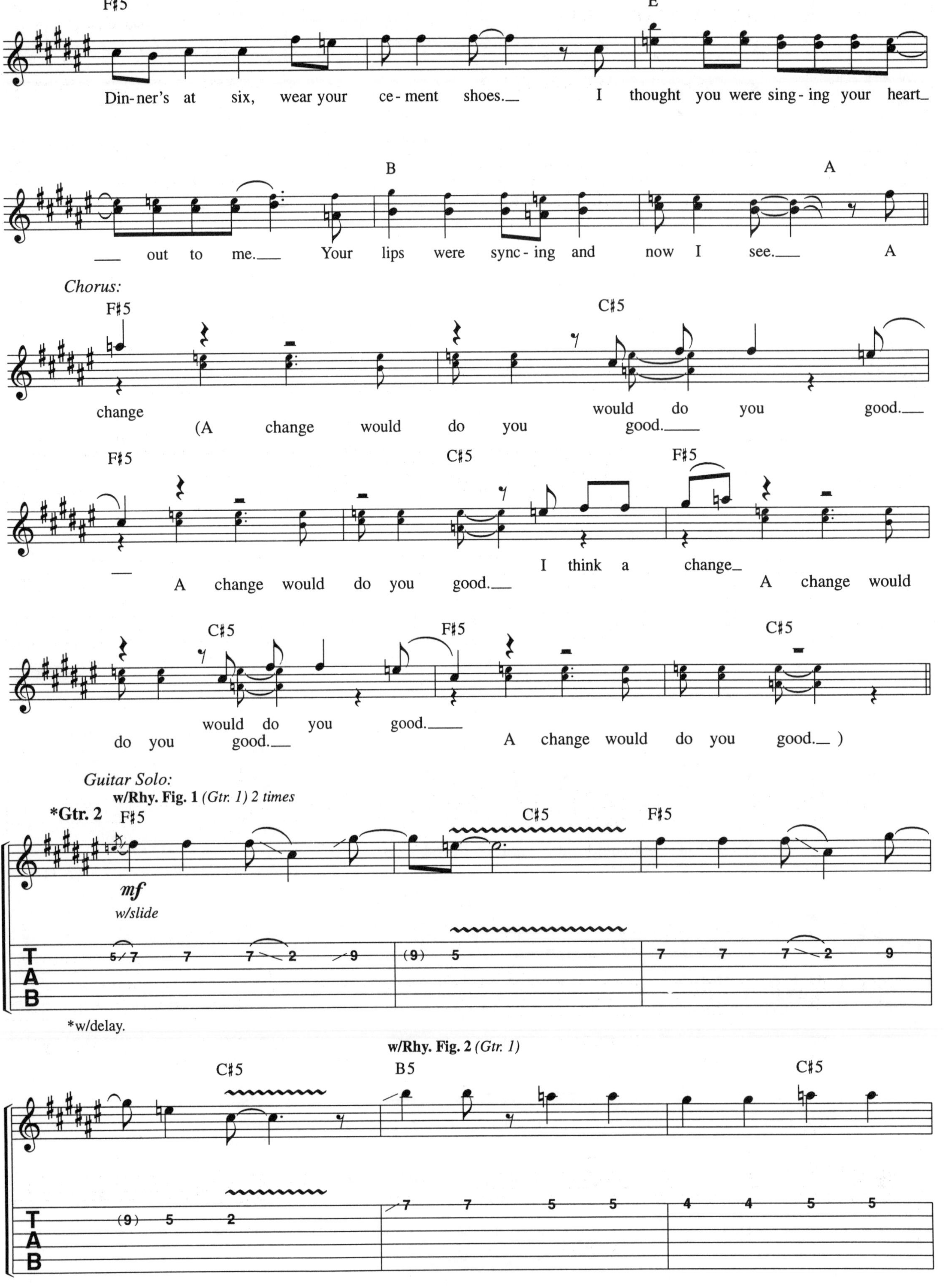
F♯5
E
Din-ner's at six, wear your ce-ment shoes. I thought you were sing-ing your heart
B
A
out to me. Your lips were sync-ing and now I see. A
Chorus:
F♯5
C♯5
change
would do you good.
(A change would do you good.
F♯5
C♯5
F♯5
I think a change
A change would do you good.
A change would
C♯5
F♯5
C♯5
would do you good.
do you good.
A change would do you good.)
Guitar Solo:
w/Rhy. Fig. 1 (Gtr. 1) 2 times
*Gtr. 2
F♯5
C♯5
F♯5
mf
w/slide
*w/delay.
w/Rhy. Fig. 2 (Gtr. 1)
C♯5
B5
C♯5

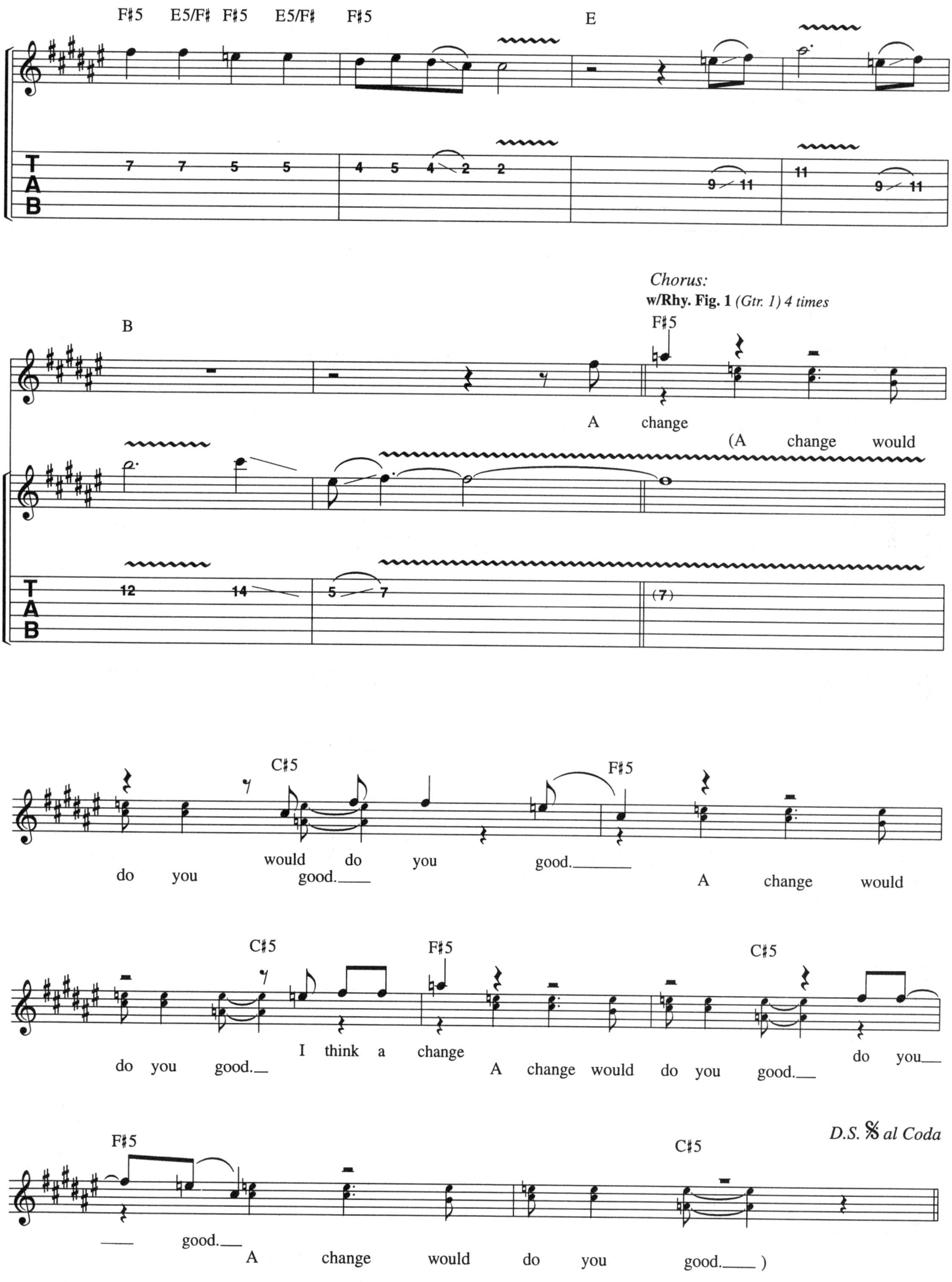

F♯5 E5/F♯ F♯5 E5/F♯ F♯5

E

B

Chorus:
w/Rhy. Fig. 1 *(Gtr. 1) 4 times*

F♯5

A change

(A change would

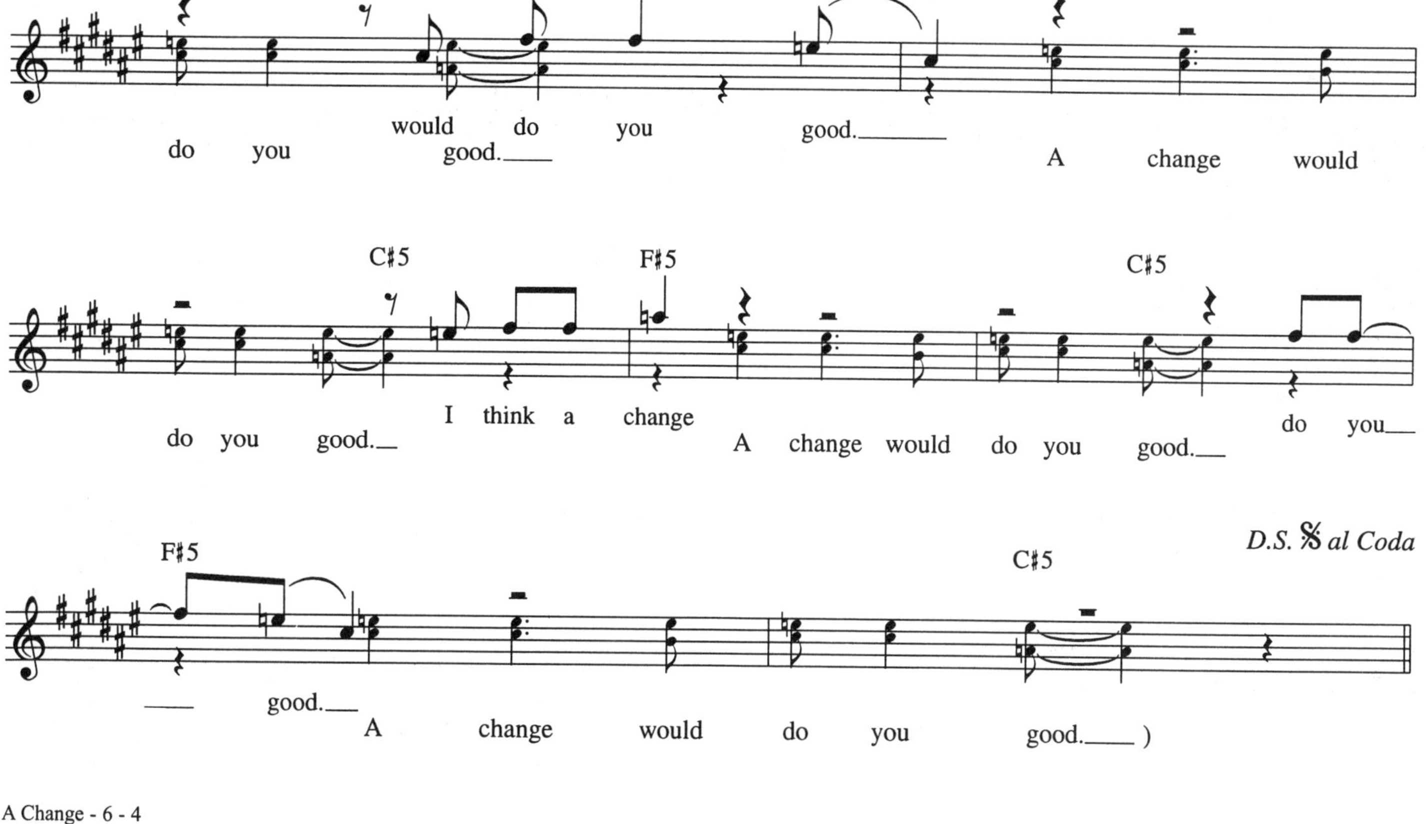

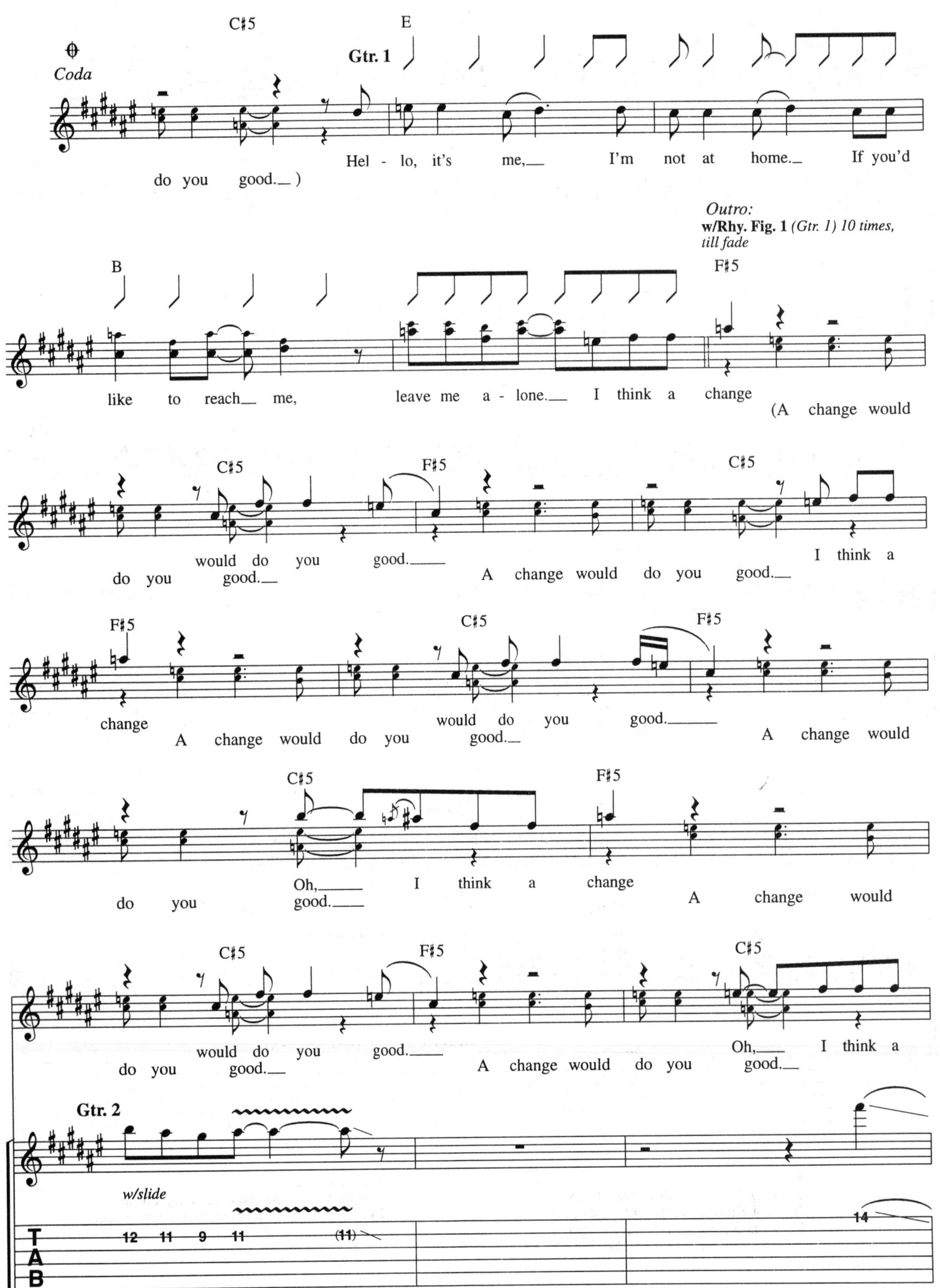
Coda
Gr. 1
C♯5
E
Hel - lo, it's me,
I'm not at home.
If you'd
do you good.)
Outro:
w/Rhy. Fig. 1 (Gtr. 1) 10 times, till fade
B
F♯5
like to reach me,
leave me a - lone.
I think a change
(A change would
C♯5
F♯5
would do you good.
do you good.
A change would do you good.
I think a
change
A change would do you good.
would do you good.
A change would
Oh,
I think a change
do you good.
A change would
would do you good.
do you good.
A change would do you good.
Oh, I think a
Gtr. 2
w/slide
T
A
B
12 11 9 11
(11)
14

Verse 3:
Chasing dragons with plastic swords.
Jack off Jimmy, everybody wants more.
Scully and Angel on the kitchen floor
And I'm calling Buddy on the Ouija board.

Pre-Chorus 2:
I've been thinking 'bout catching a train,
Leave my phone machine by the radar range.
Hello, it's me, I'm not at home.
If you'd like to reach me, leave me alone.
(To Chorus:)

COME TO MY WINDOW

Words and Music by
MELISSA ETHERIDGE

Verse:
w/Rhy. Fig. 1 (Gtr. 2, 2 times)
C(9) G/B D Dsus2 D
1. I would dial the num - bers just to lis - ten to your breath. And
2. See additional lyrics
C(9) G/B D Dsus2 D
I would stand in - side my hell and hold the hand of death.
Gtr. 1
Next 6 bars on Verse 2 only
C(9) G/B D Dsus2 D
You don't know how far I'd go to use this pre - cious ache. And
C(9) G/B D Dsus2 D
you don't know how much I'd give or how much I can take. Just to reach
Em C(9) D Dsus D Dsus D
you. Just to reach you. Oh, to

Em
C(9)
D
Dsus
D
Dsus2
D
— reach — you, — oh.
T
A
B
Chorus:
Rhy. Fig. 2
G
C(9)
A7sus
Dsus
D
Dsus2
D
Riff A
Come to my win - dow.
(end Rhy. Fig. 2)
Crawl in - side, wait — by the light — of the moon.
(end Riff A)
w/Rhy. Fig. 2 (Gtr. 2) & Riff A (Gtr. 1)
1.
— Come to my win - dow, I'll — be home soon. —

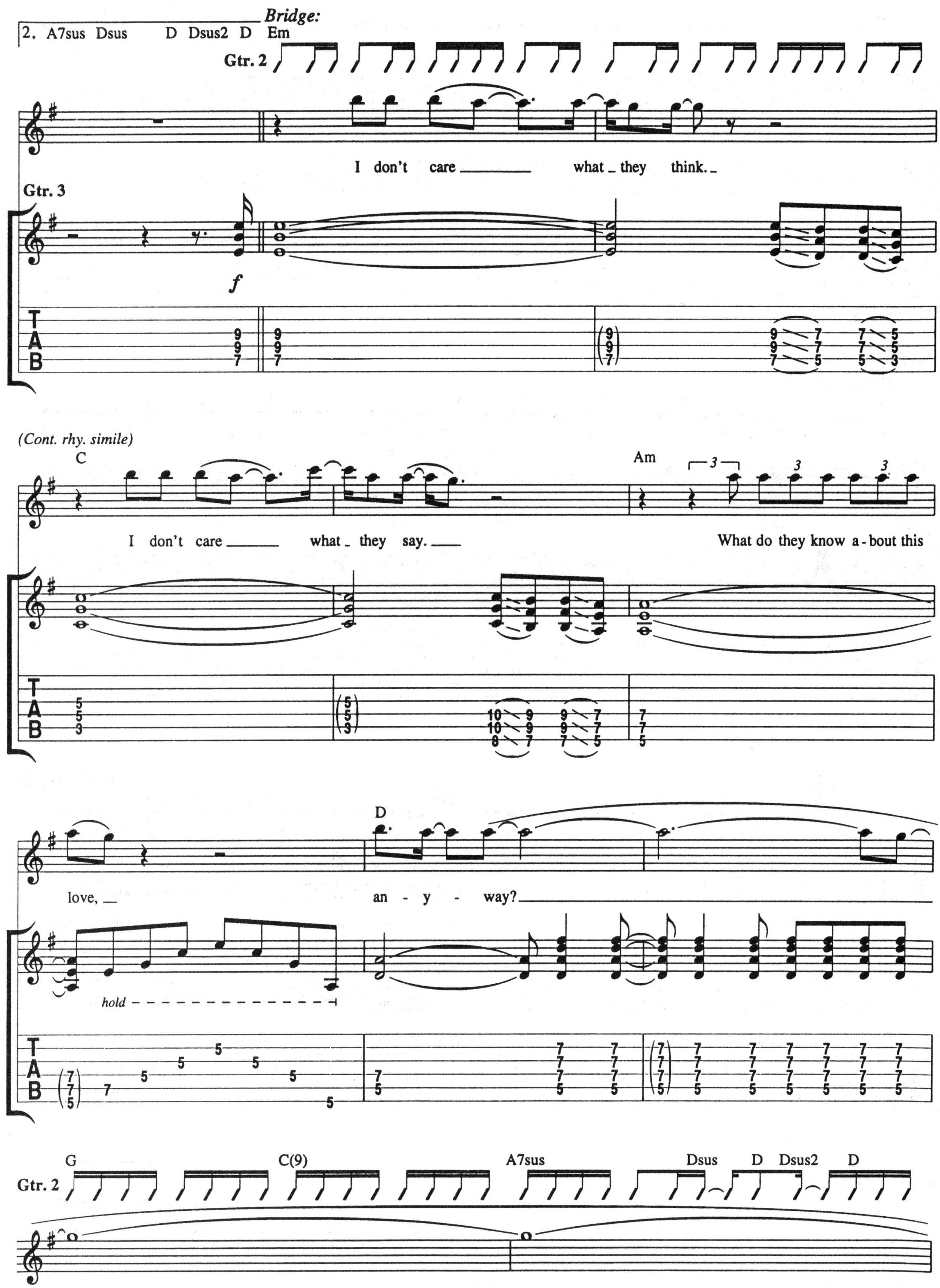

2. A7sus Dsus D Dsus2 D Em
Bridge:
Gtr. 2
I don't care what they think.
Gtr. 3
(Cont. rhy. simile)
C
I don't care what they say.
Am
What do they know about this
love,
D
an - y - way?
hold
G
C(9)
A7sus
Dsus D Dsus2 D

Verse 2:
Keeping my eyes open, I cannot afford to sleep.
Giving away promises I know that I can't keep.
Nothing fills the blackness that has seeped into my chest.
I need you in my blood, I am forsaking all the rest.
Just to reach you,
Just to reach you.
Oh, to reach you.
(To Chorus:)

DON'T SPEAK

Words and Music by
GWEN STEFANI and ERIC STEFANI

Cm Gm Fm B♭ E♭ B♭ C
as though your let-ting go. And if it's real, then I don't want to know.
Chorus:
Fm B♭m E♭ C
Gtr. 2 (Acous.)
Rhy. Fig. 2
Don't speak, I know just what you're say - ing. So, please stop ex - plain-
Gtr. 1
B♭m C Fm B♭m C
- ing. Don't tell me 'cause it hurts.

Fm
B♭m
E♭
C
Don't speak, I know what your think - ing. I don't need your rea -
T
A
B
B♭m
C
Fm
B♭m C
end Rhy. Fig. 2
- sons. Don't tell me 'cause it hurts.
2. Our
Verse 2:
w/Rhy. Fig. 1 (Gtr. 1)
Cm
Gm
Fm
B♭
mem-o-ries, they can be in-vit-ing, but some are al-to-geth - er might - y fright - 'ning. As
Gtr. 2
we die, both you and I.
Gtr. 1

E♭
B♭
C
With my head in my hands, I sit and cry.
T
A
B
8 8 8 10
8 8 8 10
8 8 8 10
8 8 8 10
7 8 8 6
Chorus:
w/Rhy. Fig. 2 (Gtr. 2) 1st 7 bars only
Fm
B♭m
E♭
C
Don't speak, I know just what your say - ing. So, please stop ex - plain-
Rhy. Fig. 3
Gtr. 1
10 10 8
6 8 8 6
8 8 8 6
5 5 3
B♭m
C
Fm
B♭m
C
Fm
B♭m
- ing. Don't tell me 'cause it hurts. No, no, no. Don't speak, I know what your think-
end Rhy. Fig. 3
3 3 1
5 5 3
10 10 8
6 6 4
5 5 3
10 10 8
8 8 6

To Coda
F5 E♭5 C5 A♭5
Gtr. 2
E♭ C B♭m C
- ing. And I don't need your rea - sons. Don't tell me 'cause it hurts.
Gtr. 1
Bridge:
D♭ A♭ C♭ G♭
It's all end - ing. I got - ta stop pre - tend - ing who we
D♭sus2/A D♭sus2 D♭sus2/E♭ D♭sus2 D♭sus2/E♭ A♭
are.

Guitar Solo:
Cm Gm Fm B♭ Cm Gm Fm B♭
Gtr. 2
Gtr. 3 (Acous.)
mf
rake -|
Gtr. 1
Cm Gm Fm B♭ Gm Cm Fm
rake -|

Interlude:
D.S. 𝄋 al Coda
Cm Gm Fm B♭ Fm B♭
You and me, I can see us dy - ing. Are we?
Gtr. 1
Gtr. 2 (w/slight dist.)
Gtr. 4 out
mf
w/last bar of Rhy. Fig. 2 (Gtrs. 1 & 2)
w/Rhy. Fig. 2 (Gtr. 2)
w/Rhy. Fig. 3 (Gtr. 1) 2 times
Coda
Fm B♭m C Fm B♭m
Don't tell me 'cause it hurts. *I know what you're say-
(Ah, ee, ah, ee, ah. Ah.
*Vocal ad lib. on repeats.
E♭ C B♭m C Fm B♭m C
- ing. So, please stop ex - plain - ing. Don't speak. Don't speak. Don't speak. No.
Ah. Ah.
Fm B♭m E♭ C
I know what you're think - ing. And I don't need your rea -
Ah, ee, ah, ee, ah. Ah. Ah.
Repeat and fade
B♭m C Fm B♭m C
- sons. I know you're good. I know you're good. I know you're real good. Oh.
)

DIVINE HAMMER

Words and Music by
KIM DEAL

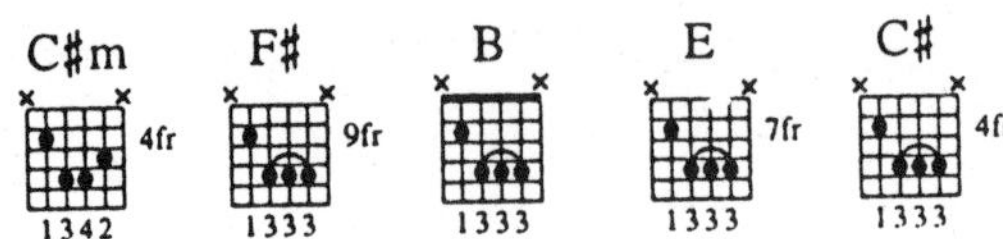

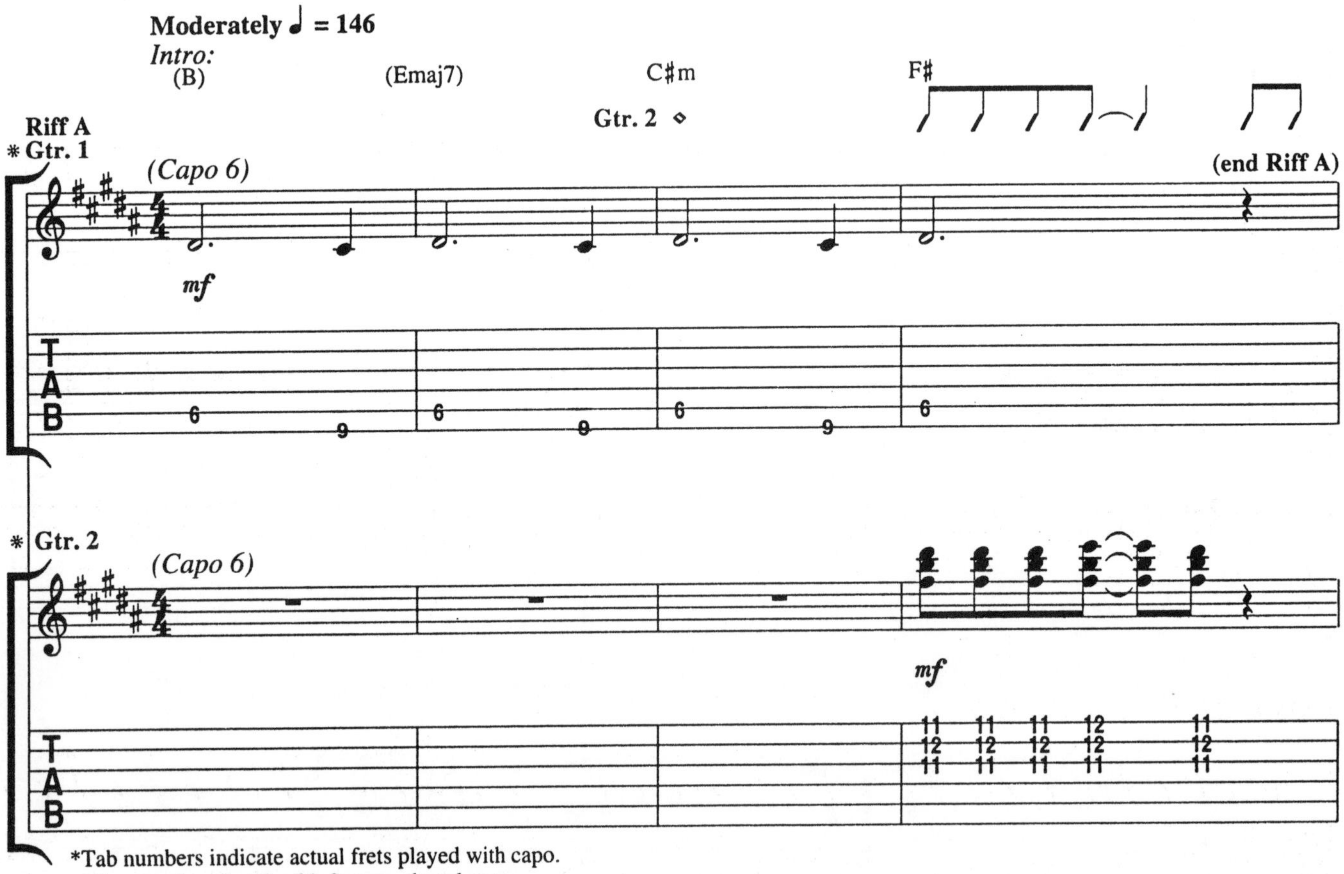

Moderately ♩ = 146
Intro:
(B) (Emaj7) C#m F#

Gtr. 2 ◇

Riff A
*** Gtr. 1**
(Capo 6)
(end Riff A)
mf

*** Gtr. 2**
(Capo 6)
mf

*Tab numbers indicate actual frets played with capo.
All notes played at the 6th fret are played open.

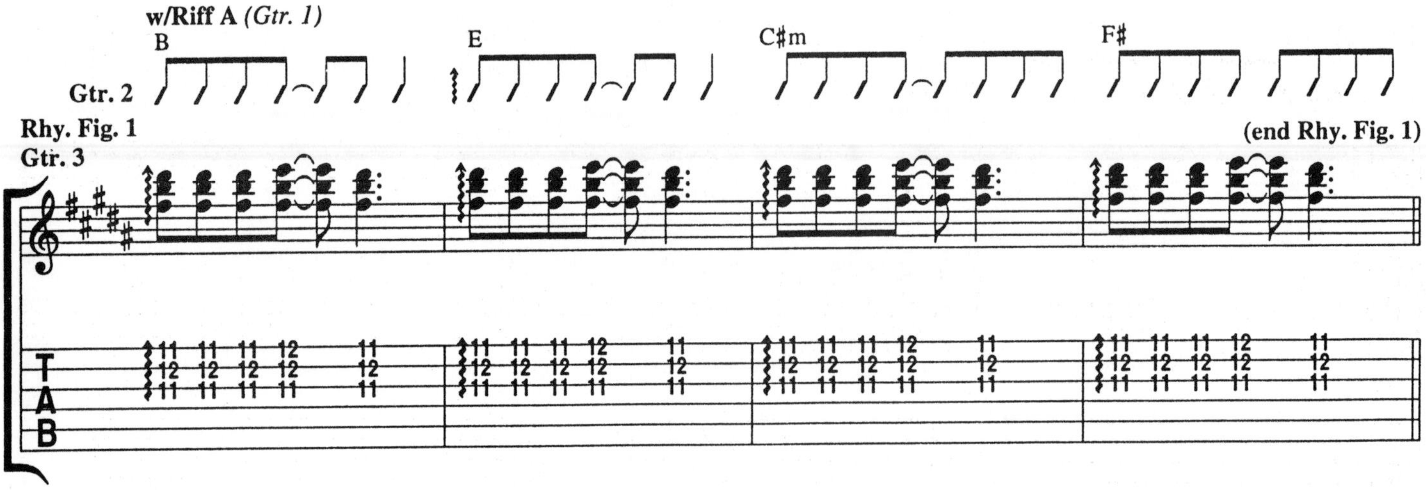

w/Riff A *(Gtr. 1)*
B E C#m F#
Gtr. 2
Rhy. Fig. 1
Gtr. 3
(end Rhy. Fig. 1)

Verse:
B
E
C#m
F#
Gtr. 2
1. I'm just look-ing, just look-ing for a way a - round. It dis-ap-pears this
2.3. See additional lyrics
*Gtr. 3
*2 gtrs. arr. for 1
near. You're the rod, I'm wa - ter.
Rhy. Fig. 2
(end Rhy. Fig. 2)
hold
w/Riff A (Gtr. 1) & Rhy. Fig. 2 (Gtr. 3)
I'm just look-ing for one di - vine ham - mer.
Chorus:
To Coda
Cont. rhy. simile
One di - vine ham - mer. one di - vine ham - mer.
Gtr. 3

Instrumental Solo I:
E C# E B
Gtrs. 2 & 3
w/Riff A (Gtr. 1) & Rhy. Fig. 1 (Gtr. 3) both 2 times
B E G#m F#
Gtr. 2
D.S. 𝄋 al Coda
B E C#m F#
Cont. rhy. simile
Coda
Instrumental Solo II:
E C# E B
Gtrs. 2 & 3
Cont. rhy. simile
Chorus:
E B
Gtr. 2
One di - vine ham - mer,
one di - vine ham - mer.
Gtr. 3
T
A
B
E

Verse 2:
I'm just looking for one divine hammer,
I'd bang it all day.
And, the carpenter goes
Bang, bang, bang.
I'm just looking for one divine hammer.
(To Chorus:)

Verse 3:
I'm just looking for a faith,
Waiting to be followed.
It disappears this near.
You're the rod, I'm water.
I'm just looking for one divine hammer.
(To Chorus:)

FOOLISH GAMES

Words and Music by
JEWEL KILCHER

w/Rhy. Fig. 2 (Gtr. 1)
Dm
B♭
And I watched from my win - dow, al-ways felt I was
F
C
1.3.
2.4.
out - side look - ing in on you.
*Pre-Chorus:
Gm
B♭
1. Well, in case you failed to no-tice, in case you failed to see,
2. See additional lyrics
*Gtr. 1 cont. ad lib. simile, see chord frames.
F
C
this is my heart bleed-ing be-fore you, this is me down on my knees.
Chorus:
B♭
C
These fool - ish games are
F
C/E
Dm
tear - ing me a - part, and
B♭
C
your thought - less words are
F
C/E
To Coda
B♭
break - ing my heart. You're break - ing my

w/Rhy. Fig. 1 (Gtr. 1)
D.S. 𝄋 al Coda
Dm
6
heart.
Coda
B♭
Dm
3
heart.
You're break - ing my heart.
B♭
F
C
Dm

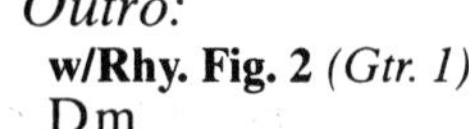

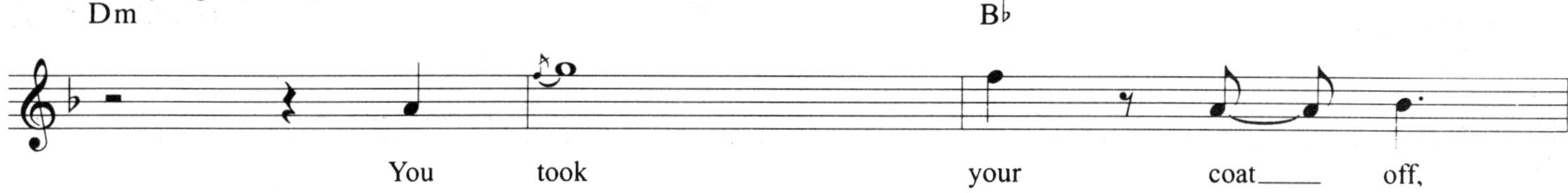

Verse 2:
You're always the mysterious one with
Dark eyes and careless hair,
You were fashionably sensitive
But too cool to care.
You stood in my doorway with nothing to say
Besides some comment on the weather.

Verse 3:
You're always brilliant in the morning,
Smoking your cigarettes and talking over coffee.
Your philosophies on art, Baroque moved you.
You loved Mozart and you'd speak of your loved ones
As I clumsily strummed my guitar.

Verse 4:
You'd teach me of honest things,
Things that were daring, things that were clean.
Things that knew what an honest dollar did mean.
I hid my soiled hands behind my back.
Somewhere along the line, I must have gone
Off track with you.

Pre-Chorus 2:
Excuse me, think I've mistaken you for somebody else,
Somebody who gave a damn, somebody more like myself.
(To Chorus:)

HAND IN MY POCKET

Lyrics by
ALANIS MORISSETTE

Music by
ALANIS MORISSETTE and GLEN BALLARD

G/F
Cadd9
G
G5/D
Gtype2
G/B
C
Gtype3
Intro
Moderate Rock ♩ = 92
Gtr. 1
(slight dist.)
mf w/ chorus effect
let ring throughout
Verse
Gtr. 3: w/ Rhy. Fill 1, 7 times, 2nd time
1. I'm broke but I'm hap-py, I'm poor but I'm kind, I'm
free but I'm fo-cused, I'm green but I'm wise, I'm
Rhy. Fig. 1
short but I'm health - y, yeah. I'm high but I'm ground-ed, I'm
hard but I'm friend - ly, ba - by. I'm sad but I'm laugh-ing, I'm
Rhy. Fill 1
Gtr. 3
mp
slight P.M.

sane but I'm o - ver - whelmed, I'm lost but I'm hope - ful, ba -
brave but I'm chick-en - shit, I'm sick but I'm pret - ty, ba -

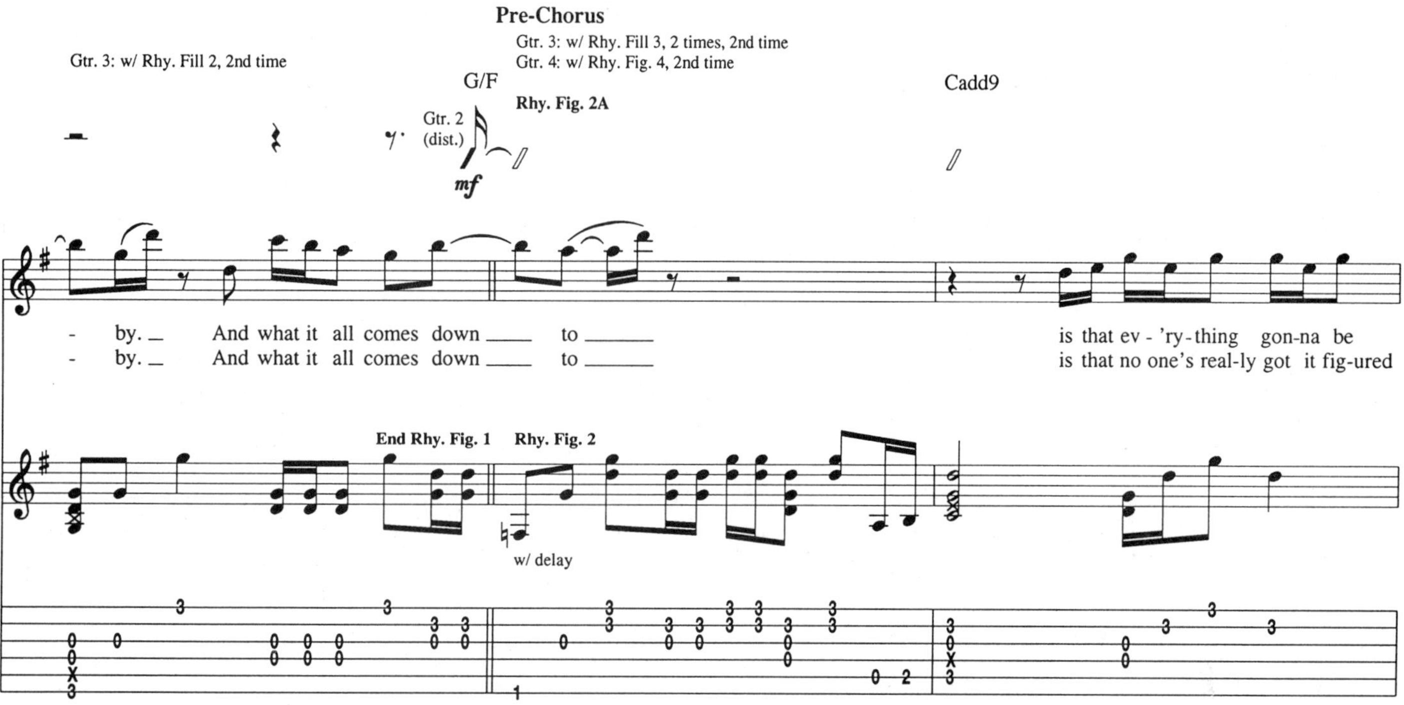

Pre-Chorus
Gtr. 3: w/ Rhy. Fill 2, 2nd time
Gtr. 3: w/ Rhy. Fill 3, 2 times, 2nd time
Gtr. 4: w/ Rhy. Fig. 4, 2nd time
G/F
Cadd9
Gtr. 2 (dist.)
Rhy. Fig. 2A
mf
- by. And what it all comes down to is that ev - 'ry-thing gon-na be
- by. And what it all comes down to is that no one's real-ly got it fig-ured
End Rhy. Fig. 1
Rhy. Fig. 2
w/ delay

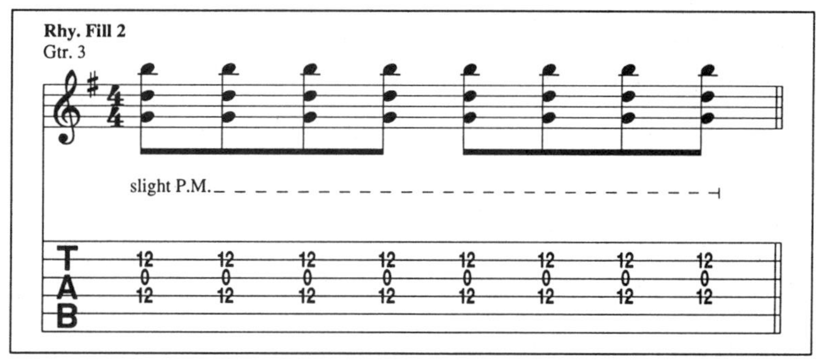

Rhy. Fill 2
Gtr. 3
slight P.M.

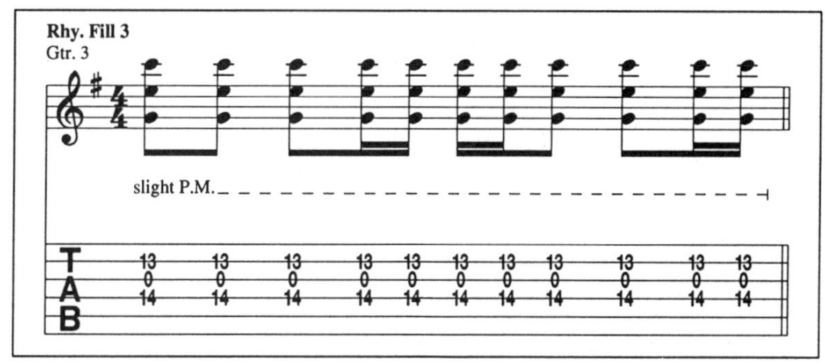

Rhy. Fill 3
Gtr. 3
slight P.M.

Gtr. 3: w/ Riff A, 1st time; w/ Rhy. Fill 4, 2nd time
Chorus
Gtr. 3: w/ Rhy. Fill 3, 2 times, 2nd time
End Rhy. Fig. 2A
Rhy. Fig. 3A
fine, fine, fine,
out just yet
'cause I've got a one hand in my pock - et and the
End Rhy. Fig. 2
Rhy. Fig. 3
* w/ bar
To Coda
Gtr. 3: w/ Riff A
End Rhy. Fig. 3A
oth-er one is giv-in' a high five.
play-in' a pi - an - o.
2. I feel
End Rhy. Fig. 3
Verse
Gtr. 1: w/ Rhy. Fig. 1
drunk but I'm so - ber, I'm young and I'm un - der - paid. I'm
Gtr. 4 (slight dist.)
Riff B
End Riff B
let ring
Rhy. Fill 4
Gtr. 3
slight P.M.
Riff A
Gtr. 3 (slight dist.)
w/ delay

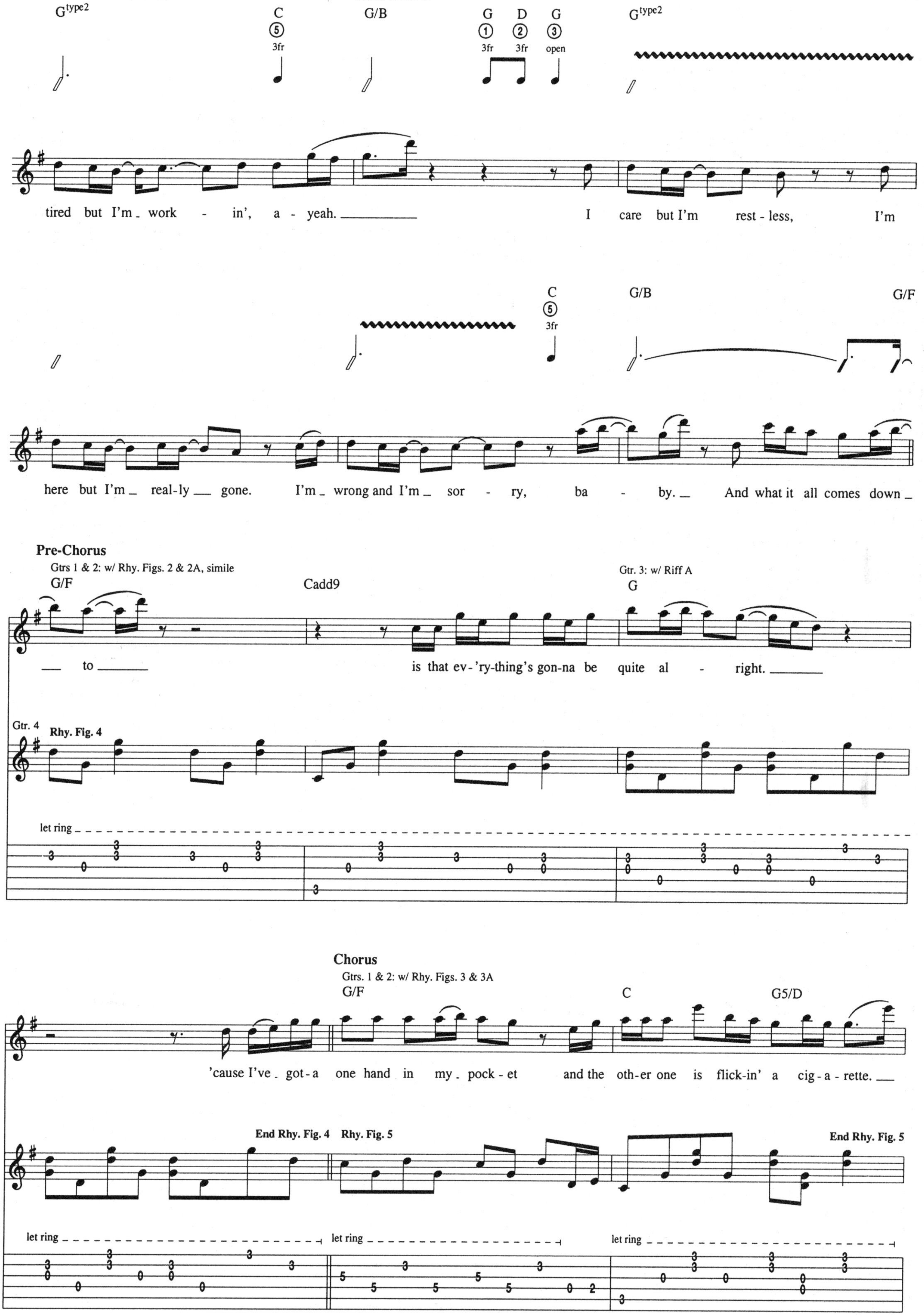

Gtr. 4: w/ Riff B, 3 times
Gtr. 3: w/ Riff A

G^type2 C G/B G D G G^type2

tired but I'm work - in', a - yeah. I care but I'm rest - less, I'm

C G/B G/F

here but I'm real-ly gone. I'm wrong and I'm sor - ry, ba - by. And what it all comes down

Pre-Chorus

Gtrs 1 & 2: w/ Rhy. Figs. 2 & 2A, simile
Gtr. 3: w/ Riff A

G/F Cadd9 G

to is that ev-'ry-thing's gon-na be quite al - right.

Gtr. 4 Rhy. Fig. 4

let ring

Chorus

Gtrs. 1 & 2: w/ Rhy. Figs. 3 & 3A

G/F C G5/D

'cause I've got-a one hand in my pock-et and the oth-er one is flick-in' a cig-a-rette.

End Rhy. Fig. 4 Rhy. Fig. 5 End Rhy. Fig. 5

let ring let ring let ring

Solo

G | Gtr. 1: w/ Rhy. Fig. 1 | G^{type2} | E (4) 2fr | G^{type2}

Gtr. 2

Gtr. 5

8va

* Harmonica arr. for gtr.

Gtr. 3

Gtr. 4

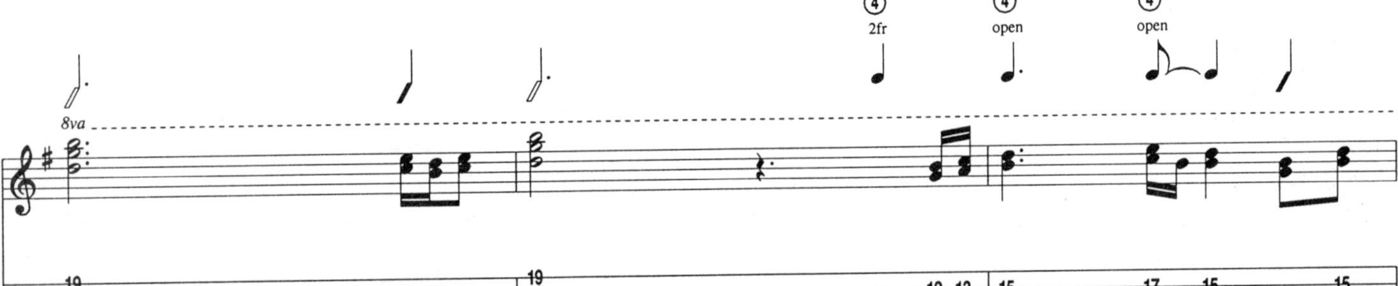

G/B | C | G^{type2} | E (4) 2fr | D (4) open | D (4) open | C

8va

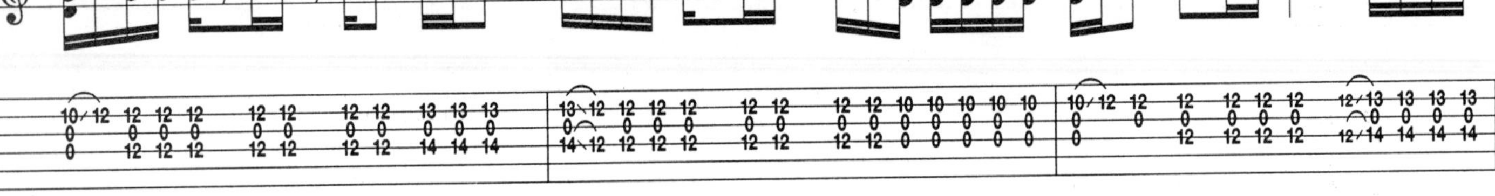

G/B
E
4
2fr
Gtype2
C
Gtype2
And what it all comes down
8va
Pre-Chorus
Gtr. 5 tacet
Gtrs. 1 & 2: w/ Rhy. Figs. 2 & 2A
Gtr. 4: w/ Rhy. Fig. 4
G/F
Cadd9
to
is that I have-n't got it all fig-ured
Gtr. 3
let ring
Gtr. 3 tacet
G
Chorus
Gtrs. 1 & 2: w/ Rhy. Figs. 3 & 3A
Gtr. 4: w/ Rhy. Fig. 5
G/F
out just yet
'cause I've got-a one hand in my pock-et and the
C
G5/D
G
D.S. al Coda
oth-er one is giv-in' a peace sign.
3. I'm

⊕ Coda

Gtr. 3: w/ Rhy. Fill 1
Gtype3
Gtr. 2

Gtr. 3: w/ Rhy. Fill 2

Pre-Chorus
Gtr. 4: w/ Rhy. Fig. 4
G/F

And what it all comes down __ to my_ friends, yeah, _

Gtr. 1

Cadd9
Gtype3

__ is that ev-'ry-thing's _ just fine, fine, __________ fine. __________ 'Cause I've got-a

Gtr. 4: w/ Rhy. Fig. 5
F G/F
⑥ 1fr
C Cadd9 G Gtype2
⑤ 3fr

one hand in my pock - et and the oth-er one is hail-ing a tax - i - cab. ______

Outro

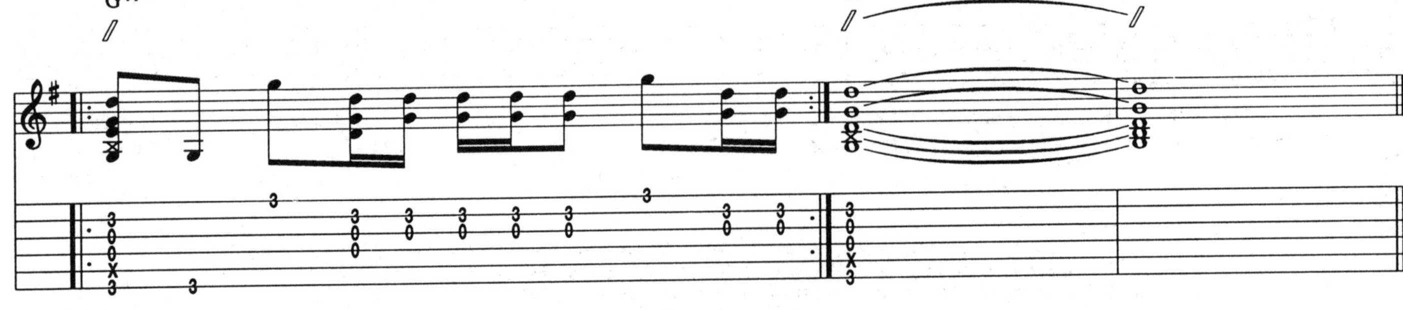

HANDS

Words and Music by
JEWEL KILCHER and PATRICK LEONARD

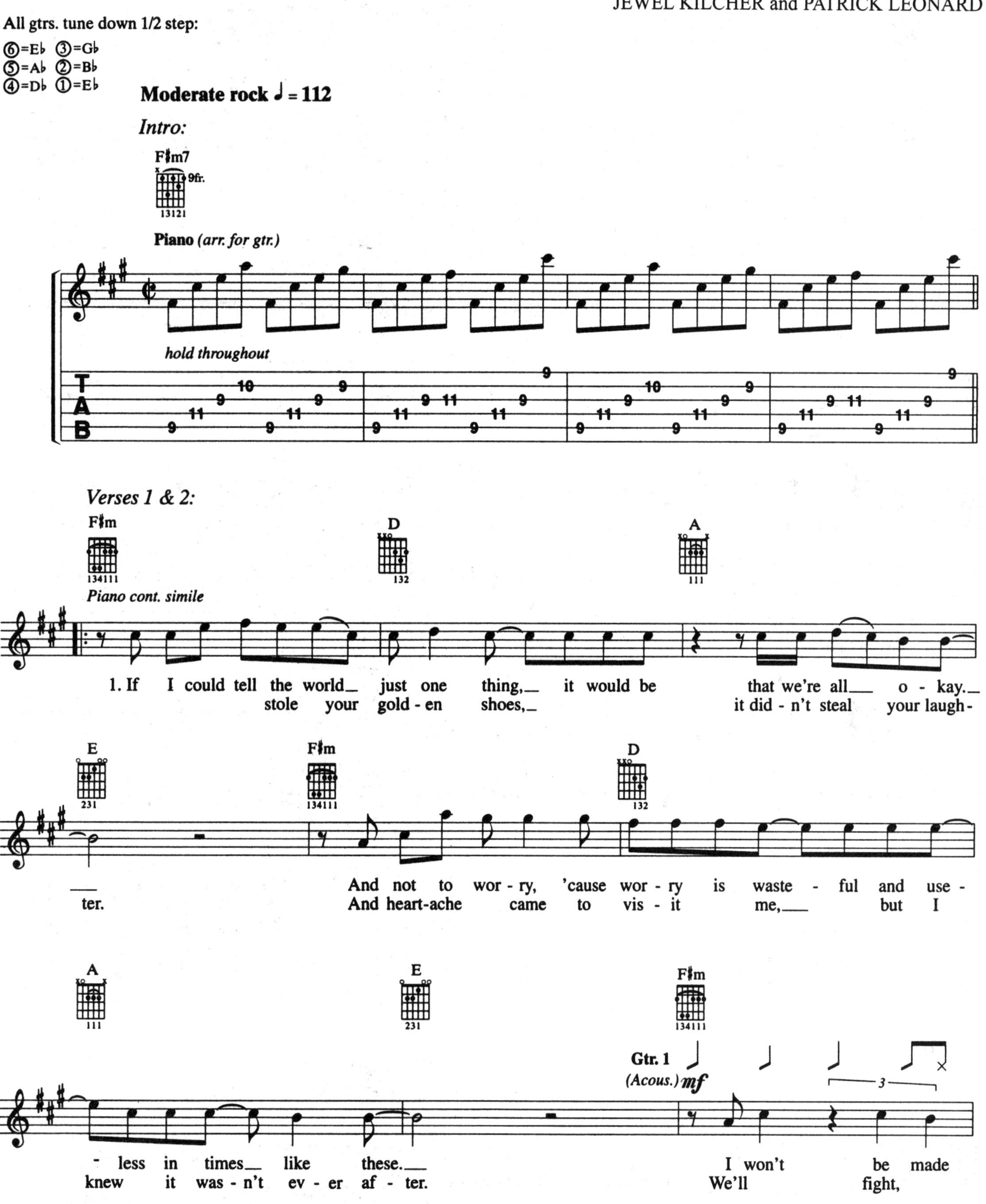

D
132
A
111
E
231
Cont. rhy. simile
use - less.
I won't be i - dle with de - spair.
not out of spite, for some - one must stand up for what's right. 'Cause
F♯m
134111
D
132
I'll gath - er my - self a - round my faith,
for
where there's a man who has no voice,
A
111
E
231
light does the dark - ness most fear.
there our's shall go sing - ing.
Chorus:
A
111
E
231
Bm
13421
Gtr. 1
My hands are small, I know. But they're
A
111
E
231
D
132
A
111
E
231
Cont. rhy. simile
not yours, they are my own. But they're not yours, they are

1.
Bm
A
E/G♯
F♯m7
9fr.
Gtr. 1
Gtr. 1 cont. in notation
__ my own.__ And I am nev - er bro - ken.
Piano (arr. for gtr.)
hold throughout
2.
A
E/G♯
F♯m
Gtr. 1
2. Pov - er- ty I am nev - er bro - ken.___
Gtr. 1

Bridge:
A
E
F♯m
D
Gtr. 1
Cont. rhy. simile
In the end, on - ly kind - ness mat - ters.
A
E
F♯m
D
Gtr. 1
In the end, on - ly kind - ness mat - ters.
Verse 3:
F♯m7
9fr.
D
5fr.
A
E
Gtr. 1 tacet
I will get down on my knees and I will pray.
Piano (arr. for gtr.)
hold throughout
F♯m7
9fr.
D
5fr.
A
E
I will get down on my knees and I will pray.

F♯m7
9fr.
13121
D
5fr.
1333
A
111
E
231
I will get down on my knees and I will pray.
Chorus:
A
E
Bm
13421
Gtr. 1
My hands are small, I know. But they're
Cont. rhy. simile
D
132
not yours, they are my own. But they're not yours, they are
my own. And I am nev - er bro - ken.
1.
E/G♯
2 134
F♯m
134111
2.
I am nev-er bro - ken. We are nev - er bro - ken.

Outro:
F♯m
134111
D
132
E
231
Gtr. 1
Cont. rhy. simile
Gtr. 2
We are God's eyes,
God's hands,
God's mind.
We are God's eyes,

F♯m
D
E
134111
132
231
God's
hands,
heart.
Begin fade
We are
eyes.
Fade
T
A
B

I THINK I'M PARANOID

Words and Music by
DOUG ERIKSON, SHIRLEY MANSON,
STEVE MARKER and BUTCH VIG

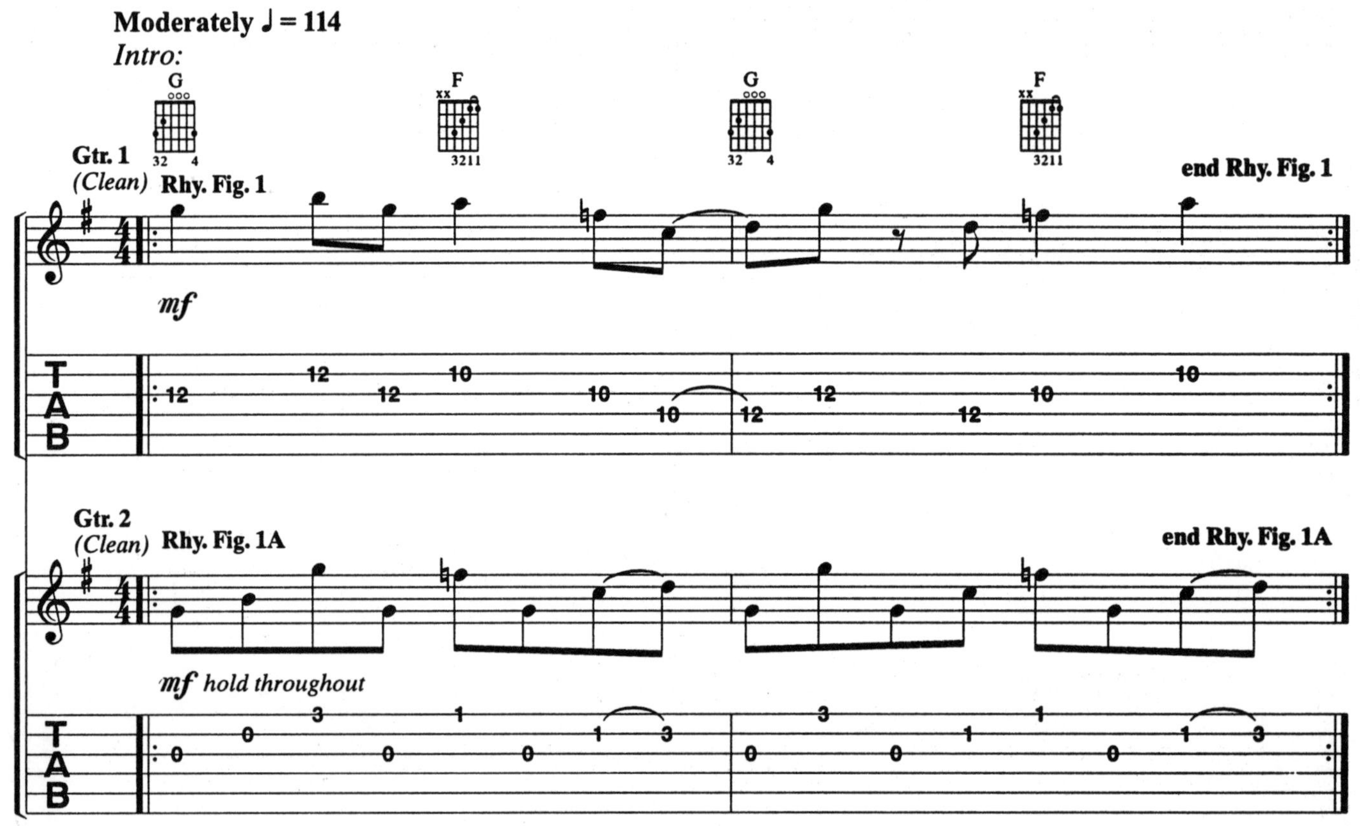

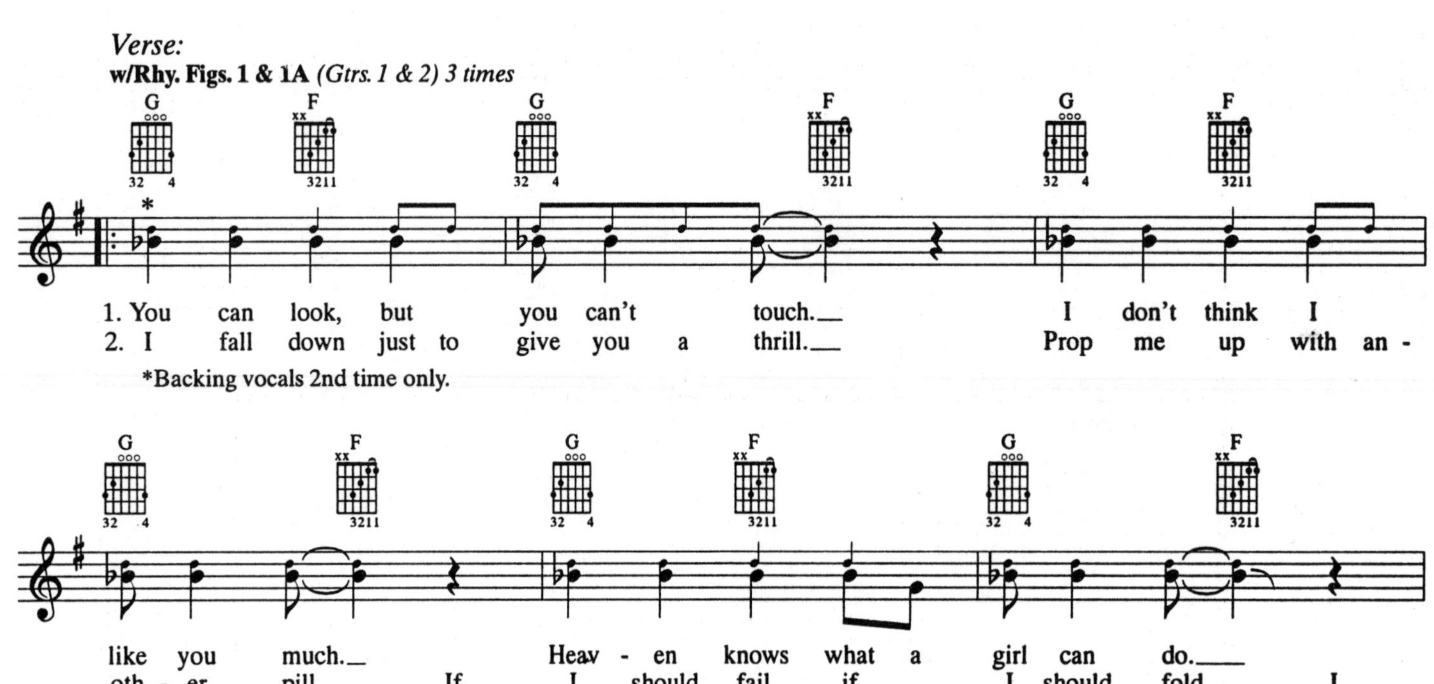

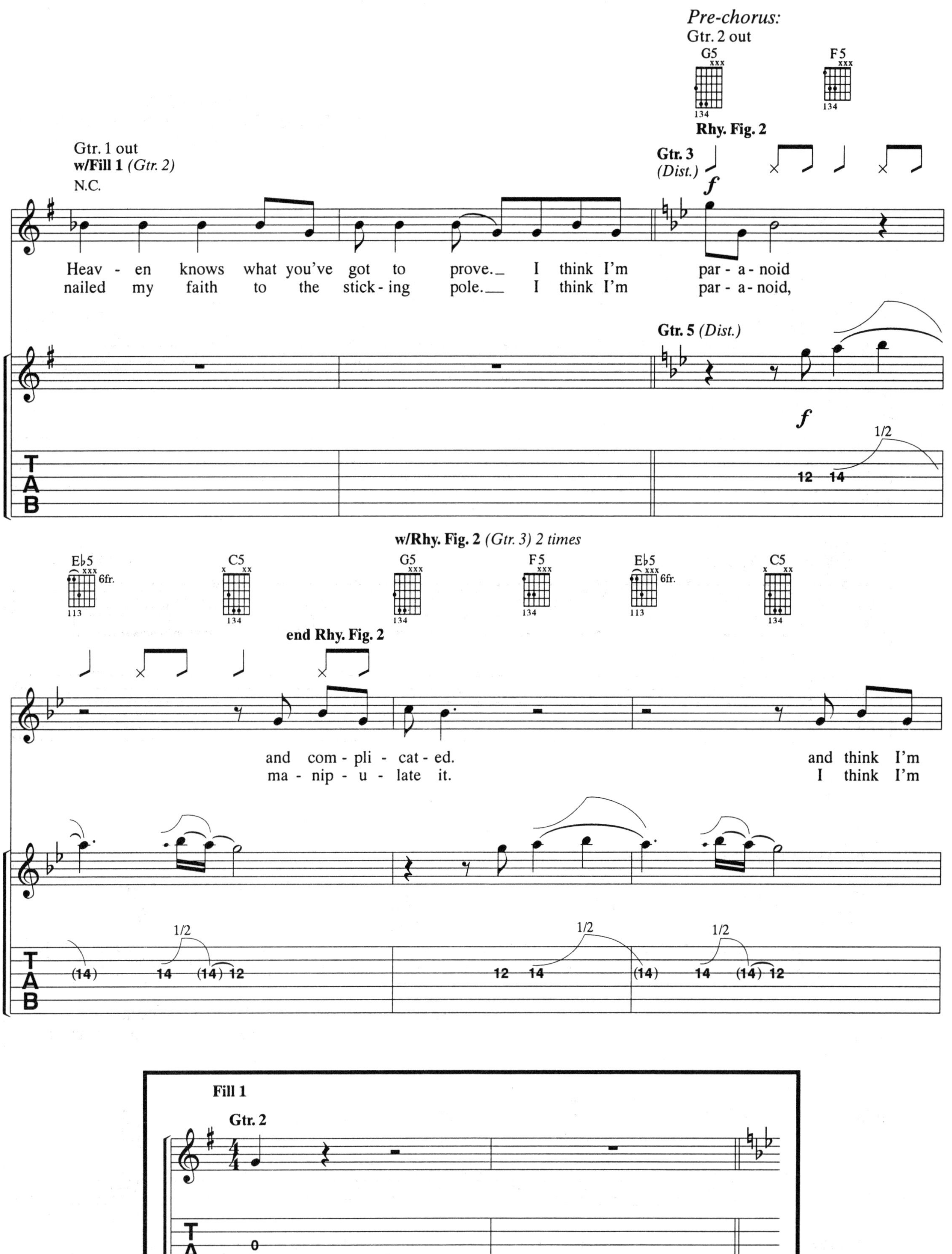
Pre-chorus:
Gtr. 2 out
G5
F5
Rhy. Fig. 2
Gtr. 1 out
w/Fill 1 (Gtr. 2)
N.C.
Gtr. 3
(Dist.)
Heav - en knows what you've got to prove. I think I'm par - a - noid
nailed my faith to the stick - ing pole. I think I'm par - a - noid,
Gtr. 5 (Dist.)
1/2
w/Rhy. Fig. 2 (Gtr. 3) 2 times
E♭5
C5
G5
F5
E♭5
C5
6fr.
end Rhy. Fig. 2
and com - pli - cat - ed. and think I'm
ma - nip - u - late it. I think I'm
Fill 1
Gtr. 2

G5
F5
E♭5
6fr.
C5
G5
F5
Gr. 3
par - a - noid
par - a - noid
ma - nip - u - late it.
and com - pli - cat - ed.
Gtr. 5
1/2
1/2
1/2
12 14
(14) 14 (14) 12
12 14
E♭5
6fr.
C5
𝄋 Chorus:
B♭5
Gtr. 3
Bend me, break me, an -
Gtr. 1
13 14 11 13 14
11 13 14 11
5 6 5 6 5
Gtr. 5
Gtr. 5 out
(14)
12

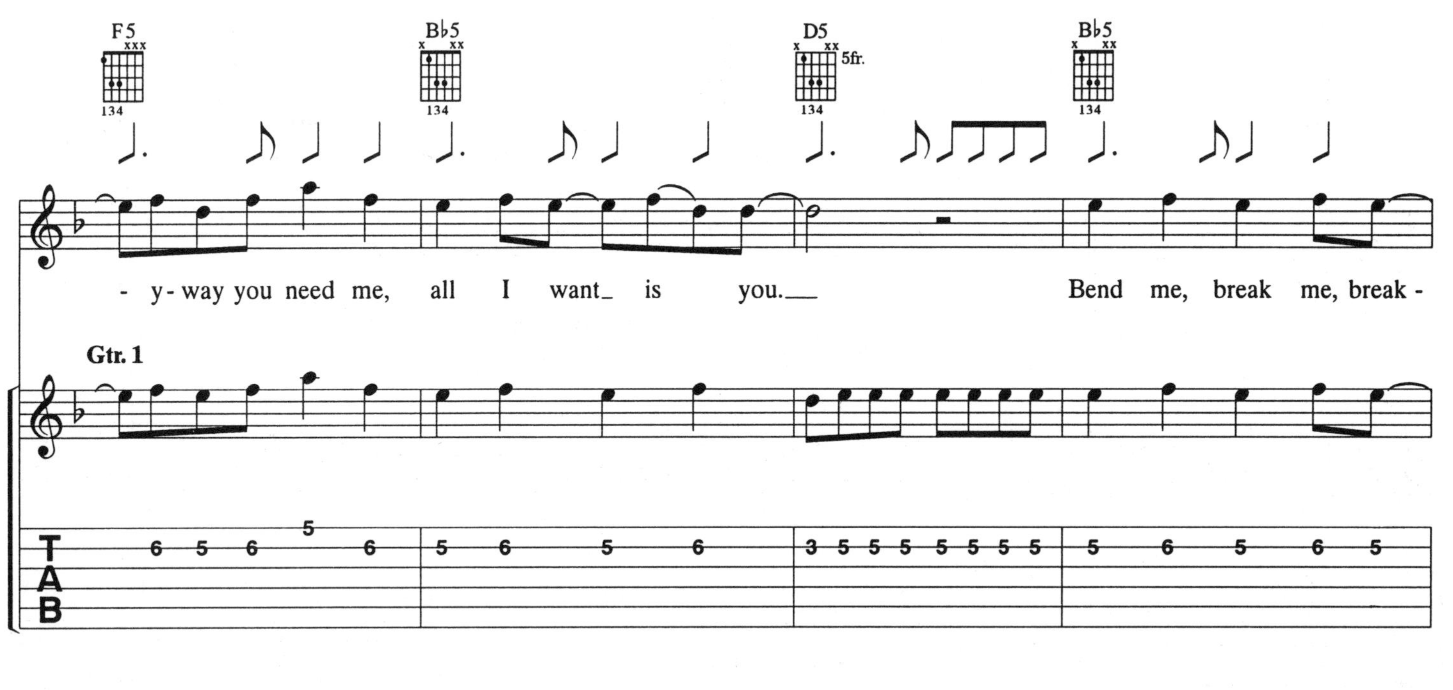
F5
B♭5
D5
5fr.
B♭5
- y- way you need me, all I want_ is you.___ Bend me, break me, break -
Gtr. 1

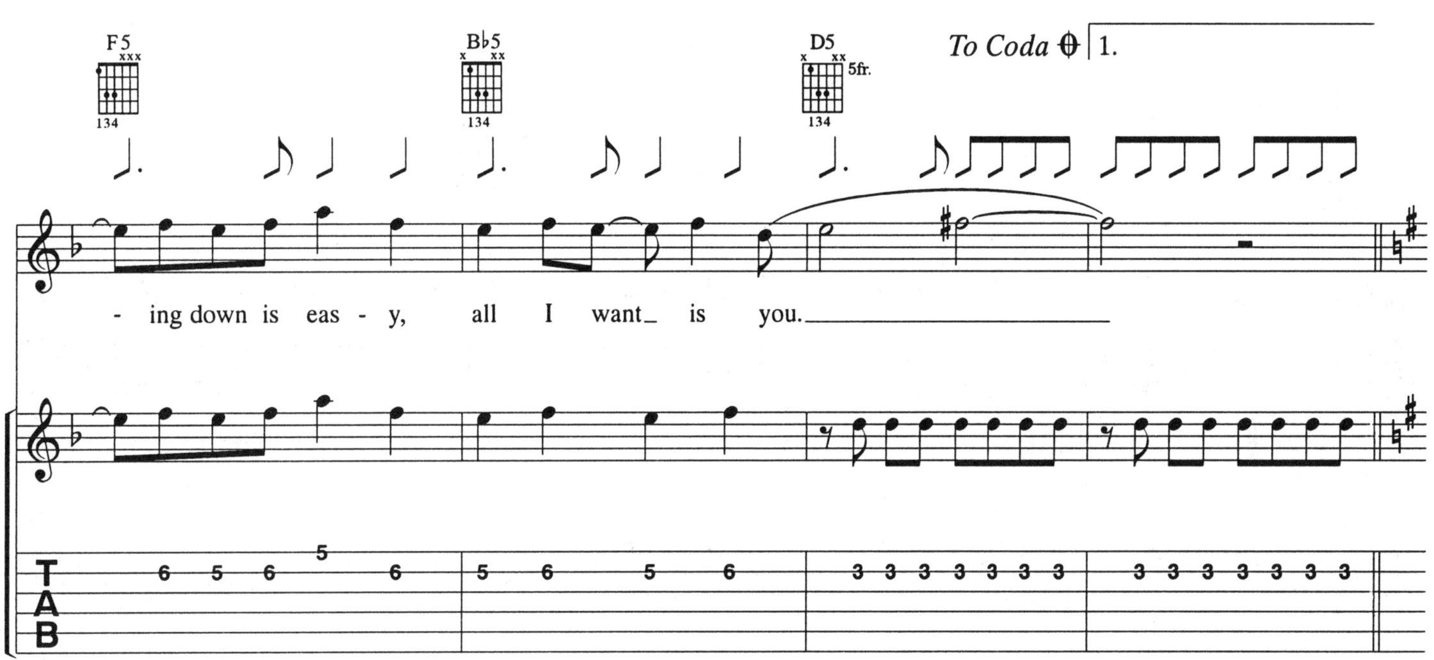
F5
B♭5
D5
5fr.
To Coda ⊕
1.
- ing down is eas - y, all I want_ is you.

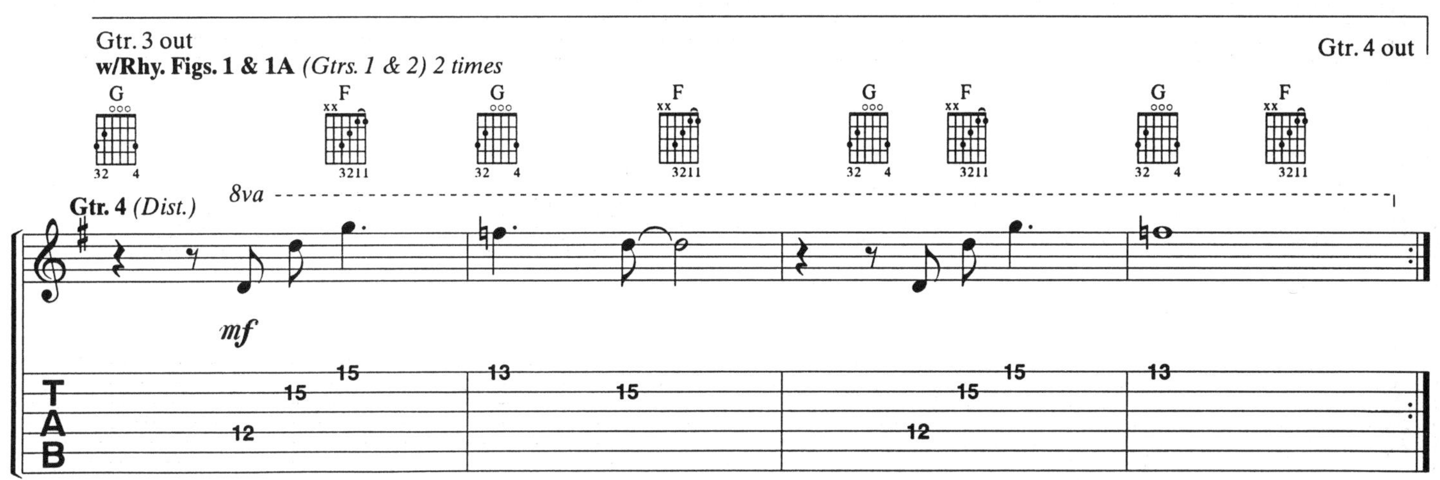
Gtr. 3 out
w/Rhy. Figs. 1 & 1A (Gtrs. 1 & 2) 2 times
Gtr. 4 out
G
F
Gtr. 4 (Dist.)
8va
mf

Interlude:
Gtr. 3 out
2.
Gtr. 3
E5
D5
— I, I, I, I, I, oh.
I think I'm par - a - noid.
Gtr. 1
Gtr. 6 (Dist.)
f
C5/G
E5
D5
I think I'm par - a - noid.
Gtr. 6

2.
C5/G
3fr.
113

N.C.

D.S. 𝄋 al Coda

𝄌 *Coda*

Gtr. 3

Gtr. 1

13 14 11 13 14 | 11 13 14

Gtr. 1

3 3 3 3 3 3 3

Gtr. 6

Gtr. 6 out

5 3 3

Gtr. 5

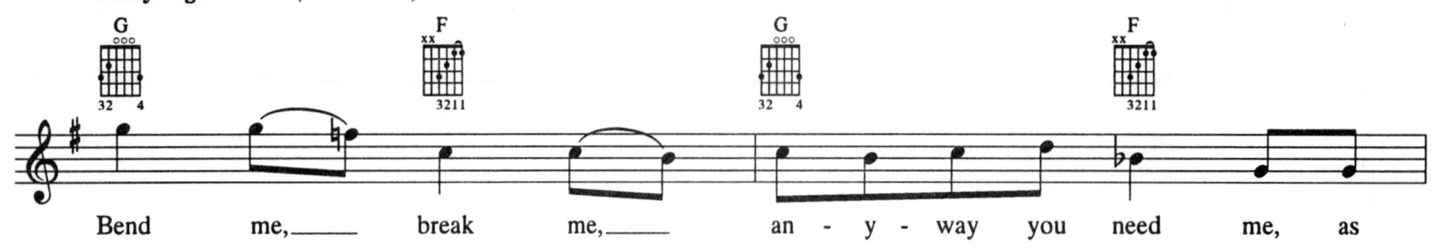
Gtrs. 3 & 5 out
w/Rhy. Figs. 1 & 1A (Gtrs. 1 & 2) 3½ times
G
F
G
F
Bend me, break me, an - y - way you need me, as

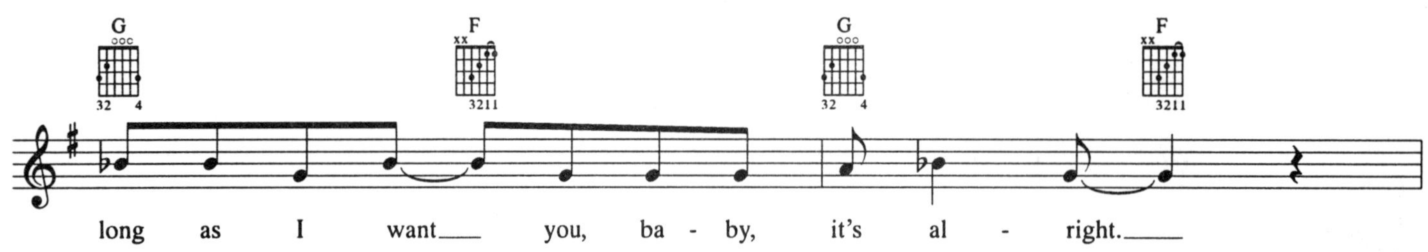
G
F
G
F
long as I want you, ba - by, it's al - right.

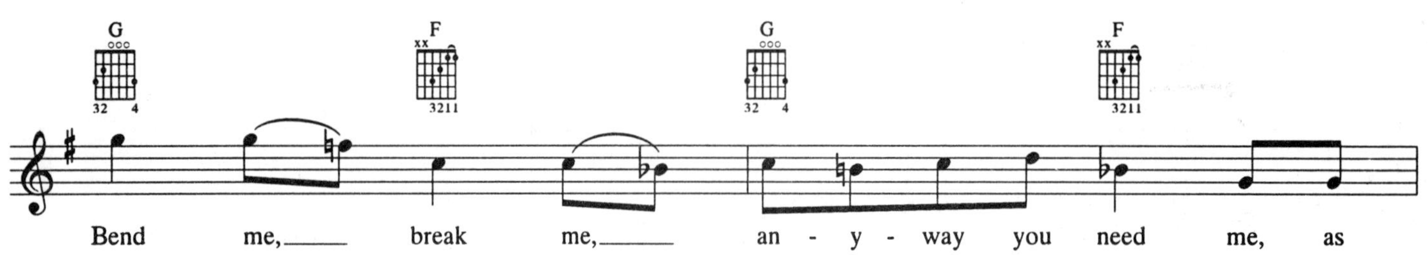
G
F
G
F
Bend me, break me, an - y - way you need me, as

G
F
Gtr. 1 out
w/Fill 2 (Gtr. 2)
N.C.
long as I want you, ba - by, it's al - right.
rit.

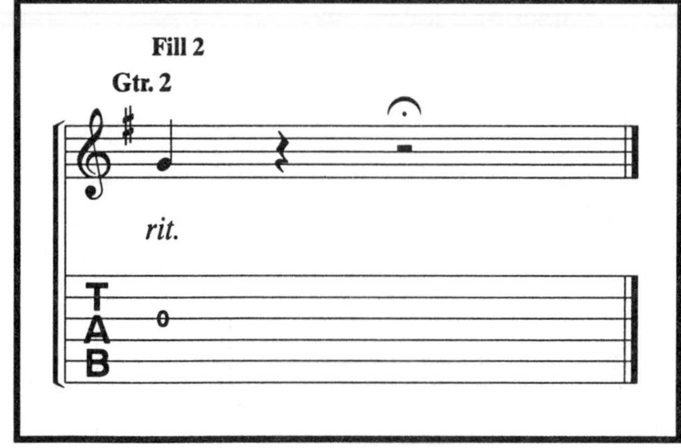
Fill 2
Gtr. 2
rit.
T
A
B
0

I WILL REMEMBER YOU

Words and Music by SARAH McLACHLAN,
SEAMUS EGAN and DAVID MERENDA

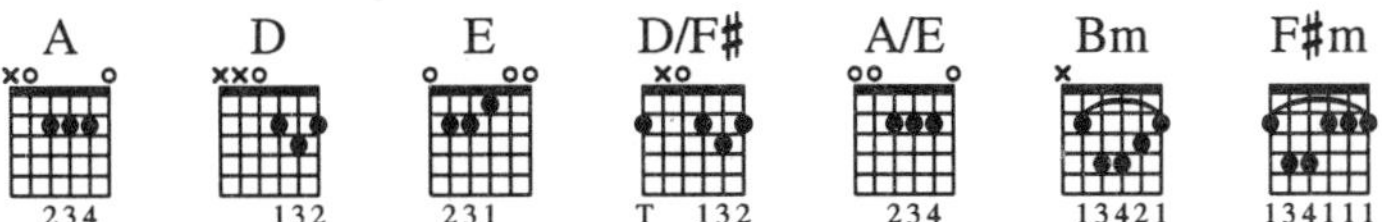

Moderately slow ♩ = 78

Intro:

A D E A D E

I will re-mem-ber you. Will you re-mem-ber me? Don't

w/Fill 1 *(Acous. Gtr. 1)*

A D/F♯ A/E Bm A D

let your life pass you by. Weep not for

E A

Acous. Gtr. 1

mem-o-ries.

𝄋 *Verse:*

Acous. Gtr. 1 tacet 1st 4 meas. Verse 2

A D

Cont. rhy. simile

1. I'm so tired but
so a-fraid to love you, but

E A D E F♯m

I can't sleep. Stand-ing on the edge of some-thing much too deep. It's
more a-fraid to lose. Cling-ing to a past that does-n't let me choose. But

A D E A D/F♯

fun-ny how we feel so much, but can-not say a word. Though we are scream-ing in-side, oh,
once there was a dark-ness, a deep and end-less night. You gave me ev-'ry-thing you had,

Fill 1
Acous. Gtr. 1

mf *hold* *cont. in slashes*

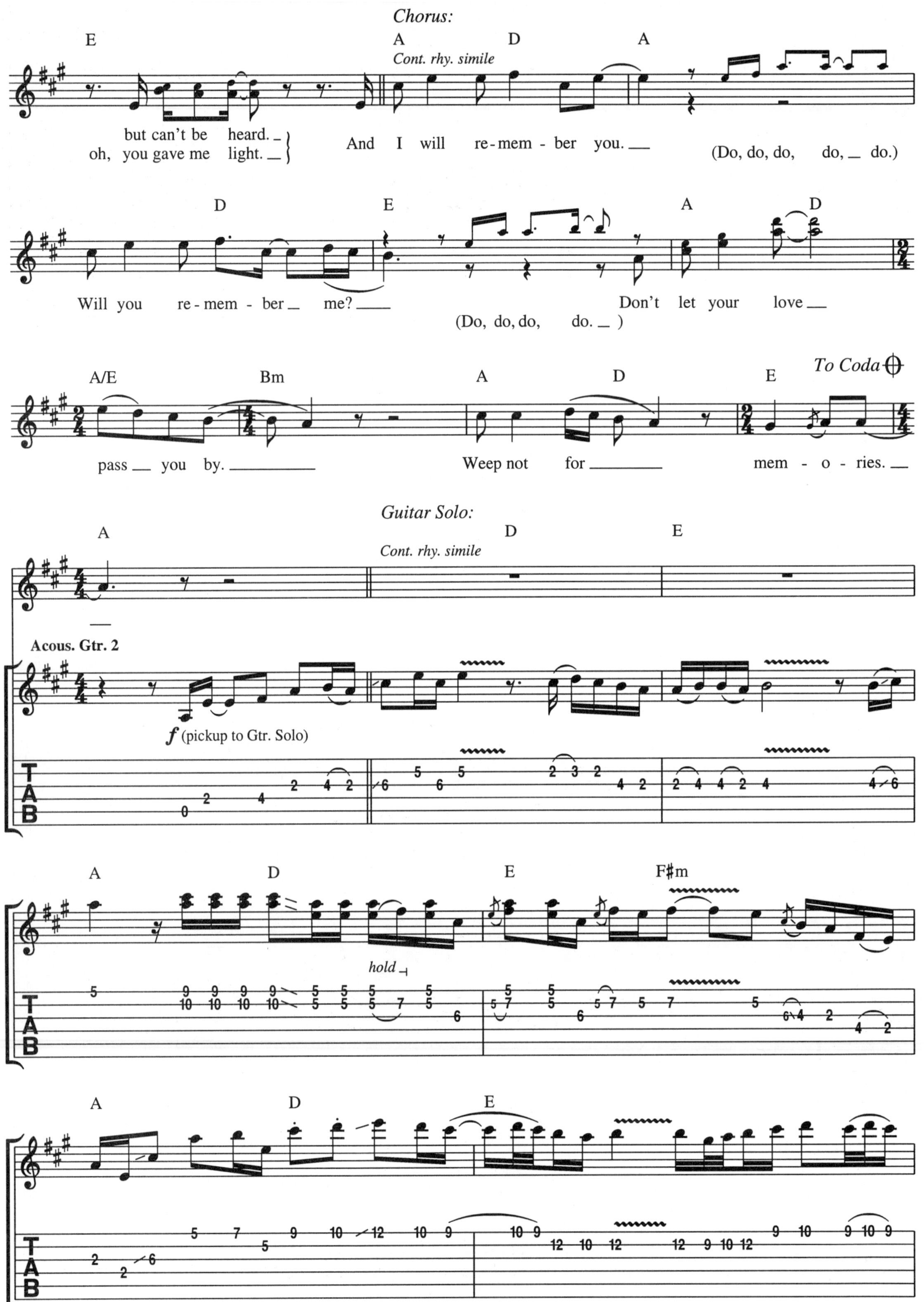
Chorus:
E
A
D
A
Cont. rhy. simile
but can't be heard.
oh, you gave me light.
And I will re-mem - ber you.
(Do, do, do, do, do.)
D
E
A
D
Will you re-mem - ber me?
Don't let your love
(Do, do, do, do.)
A/E
Bm
A
D
E
To Coda
pass you by.
Weep not for
mem - o - ries.
Guitar Solo:
A
D
E
Cont. rhy. simile
Acous. Gtr. 2
f (pickup to Gtr. Solo)
A
D
E
F#m
hold
A
D
E

A
D/F♯
E
D.S. 𝄋 al Coda
2. I'm
9
10
9 7 6
7
7
9
7 9 11
9
9
12 14 12

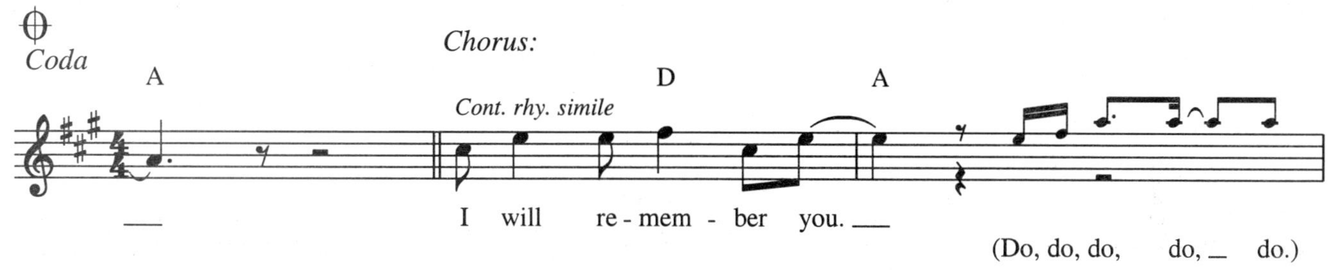
Coda
Chorus:
A
D
A
Cont. rhy. simile
I will re - mem - ber you.
(Do, do, do, do, do.)

D
E
A
D
Will you re - mem - ber me?
Don't let your love
(Do, do, do, do.)

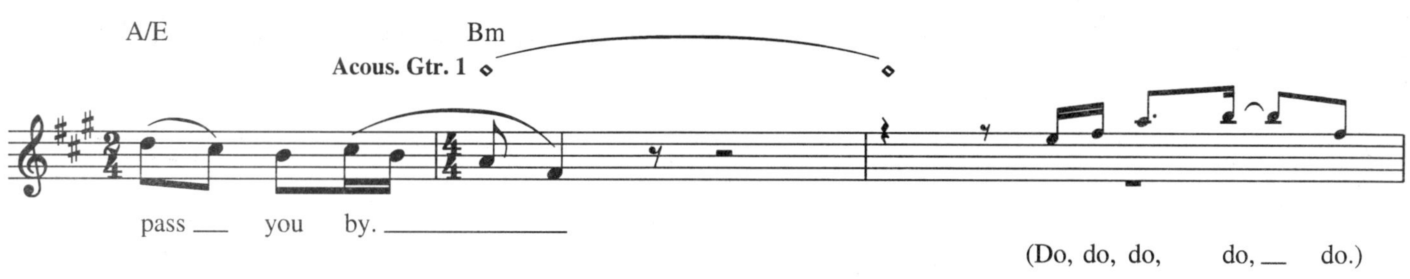
A/E
Bm
Acous. Gtr. 1
pass you by.
(Do, do, do, do, do.)

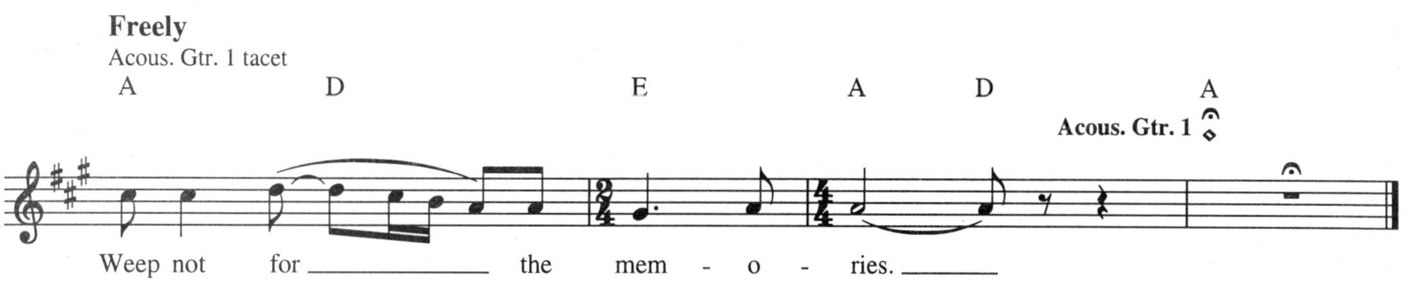
Freely
Acous. Gtr. 1 tacet
A
D
E
A
D
A
Acous. Gtr. 1
Weep not for the mem - o - ries.

I WANT TO COME OVER

Words and Music by
MELISSA ETHERIDGE

*D
A
E
You know I'm here.
The night is thin.
Gtr. 3
**
hold
hold
* Chords implied by bass/keybd.
** On 2nd verse.
I know you're a - lone,
I watched the car leave.
Your lov-er is gone,
To Coda
D
A
E
Asus2
and let me in.
Gtr. 3
hold
mf
hold
B
O - pen your back door, I just need to
hold
hold

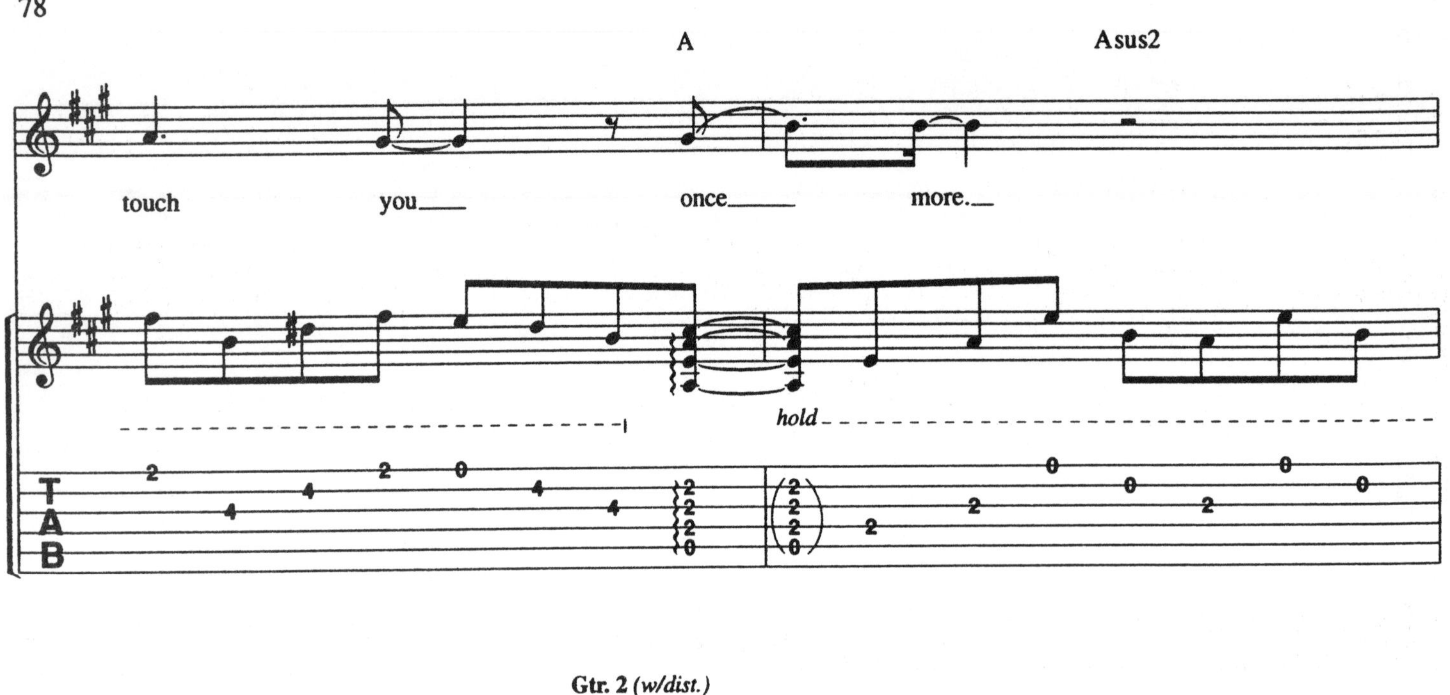
A
Asus2
touch
you
once
more.
hold
TAB

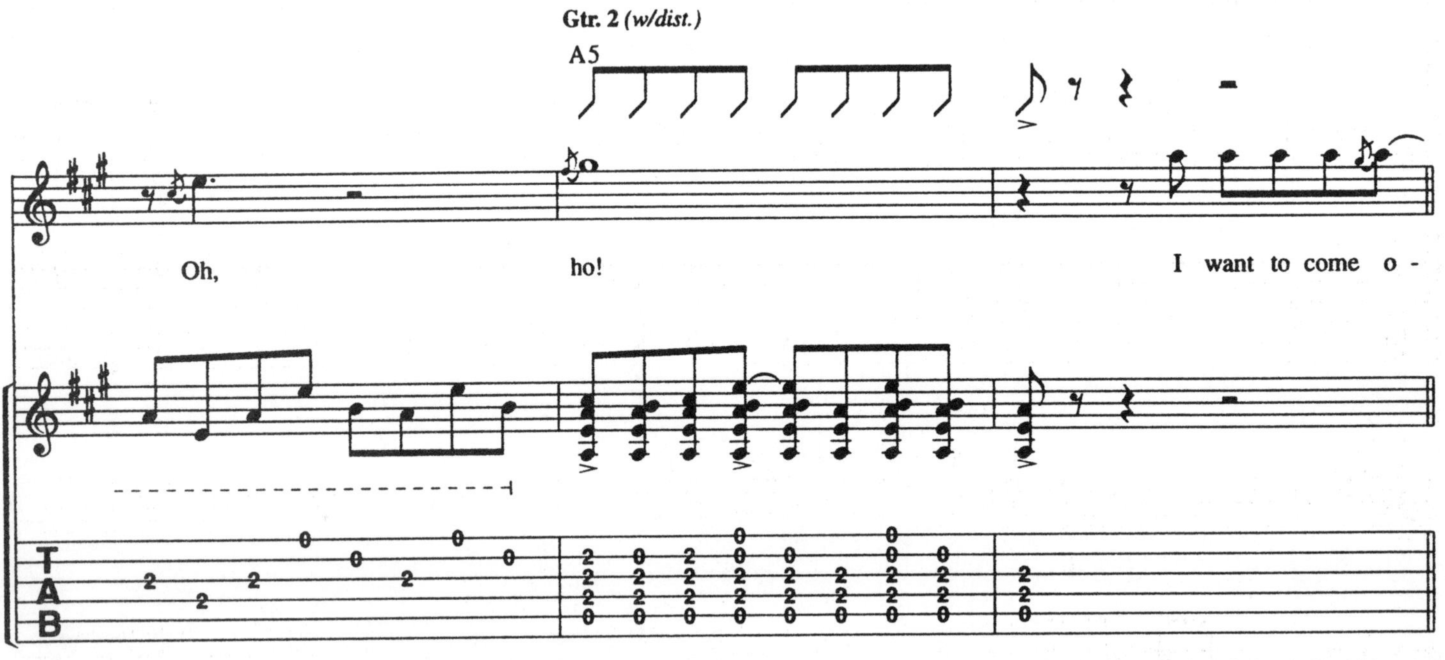
Gtr. 2 (w/dist.)
A5
Oh,
ho!
I want to come o -
TAB

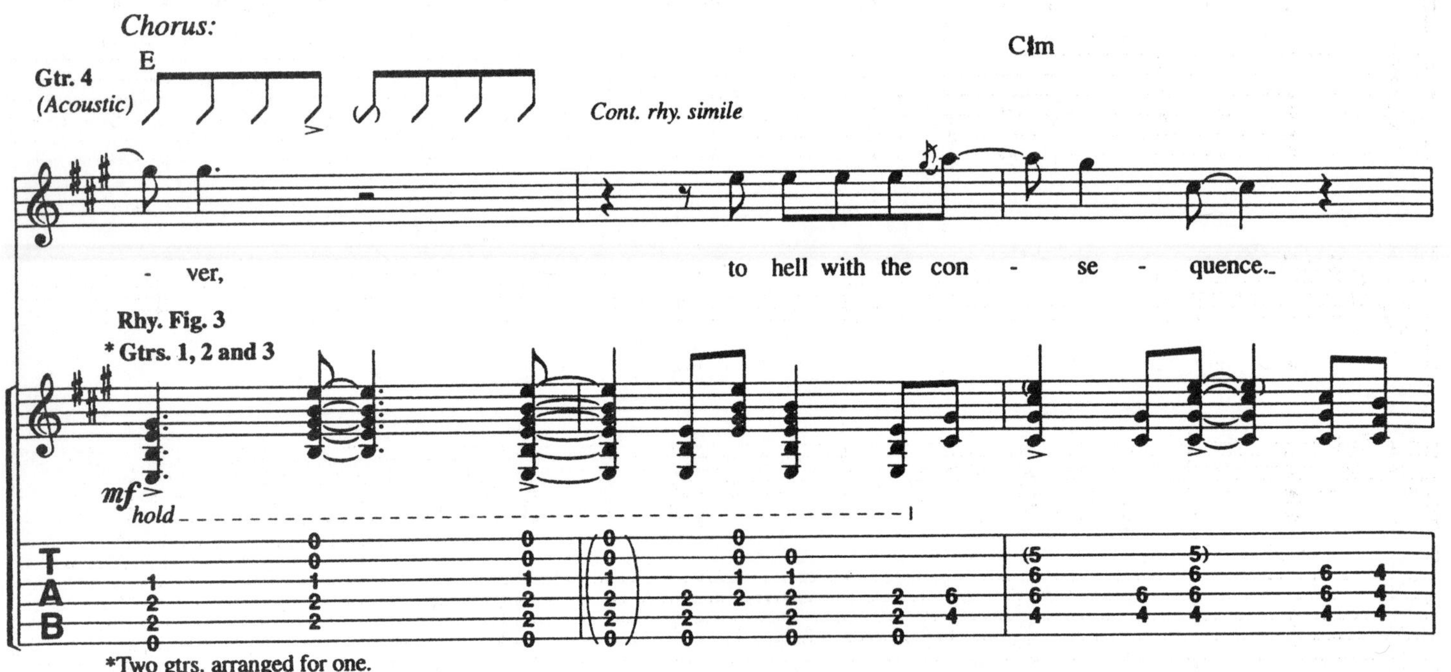
Chorus:
Gtr. 4
(Acoustic)
E
C♯m
Cont. rhy. simile
- ver,
to hell with the con - se - quence.
Rhy. Fig. 3
* Gtrs. 1, 2 and 3
mf
hold
TAB
*Two gtrs. arranged for one.

A
You told me you loved me, that's all I
hold
D A E
believe. I want to come o - ver.
hold
(F♯5) G♯m
It's a need I can't ex - plain; to
end Rhy. Fig. 3
hold
hold
A D A E
1. w/Rhy. Fig. 1 (Gtr. 1) 2 times, simile
Gtr. 4 tacet
see you a - gain. I want to come o - ver.
hold

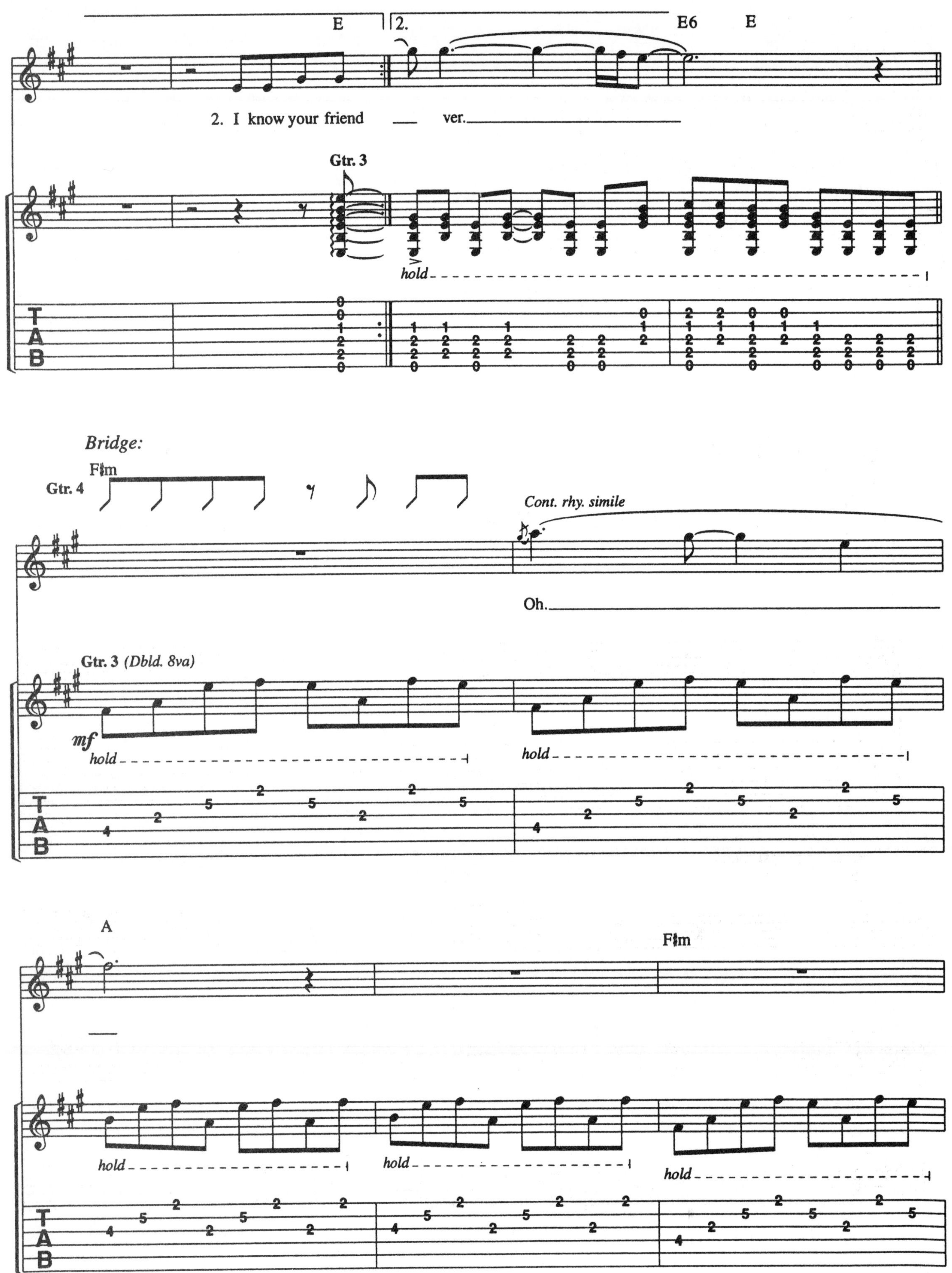
E
2.
E6
E
2. I know your friend
ver.
Gtr. 3
hold
Bridge:
F♯m
Gtr. 4
Cont. rhy. simile
Oh.
Gtr. 3 (Dbld. 8va)
mf
hold
A
F♯m

A
D.C. al Coda
Oh.
hold
Gtr. 4
A6
A
Band tacet
Drums
Coda
Let me in.
I want to come o -
Gtr. 3
hold
Chorus:
w/Rhy. Fig. 3 (All Gtrs.)
E
C♯m
- ver, to hell with the con - se - quence.
You told me you loved
A
D
A
me, that's all I be - lieve.
I want to come o -
E
(F♯5) G♯m
- ver. It's a need I can't ex - plain;

Gtr. 4
G♯m
A5
Cont. rhy. simile
I want to come o - ver
Rhy. Fig. 3A
Gtrs. 1, 2 and 3
D
Gtrs. 1 and 4
A(5)
end Rhy. Fig. 3A
(G)
to see you, to see you a -
Gtr. 2 (w/dist., no delay)
mp
hold
Outro:
w/Rhy. Fig. 3 (Gtrs. 2, 3 and 4)
E
C♯m
- gain.
Gtr. 1 (w/dist., no delay)
mf
A
D
1/2

Verse 2:
I know your friend.
You told her about me.
She filled you with fear,
Some kind of sin.
How can you turn,
Denying the fire?
Lover I burn,
Let me in.
(To Chorus:)

Verse 3:
I know you're confused,
I know that you're shaken,
You think we'll be lost
Once we begin.
I know you're weak.
I know that you want me.
Lover don't speak,
Let me in.
(To Chorus:)

I'M THE ONLY ONE

Lyrics and Music by
MELISSA ETHERIDGE

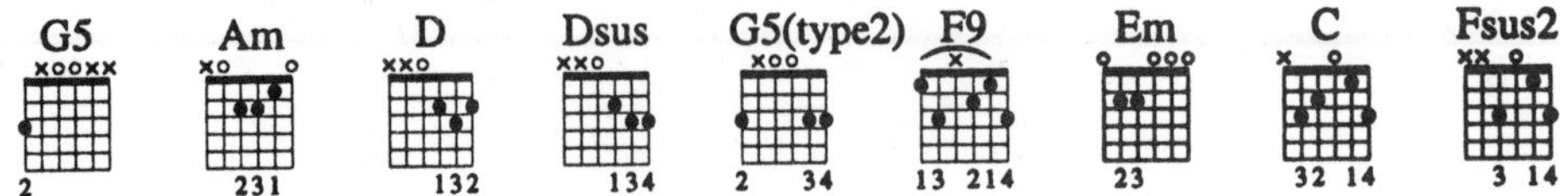

*When played on 12 string guitar some notes will sound one octave higher than written.

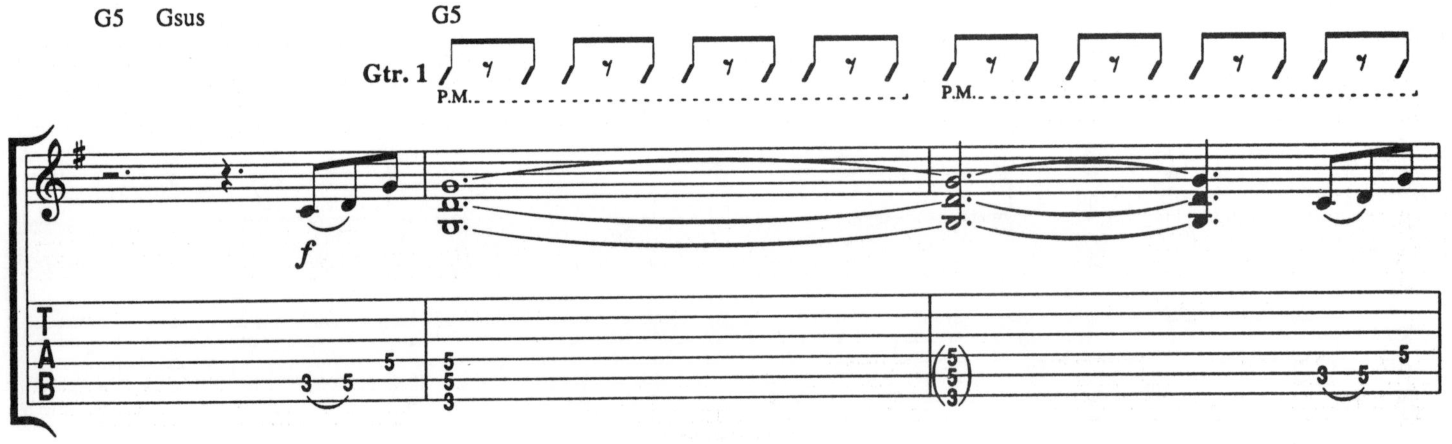

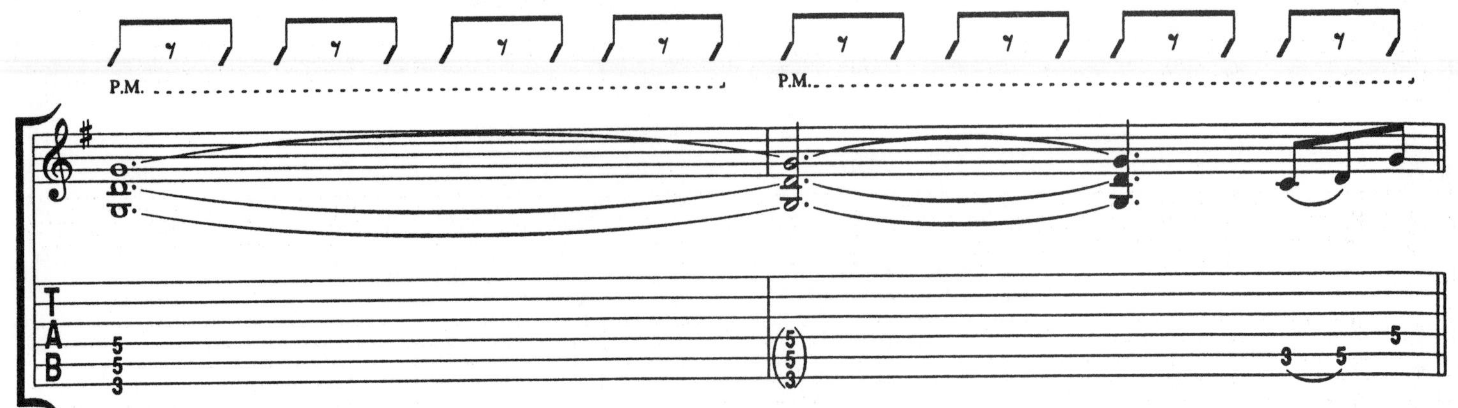

Verse:
G5
Gtr. 1
P.M.
1. Please ba - by, can't you see my mind's a burn-ing hell? I got
2. See additional lyrics.
P.M.
Rhy. Fig. 2a
(P.M.)
ra - zor's a - rip - pin' and tear - in' and strip-pin' my heart a - part as well.
Rhy. Fig. 2
(P.M.)
w/ Rhy. Figs. 2 (Gtr. 2) & 2a (gtr. 1) both 2 times
To - night you told me that you ache for some-thing new. And
some oth - er wom - an is look - in' like some-thing that might be good for you.
Pre-Chorus:
Am
Gtr. 1
D
Dsus
(Cont. rhy. simile)
Go on and hold her 'til the scream - ing is gone.
Gtr. 2
hold

Am
D
Go on be - lieve her when she tells you noth - ing's wrong.
hold
hold
Chorus:
G5(type2)
F(9)
Rhy. Fig. 3a
(Cont. rhy. simile)
But I'm the on - ly one who'll walk a - cross the fire for you.
Rhy. Fig. 3
w/Fill 1 (Gtr. 3)
Em
G5(type2)
And I'm the on - ly one who'll
Fill 1
Gtr. 3
f

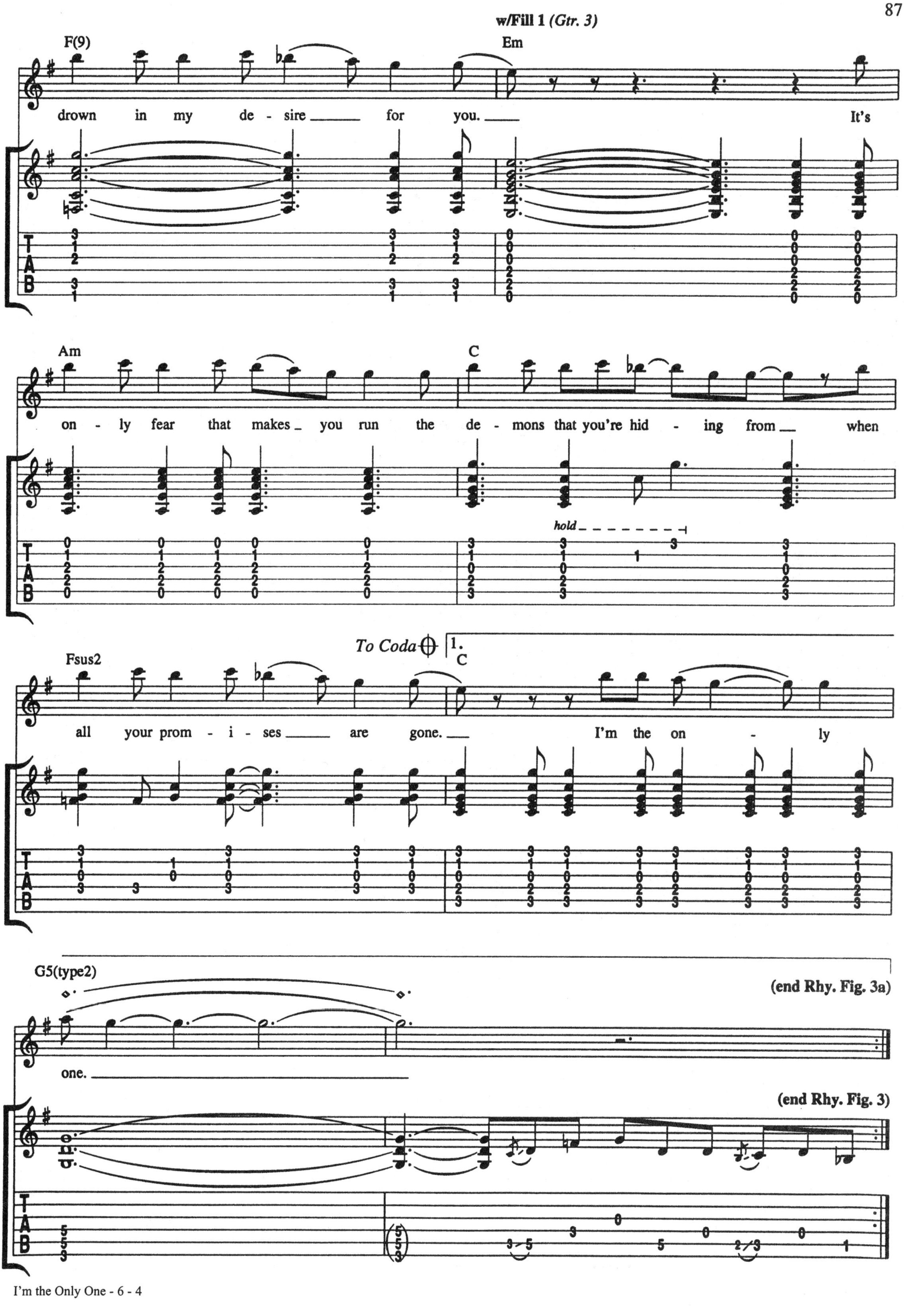

w/Fill 1 (Gtr. 3)
F(9)
Em
drown in my de - sire for you. It's
Am
C
on - ly fear that makes you run the de - mons that you're hid - ing from when
hold
To Coda
1.
Fsus2
C
all your prom - i - ses are gone. I'm the on - ly
G5(type2)
(end Rhy. Fig. 3a)
one.
(end Rhy. Fig. 3)

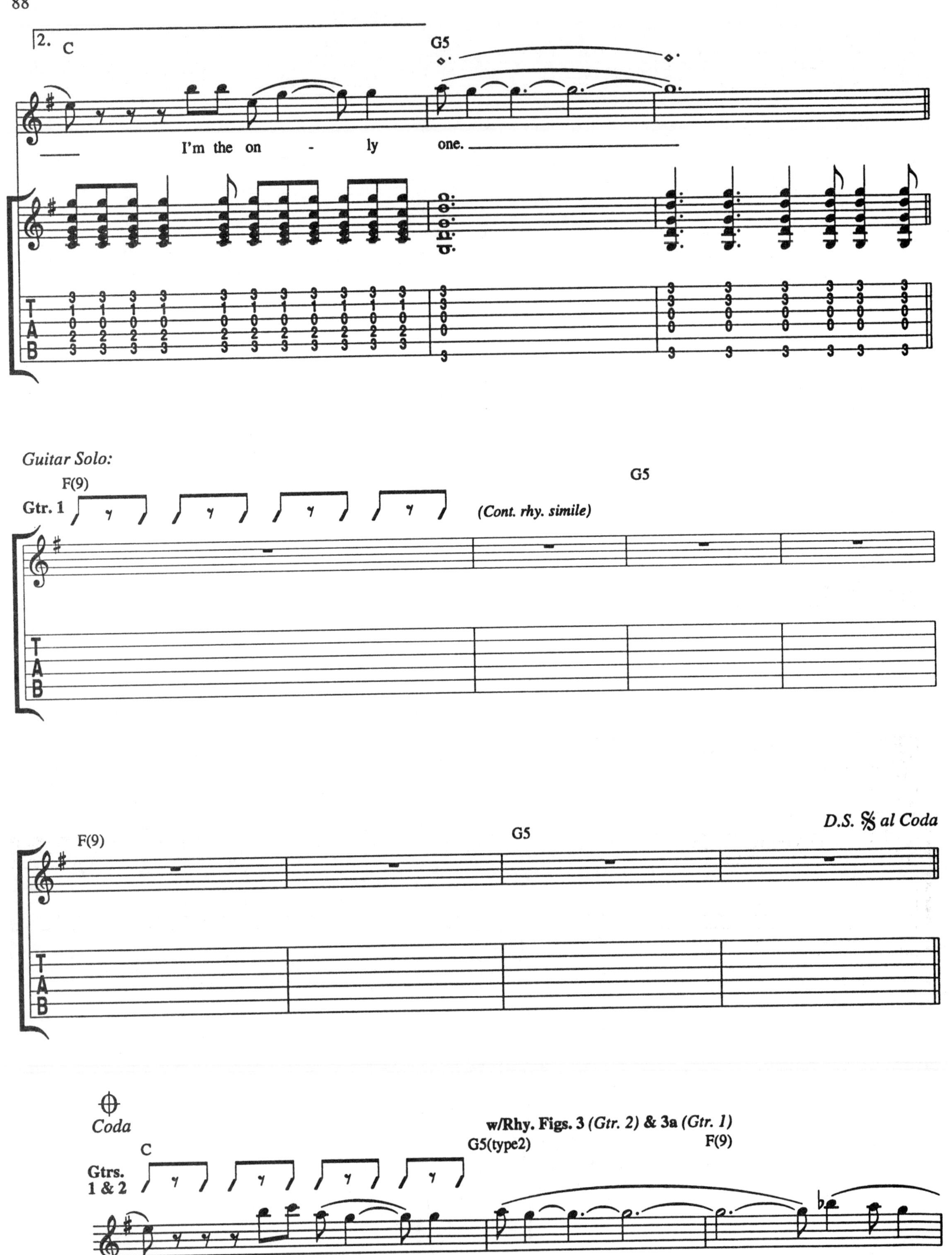
2.
C
G5
I'm the on - ly one.
Guitar Solo:
F(9)
Gtr. 1
(Cont. rhy. simile)
G5
F(9)
G5
D.S. 𝄋 al Coda
Coda
w/Rhy. Figs. 3 (Gtr. 2) & 3a (Gtr. 1)
C
G5(type2)
F(9)
Gtrs. 1 & 2
I'm the on - ly one, yeah.

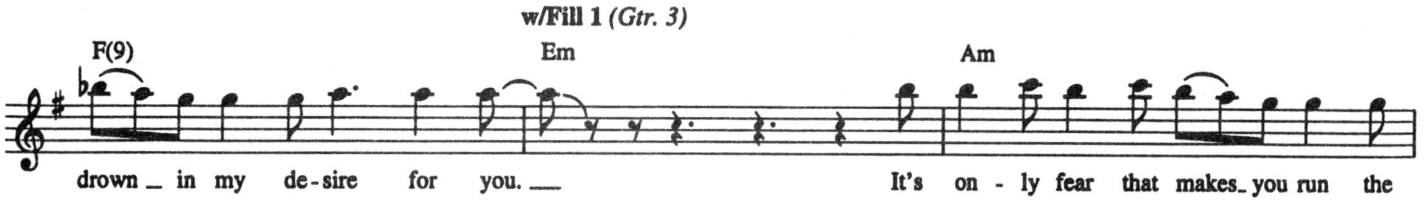

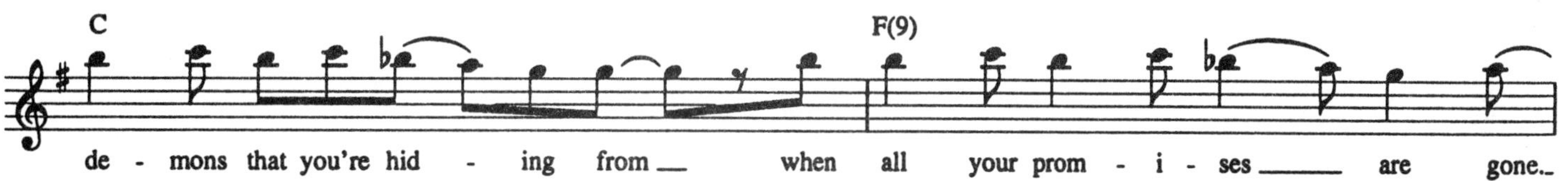

Verse 2:

Please baby, can't you see I'm trying to explain.
I've been here before and I'm locking the door and
I'm not going back again.
Her eyes and arms and skin won't make it go away.
You'll wake up tomorrow and wrestle the sorrow
that holds you down today.

(To Pre-Chorus:)

IF IT MAKES YOU HAPPY

Words and Music by
SHERYL CROW and JEFF TROTT

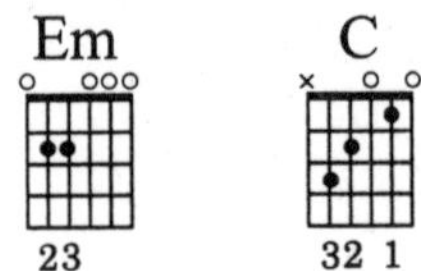

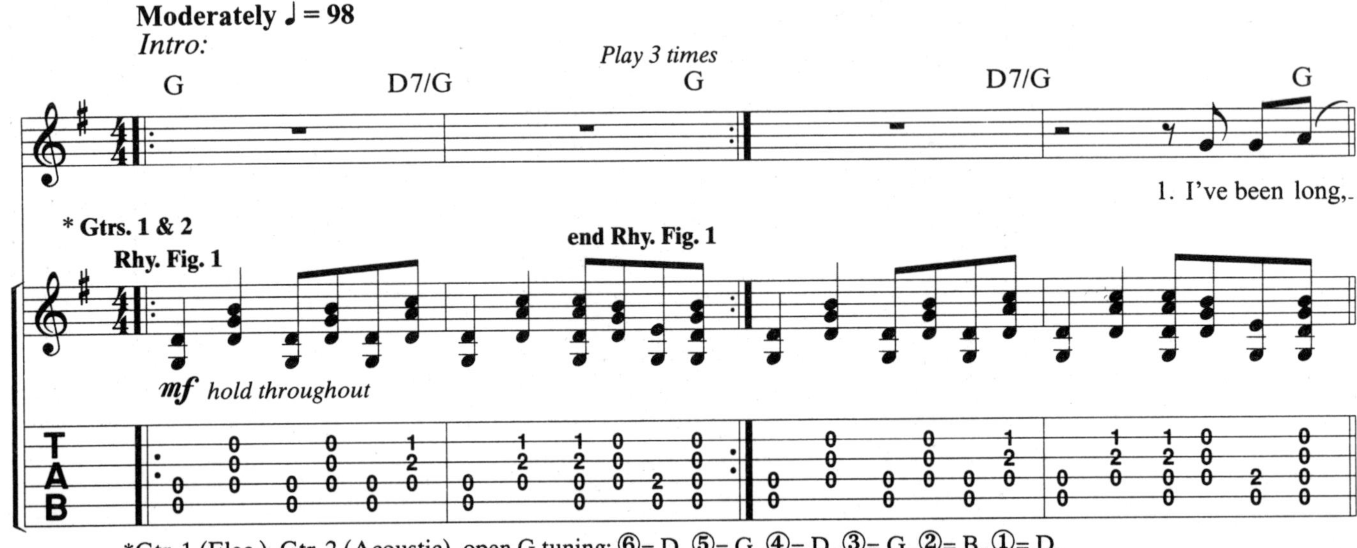

*Gtr. 1 (Elec.), Gtr. 2 (Acoustic), open G tuning: ⑥= D, ⑤= G, ④= D, ③= G, ②= B, ①= D.

* Open G tuning: ⑥= D, ⑤= G, ④= D, ③= G, ②= B, ①= D.

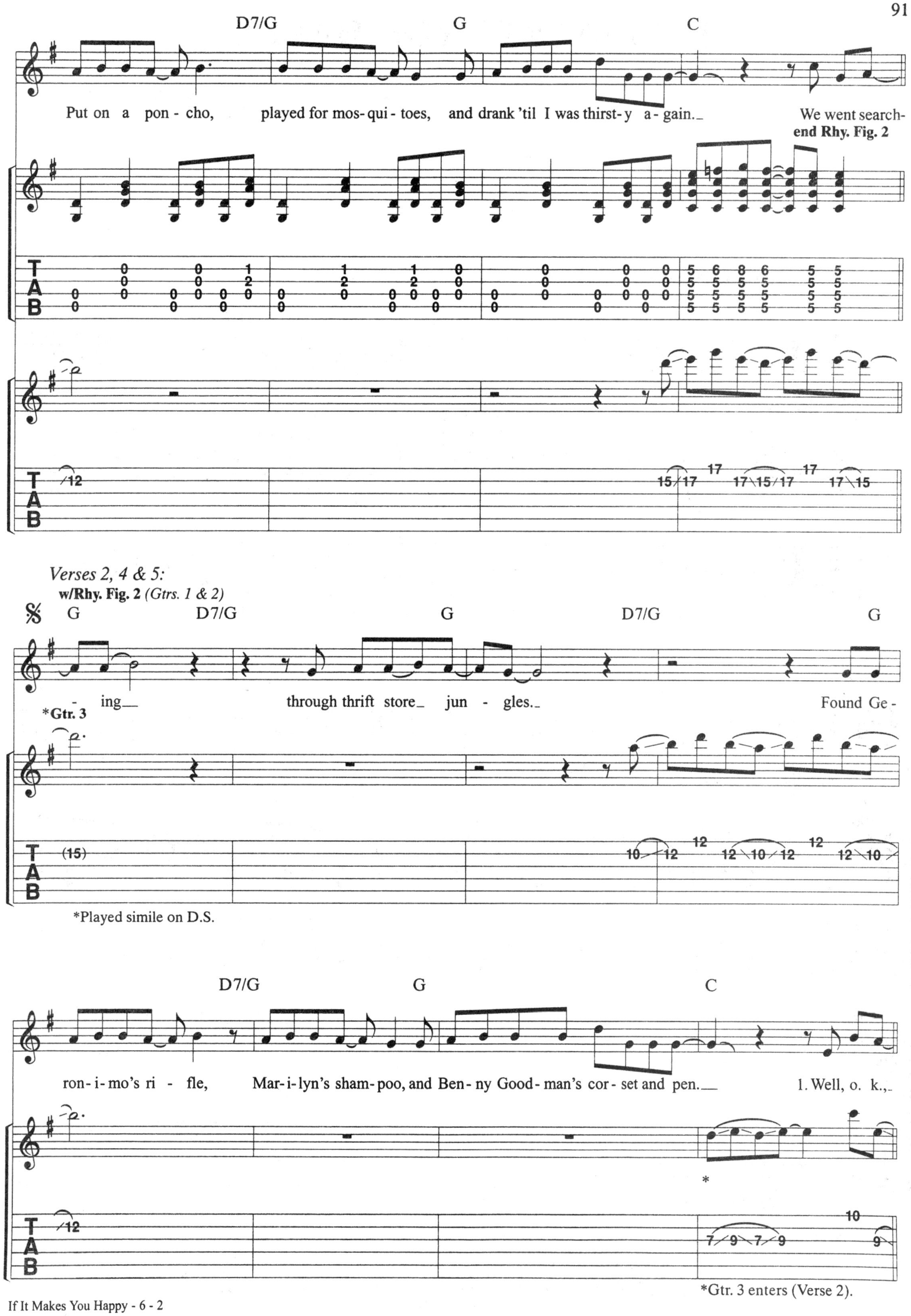

D7/G G C

Put on a pon - cho, played for mos- qui - toes, and drank 'til I was thirst- y a- gain._ We went search-

end Rhy. Fig. 2

Verses 2, 4 & 5:

w/Rhy. Fig. 2 *(Gtrs. 1 & 2)*

G D7/G G D7/G G

- ing_ through thrift store_ jun - gles._ Found Ge -

*Gtr. 3

*Played simile on D.S.

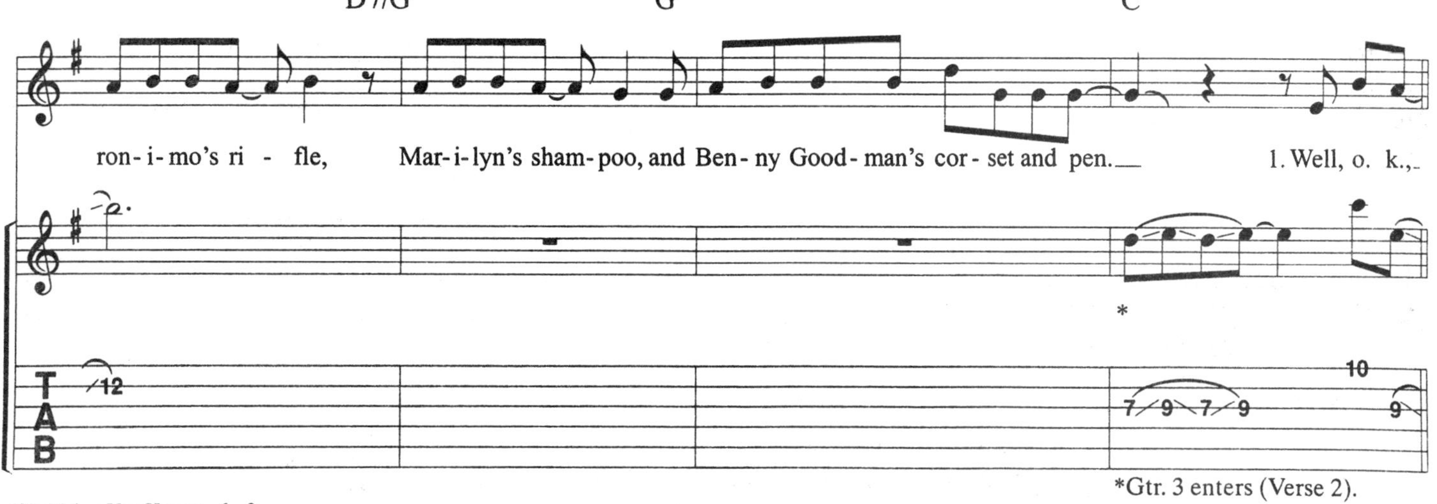

Pre-Chorus:

D C D

— I made this up. I prom- ised you I'd nev- er give up.— If it makes you hap-

2.3. *See additional lyrics*

Gtrs. 1 & 2

Gtr. 3

Gtr. 3 out

Chorus:

2.3.
D7/G
G
3. You get down, sad?
If it makes you hap-
w/Rhy. Fig. 3 (Gtrs. 1 & 2)
Am
C
G
py,
it can't be that bad.
D
Am
C
To Coda
If it makes you hap - py,
then why the hell are you so
Bridge:
Em
C
Gtr. 2
sad?
Gtr. 1 out
Gtr. 4 (Elec.)
mf w/tremolo
Gtr. 5 (Acoustic)
Riff A
end Riff A
P.M. throughout

w/Riff A (Gtr. 5)
Em
C
Gtr. 2
Gtr. 4
w/Rhy. Fig. 1 (Gtrs. 1 & 2)
D.S. 𝄋 al Coda
G
D7/G
G
D7/G
5. We've been far,
Gtr. 4
Gtr. 4 out
Coda
G
Outro:
w/Rhy. Fig. 3 (Gtrs. 1 & 2)
Am
C
sad?
Gtrs. 1 & 2
Gtr. 6 (Elec.)
mf w/slight dist.

Verse 3:
You get down, real low down.
You listen to Coltrane, derail your own train.
Well, who hasn't been there before?

Verse 4:
I come 'round, around the hard way.
Bring you comics in bed, scrape the mold off the bread,
And serve you French toast again.

Pre-Chorus 2:
Well, o.k., I still get stoned.
I'm not the kind of girl you'd take home.
(To Chorus:)

Verse 5:
We've been far, far away from here.
Put on a poncho, played for mosquitoes,
And everywhere in between.

Pre-Chorus 3:
Well, o.k., we get along.
So what if right now everything's wrong?
(To Chorus:)

IRONIC

Lyrics by
ALANIS MORISSETTE

Music by
ALANIS MORISSETTE and GLEN BALLARD

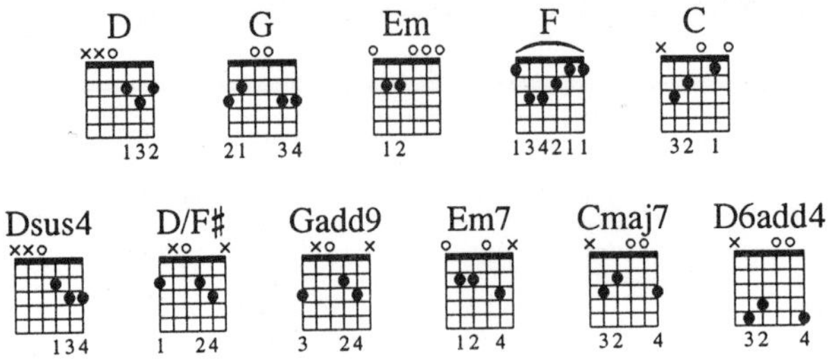

D
G
Em
F
C
Dsus4
D/F#
Gadd9
Em7
Cmaj7
D6add4

Gtrs. 1, 4 & 5: Capo IV

Intro

Moderately Slow ♩ = 86

Emaj7
*(Cmaj7)
F#6add4
(D6add4)
Emaj7
(Cmaj7)
Hey, I, I, whoa ho, I.
Gtr. 1
(acous.)
mf w/ fingers
let ring throughout

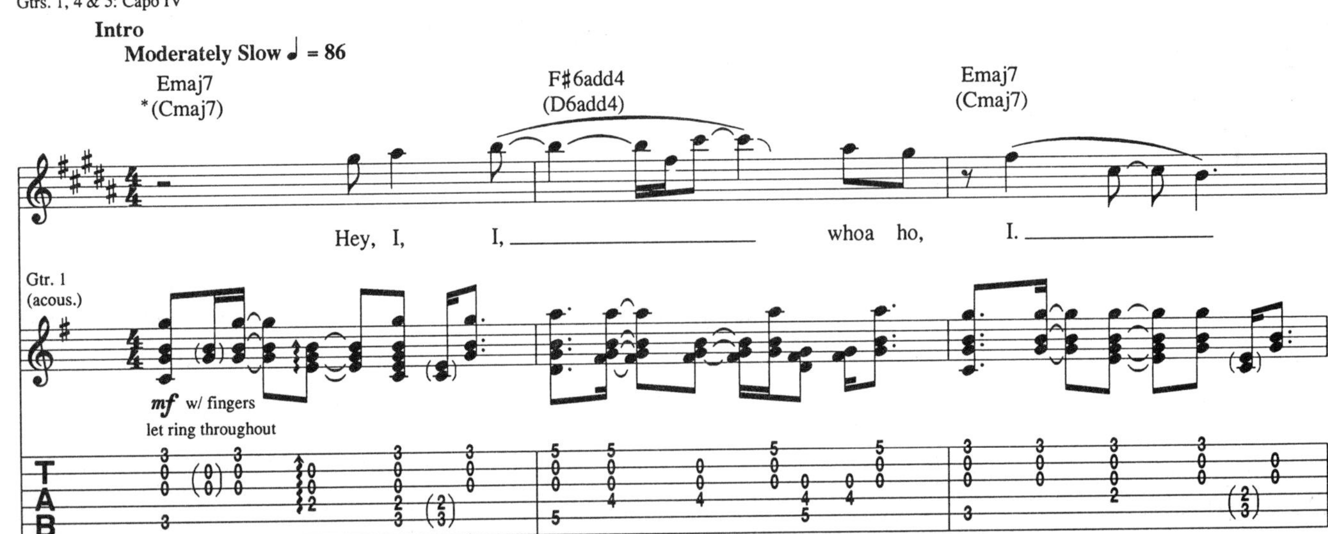

* Symbols in parentheses represent chord names respective to capoed guitars.
Symbols above reflect actual sounding chords.

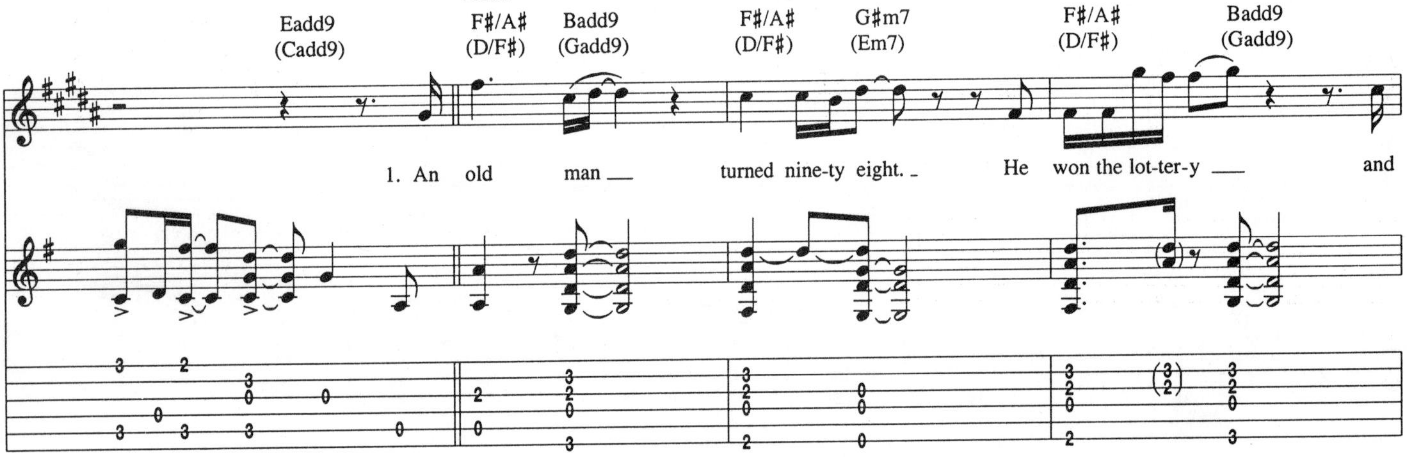

Verse
Eadd9
(Cadd9)
F#/A#
(D/F#)
Badd9
(Gadd9)
F#/A#
(D/F#)
G#m7
(Em7)
F#/A#
(D/F#)
Badd9
(Gadd9)
1. An old man turned nine-ty eight. He won the lot-ter-y and

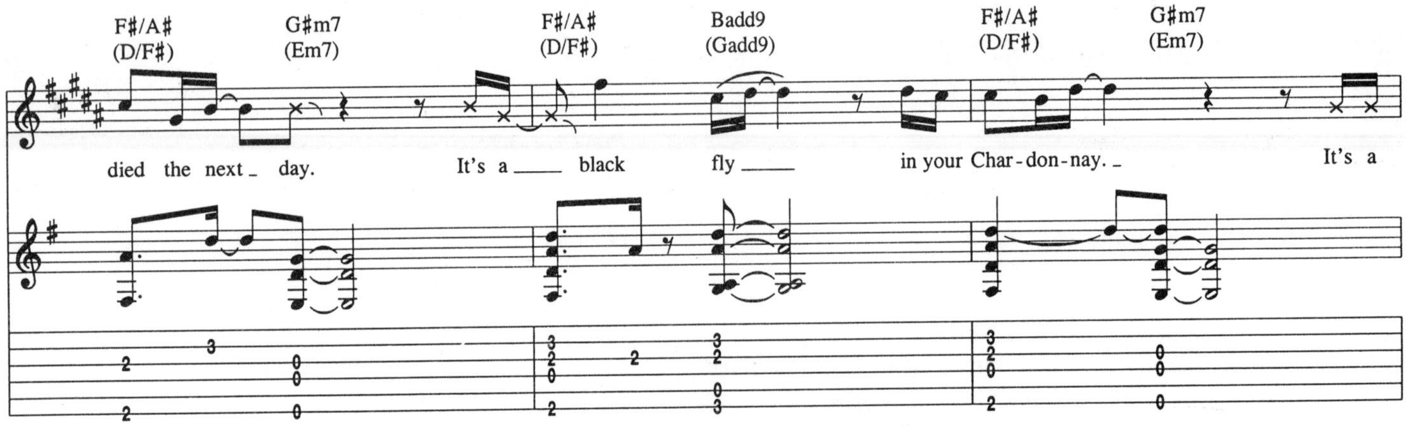

F#/A#
(D/F#)
G#m7
(Em7)
F#/A#
(D/F#)
Badd9
(Gadd9)
F#/A#
(D/F#)
G#m7
(Em7)
died the next day. It's a black fly in your Char-don-nay. It's a

Pre-Chorus
F♯/A♯
(D/F♯)
Badd9
(Gadd9)
G♯m7
(Em7)
death row par - don two min-utes too late. And is-n't it i - ron-ic? Don't cha
Chorus
D
G
Em
Rhy. Fig. 1
Gtr. 1
End Rhy. Fig. 1
think? It's like rain on your wed-ding day. It's a free ride
Rhy. Fig. 1A
Gtr. 2 (elec.)
End Rhy. Fig. 1A
(cont. in slash)
f w/ dist.
Gtrs. 1 & 2: w/ Rhy. Figs. 1 & 1A, 2 times
F♯
(D)
B
(G)
G♯m
(Em)
when you've al - read - y paid. It's the good ad - vice
that you just did - n't take. And

Verse
Gtr. 4: w/ Riff A, 5 times
F C D Dsus4 D/F# Gadd9
Rhy. Fig. 2
End Rhy. Fig. 2
Rhy. Fig. 3
Gtrs. 1 & 5 (acous.)
Gtr. 1
mf
who would of thought, it fig-ures?
2. Mis-ter Play It Safe was a-
Gtr. 2
Rhy. Fig. 2A
End Rhy. Fig. 2A
Gtr. 3 (elec.)
mf w/ dist.
divisi
Gtr. 2 tacet
Gtrs. 1 & 5: w/ Rhy. Fig. 3, 3 times, simile
D/F# Em7 F#/A# (D/F#) Badd9 (Gadd9) F#/A# (D/F#) G#m7 (Em7)
End Rhy. Fig. 3
fraid to fly. He packed his suit - case and kissed his kids good-bye. He wait-ed his
Gtr. 3
F#/A# (D/F#) Badd9 (Gadd9) F#/A# (D/F#) G#m7 (Em7) F#/A# (D/F#) Badd9 (Gadd9)
whole damn life to take that flight. And as the plane crashed down he thought, "Well
Riff A
Gtr. 4 (elec.)
mf w/ clean tone & chorus
let ring
TAB

Pre-Chorus

Gtrs. 1 & 5: w/ Rhy. Fig. 3, simile

F♯/A♯ (D/F♯) G♯m7 (Em7) F♯/A♯ (D/F♯) Badd9 (Gadd9) F♯/A♯ (D/F♯) G♯m7 (Em7)

is-n't this nice?" And is-n't it i - ron-ic? Don't cha think? It's like rain

(7) 7 9 9 9 7 7 7

Chorus

Gtrs. 3, 4 & 5 tacet
Gtrs. 1 & 2: w/ Rhy. Figs. 1 & 1A, 3 times

F♯ (D) B (G) F♯ (D) G♯m (Em) F♯ (D) B (G)

on your wed-ding day. It's a free ride when you've

F♯ (D) G♯m (Em) F♯ (D) B (G)

al - read - y paid. It's the good ad - vice that you

To Coda

Gtrs. 1 & 2: w/ Rhy. Figs. 2 & 2A, simile

F♯ (D) G♯m (Em) A (F) E (C) F♯ (D) F♯sus4 (Dsus4)

just did - nt take. And who would of thought? It fig - ures. Well,

Bridge

Gtr. 2 tacet

Cmaj7 D6add4

Rhy. Fig. 4 — End Rhy. Fig. 4

Gtr. 1

life has a fun-ny way of sneak-ing up on you when you think ev - 'ry - thing's o - kay and

Rhy. Fig. 4A — End Rhy. Fig. 4A

Gtr. 4

3	0	3	3	5	5	5	7	5
0		0	0	0	0	0	0	0
0	0	0	0	0	0	0	0	0
2	2	2	2	4	4	4	4	4
3	3	3	3	5	5	5	5	5

Gtrs. 1 & 4: w/ Rhy. Figs. 4 & 4A, 1 1/2 times, simile
Emaj7
(Cmaj7)
F♯6add4
(D6add4)
Emaj7
(Cmaj7)
ev-'ry-thing's go-ing right.
And life has a fun-ny way of helping you out
Gtr. 3
F♯6add4
(D6add4)
Emaj7
(Cmaj7)
Gtr. 1
(cont. in notation)
when you think ev-'ry-thing's gone wrong and ev-'ry-thing blows up in your face.
3. A
Gtr. 3
Gtr. 4
Gtrs. 1 & 4
Verse
Gtr. 4: w/ Riff A, 3 1/2 times
Gtrs. 1 & 5: w/ Rhy. Fig. 3, 3 1/2 times, simile
Gtr. 3 tacet
F♯/A♯
(D/F♯)
Badd9
(Gadd9)
F♯/A♯
(D/F♯)
G♯m7
(Em7)
F♯/A♯
(D/F♯)
Badd9
(Gadd9)
traf-fic jam when you're al-read-y late, a no smok - ing sign on your
Gtr. 3

F♯/A♯ (D/F♯) G♯m7 (Em7) F♯/A♯ (D/F♯) Badd9 (Gadd9)
cig - a - rette break. It's like ten thou - sand spoons when all you
F♯/A♯ (D/F♯) G♯m7 (Em7) F♯/A♯ (D/F♯) Badd9 (Gadd9)
need is a knife. It's meet - ing the man of my dreams, and then meet -
Pre-Chorus
Gtr. 4: w/ Riff A, 2 times
D/F♯ Em7 F♯/A♯ (D/F♯) Badd9 (Gadd9)
Gtrs. 1 & 5
(Gtr. 1, cont. in notation)
ing his beau - ti - ful wife. And is - n't it i - ron - ic? Don't cha
Gtr. 5
mf
let ring
Gtr. 4
w/ bar
Gtr. 1
D.S. al Coda
F♯/A♯ (D/F♯) G♯m7 (Em7) F♯/A♯ (D/F♯) Badd9 (Gadd9) F♯/A♯ (D/F♯) G♯m7 (Em7)
think? A lit - tle too i - ron - ic, and yeah I real - ly do think. It's like rain
let ring

Coda
Bridge
Gtr. 2 tacet
* Gtrs. 1 & 4: w/ Rhy. Figs. 4 & 4A, 3 1/2 times, simile
F♯ F♯sus4
(D) (Dsus4)
Emaj7
(Cmaj7)
F♯6add4
(D6add4)
Emaj7
(Cmaj7)
And _ you know life has a fun-ny way _ of sneak-ing up on
Gtr. 3
* Gtr. 1 loosely doubled by Gtr. 5, next 7 meas.
F♯6add4
(D6add4)
Emaj7
(Cmaj7)
F♯6add4
(D6add4)
Emaj7
(Cmaj7)
you. _ Ooh, life has a fun-ny, fun-ny way _ of help-ing you out, _ help-ing you
**string noise
Free Time
out.
Gtr. 3
rit.
Gtr. 5
rit.
let ring
Gtr. 1
rit.
pp
Gtr. 4
rit.
pp

ONE OF US

Words and Music by
ERIC BAZILIAN

w/Rhy. Fig. 1 (Gtrs. 1 & 2)
E5 C5 G5 G5V D5 E5 C5
Rhy. Fig. 1A
Gtr. 3
w/distortion
*Throughout Rhy. Fig. 2A & Rhy. Fill 2A, when H is indicated don't strike chord. Hammer on ④ while letting ⑤ ring.
Hey, yeah,
G5 G5V D5 E5 C5 G5 G5V D end Rhy. Fig. 1A
yeah, yeah, yeah, yeah.
(Gtr. 3 out)
Verses 1 & 2:
E5 C5 G5 G5V D5 Em C
Rhy. Fill 2A
end Rhy. Fill 2A
sl.
1. If God had a name,
God had a face,
Gtrs. 1 & 2
Rhy. Fill 2
(Gtr. 2 out)
end Rhy. Fill 2
Gtr. 1
mp
P.M.
G D5 Em C G D5
what would it be and would you call it to his face if you were faced with him in
what would it look like and would you want to see, if see - ing meant that you would

Em
C
G
D5
Em
C
all his ___ glo - ry? What would you ask if you had just one ques-tion?
have to be - lieve ___ in things like heav - en and in Je - sus and the saints and
Pre-Chorus:
2nd time w/Riff A (Gtr. 3)
G
D5
C
Csus2
D
Dsus
D
all the proph - ets? And And yeah, yeah, God is ___ great.
Rhy. Fig. 2
w/Rhy. Fill 1 (Gtr. 2)
C
Csus2
D5
C
Csus2
Dsus
D
Yeah, yeah, God is ___ good. ___ Yeah, yeah, yeah, yeah, yeah. What if
end Rhy. Fig. 2
mf
Riff A
Gtr. 3
1.
2.

Chorus:
w/Rhy. Figs. 1 (Gtrs. 1 & 2) & 1A (Gtr. 3)
w/Bkgd. Voc. Fig. 1 3rd time only
E5 C5 G5 G5V D5 E5 C5 G5 G5V D5
God was one of us, just a slob like one of us, just a
E5 C5 G5 G5V D5
stran - ger on the bus try'n' to make his way ___ home?
1.
w/Rhy. Fills 2 (Gtrs. 1 & 2) & 2A (Gtr. 3)
E5 C5 G5 G5V D5
2. If
2.
w/Rhy. Fill 3 (Gtrs. 1 & 2)
w/Rhy. Fig. 1A (Gtr. 3) 1st 2 bars only
E5 C5 G5 G5V D5
___ home? ___
1. He's try'n' to make his way ___ home, ___
2. Just try'n' to make his way ___ home, ___
w/Rhy. Figs. 1 (Gtrs. 1 & 2) (1st 2 bars only)
& 1A (Gtr. 3) (complete)
E5 C5 G5 G5V D5
back up to heav-en all a -
like a ho - ly roll-in'
w/Rhy. Fill 3 (Gtrs. 1 & 2)
E5 C5 G5 G5V D5
lone. No - bod - y call - ing on the phone,
stone. Back up to heav-en all a - lone,
w/Rhy. Fill 2
E5 C5 G5 G5V D5
To Coda
'cept for the Pope, may - be, in
just try'n' to make his way ___
Guitar Solo:
w/Rhy. Fig. 2 (Gtr. 2)
C5 D5 C5
Gtr. 3
Rome.
A.H.
(8va)
Gtr. 1
w/distortion
1/2
1/2
Bkgd. Voc. Fig. 1
Sing 7 times
Oh. ___
Rhy. Fill 3
Gtrs. 1 & 2

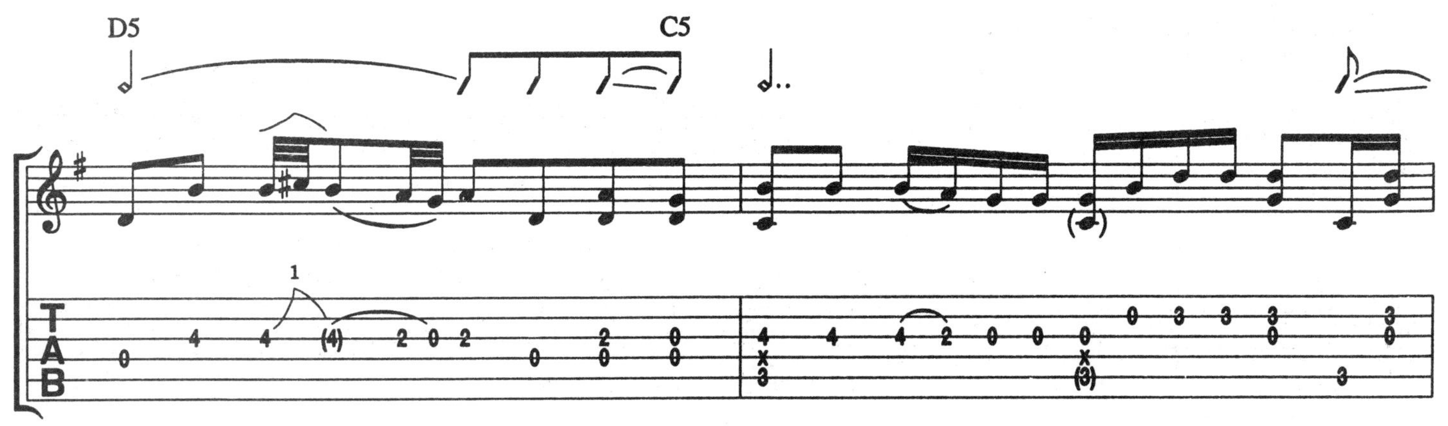
D5
C5
1

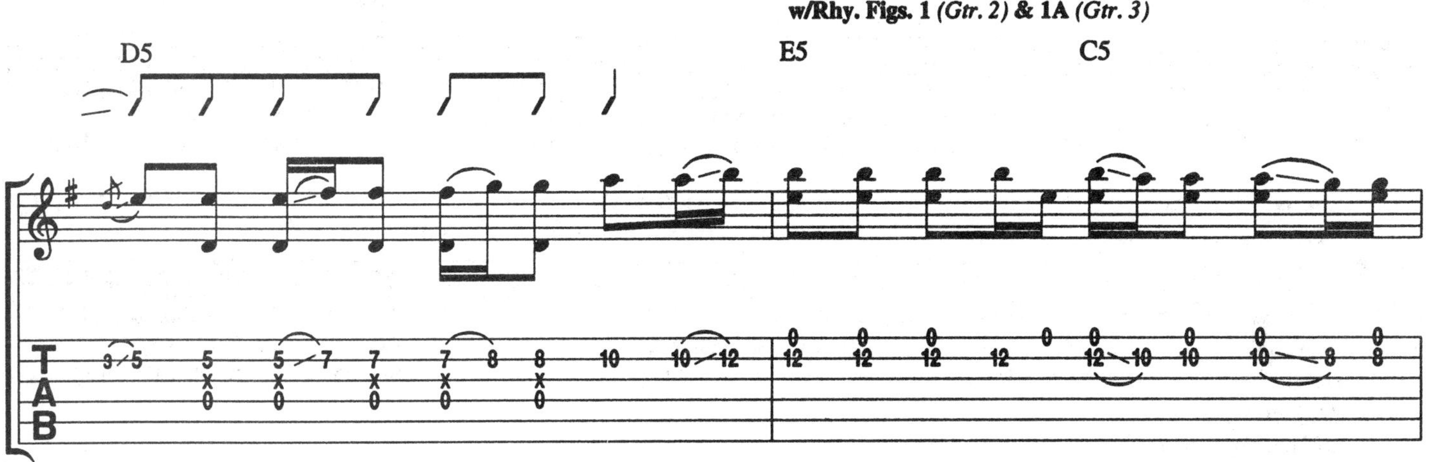
w/Rhy. Figs. 1 (Gtr. 2) & 1A (Gtr. 3)
D5
E5
C5

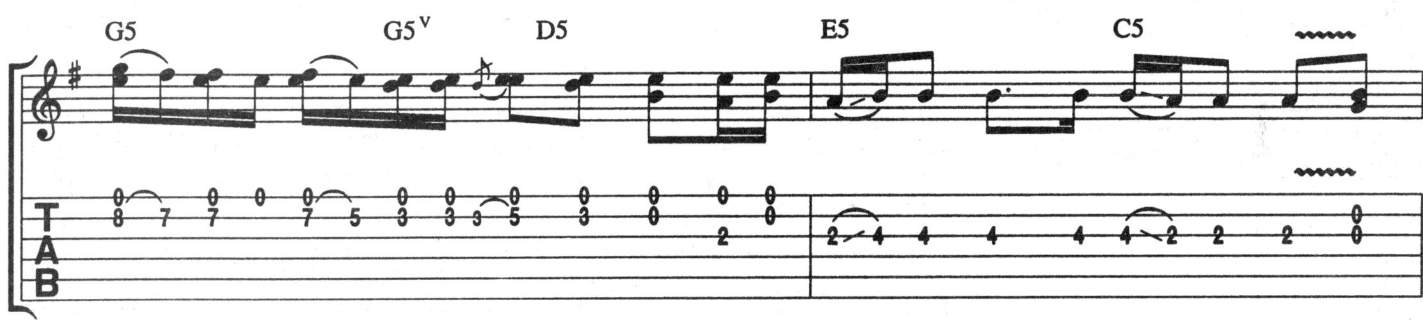
G5
G5v
D5
E5
C5

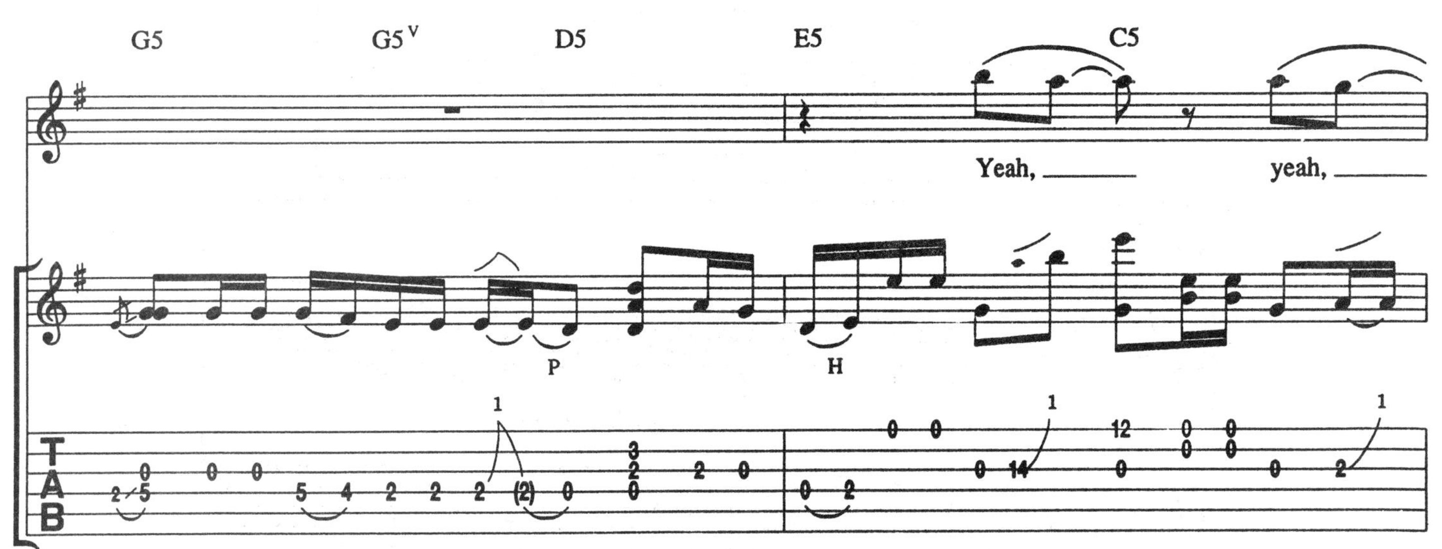
G5
G5v
D5
E5
C5
Yeah,
yeah,
P
H
1

w/Rhy. Fills 2 (Gtr. 2) & 2A (Gtr. 3)
G5
G5V
D5
E5
C5
yeah,
yeah.
Pre-Chorus:
G5
G5V
D5
Csus2
And
yeah,
yeah,
mp semi-clean tone
D5
C
Csus2
D5
God
is
great.
Yeah,
yeah,
God
is
good.
D.S. 𝄋 (take 2nd ending) al Coda
w/Rhy. Fill 1 (Gtrs. 1 & 2)
C
Csus2
Dsus
D
Yeah,
yeah,
yeah,
yeah,
yeah.
What
if

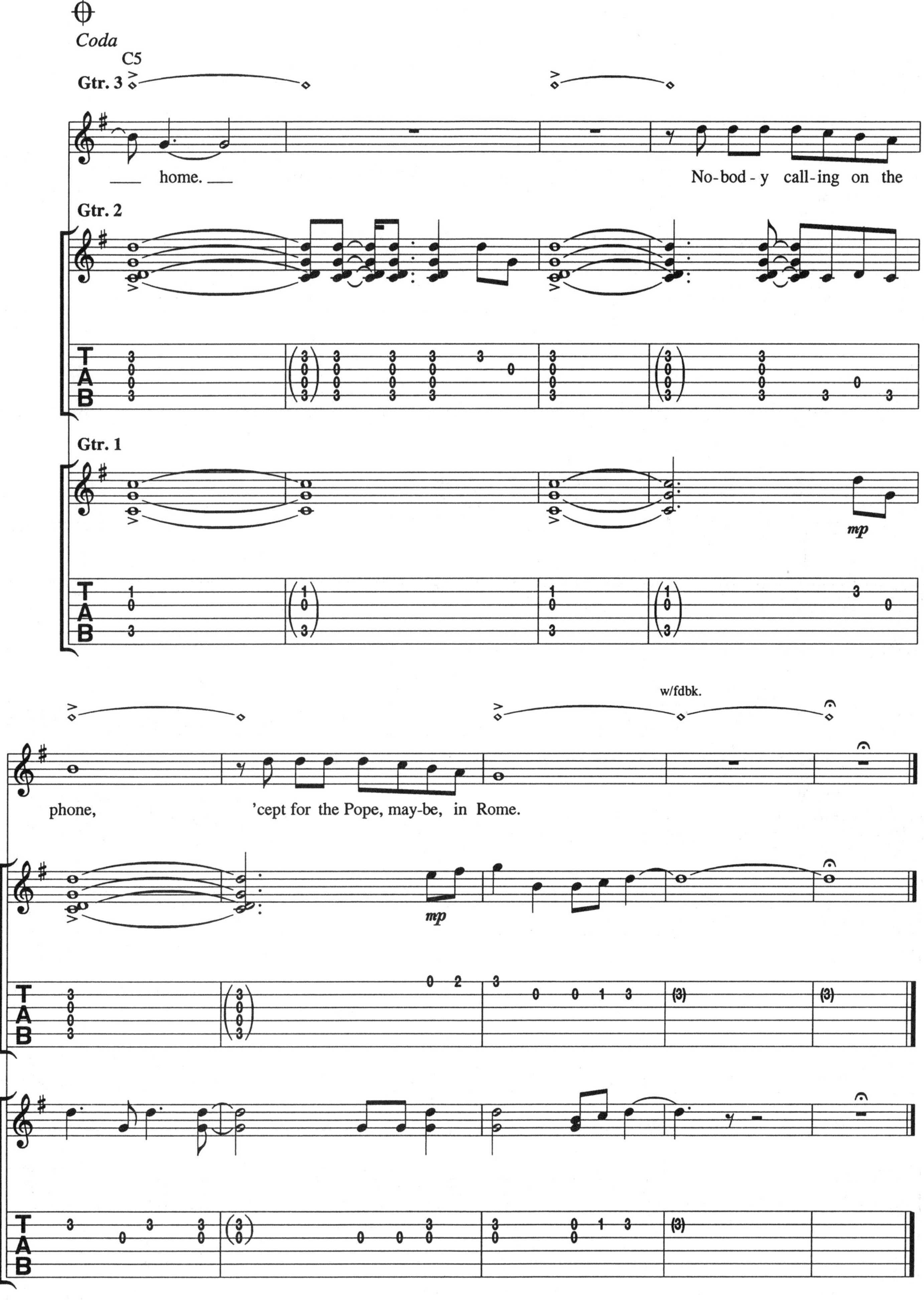
Coda
C5
Gtr. 3
home.
No-bod-y call-ing on the
Gtr. 2
Gtr. 1
mp
w/fdbk.
phone,
'cept for the Pope, may-be, in Rome.
mp

JUST A GIRL

Words and Music by
GWEN STEFANI and THOMAS DUMONT
Moderate rock ♩ = 110
Intro:
N.C.(D)
Gtr. 1 (Dist.)
Rhy. Fig. 1
end Rhy. Fig. 1
P.M.
mf
* Verses 1 & 2:
w/Rhy. Fig. 1 (Gtr. 1) 3 times
1. Take this pink rib - bon off my eyes. I'm ex - posed and it's no big sur - prise. Don't ya think I know ex - act - ly where I stand? This world is forc - ing me to hold your hand. 'Cause
2. See additional lyrics
*Cont. double-time feel from Chorus 1.
Rhy. Fig. 2
Gtrs. 1 & 2
end Rhy. Fig. 2
P.M.
Double-time feel
Chorus 1, 2 & 3:
Bm
A
G
A
I'm just a girl, oh, lit - tle ol' me. Well,
2.3. See additional lyrics
Rhy. Fig. 3
end Rhy. Fig. 3
TAB

Bm
A
G
A
don't let me out of your sight. Oh,
Rhy. Fig. 4
end Rhy. Fig. 4
w/Rhy. Fig. 3 (Gtrs. 1 & 2) 2 times, simile
Substitute w/Rhy. Fig. 4
(Gtrs. 1 & 2) 2nd and 3rd times, simile
To Coda
I'm just a girl, all pret-ty and pe - tite. So don't let me have an - y rights.
1.
G5
C5
w/Rhy. Fig. 1 (Gtr. 1)
N.C.(D)
Oh, I've had it up to here. 2. The
(Oh.)
Rhy. Fig. 5
Gtrs. 1 & 2
Gtr. 2 out
end Rhy. Fig. 5
P.M.
2.
w/Rhy. Fig. 3 (Gtrs. 1 & 2)
w/Rhy. Fig. 4 (Gtrs. 1 & 2) simile
I'm just a girl, take a good look at me. Just your typ - i - cal pro - to - type.
w/Rhy. Fig. 5 (Gtrs. 1 & 2)
Oh, I've had it up to here.
(Oh.)

Interlude:
w/Rhy. Fig. 3 (Gtrs. 1 & 2) 4 times, simile
Bm A G A Bm A G A
Riff 1
*Gtr. 3
end Riff 1
mf
*Keyboard arr. for gtr. w/envelope filter.
Bm A/C♯* G/D* A/E* Bm A G A
Gtr. 3 out
Riff 2
end Riff 2
*Chord inversions implied by bass.
end double-time feel
w/Rhy. Fig. 5 (Gtrs. 1 & 2)
G5 C5
w/Rhy. Fig. 1 (Gtrs. 1 & 2)
N.C.(D)
Oh, am I mak - ing my - self clear?
(Oh,)
Verse 3:
w/Rhy. Fig. 1 (Gtrs. 1 & 2) 2 times
3. I'm just a girl. I'm just a girl in the world.
w/Rhy. Fig. 2 (Gtrs. 1 & 2)
D.S. al Coda
That's all that you'll let me be. 3. Oh,
Chorus 4:
w/Rhy. Fig. 3 (Gtrs. 1 & 2) 4 times, simile
w/Riff 1 (Gtr. 3)
w/Riff 2 (Gtr. 3)
Coda
Bm A G A Bm A
I'm just a girl, my a - pol - o - gies. What I've be - come is so bur - den-

Verse 2:
The moment that I step outside,
So many reasons for me to run and hide.
I can't do the little things I hold so dear.
It's all those little things that I fear.

Chorus 2:
'Cause I'm just a girl, I'd rather not be,
'Cause they won't let me drive late at night.
Oh, I'm just a girl. Guess I'm some kind of freak,
'Cause they all sit and stare with them eyes. Oh, . . .
(To Interlude:)

Chorus 3:
Oh, I'm just a girl, livin' in captivity.
Your rule of thumb makes me worry some.
Oh, I'm just a girl, oh, what's my destiny?
What I've succumbed to is making me numb. Oh . . .
(To Coda)

MY SISTER

Words and Music by
JULIANA HATFIELD

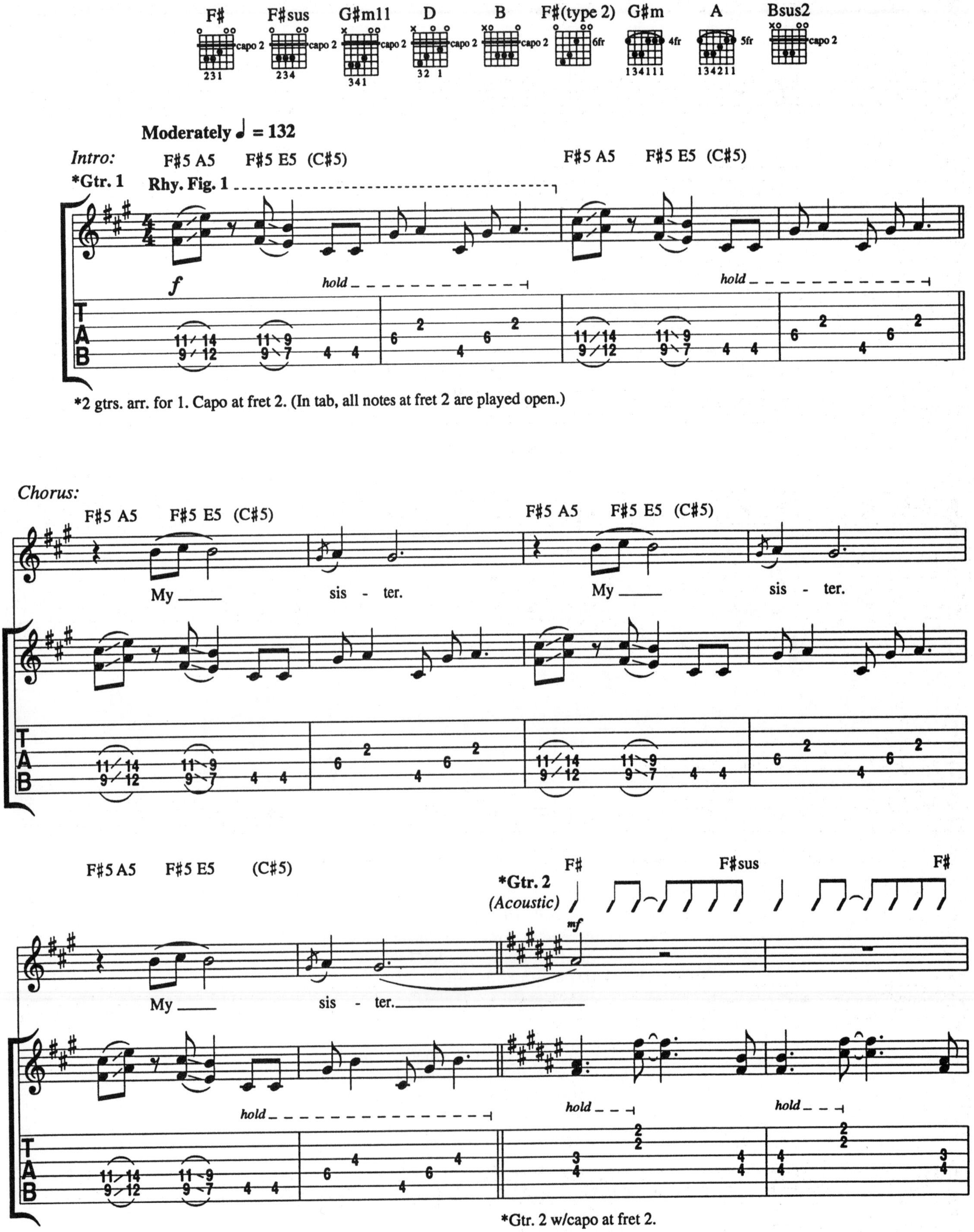

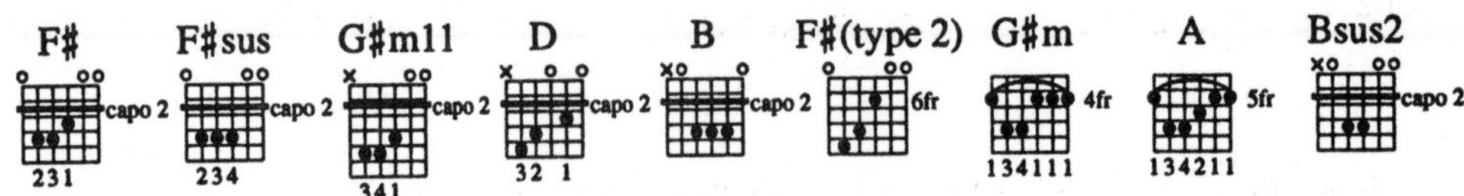

Moderately ♩ = 132

*2 gtrs. arr. for 1. Capo at fret 2. (In tab, all notes at fret 2 are played open.)

Chorus:

F♯5 A5 F♯5 E5 (C♯5) F♯5 A5 F♯5 E5 (C♯5)

My ___ sis - ter. My ___ sis - ter.

F♯5 A5 F♯5 E5 (C♯5) F♯ F♯sus F♯

*Gtr. 2 (Acoustic)

mf

My ___ sis - ter. ___

hold hold hold

*Gtr. 2 w/capo at fret 2.

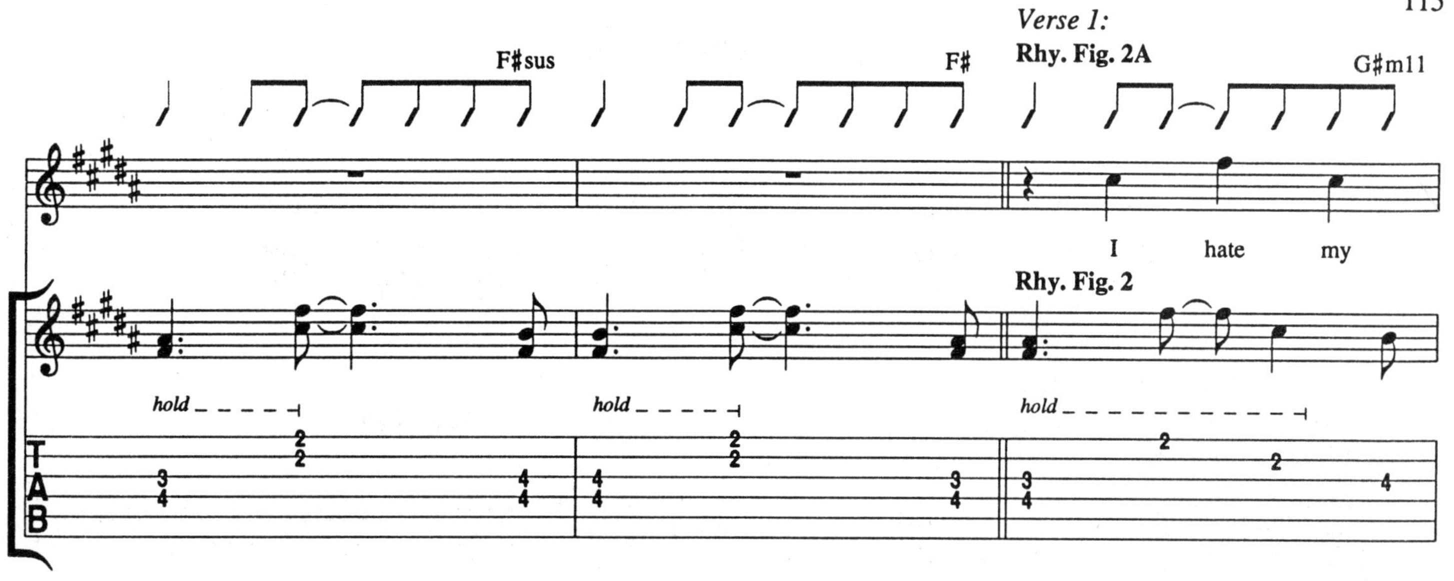
Verse 1:
Rhy. Fig. 2A
F#sus
F#
G#m11
I hate my
Rhy. Fig. 2
hold
hold
hold
T
A
B

(end Rhy. Fig. 2A)
D
B
F#
sis - - ter, she's such a bitch. She
(end Rhy. Fig. 2)
hold
hold
hold
T
A
B

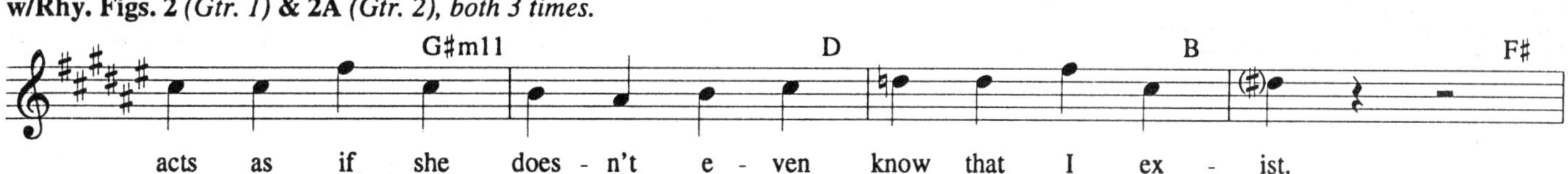
w/Rhy. Figs. 2 (Gtr. 1) & 2A (Gtr. 2), both 3 times.
G#m11
D
B
F#
acts as if she does - n't e - ven know that I ex - ist.

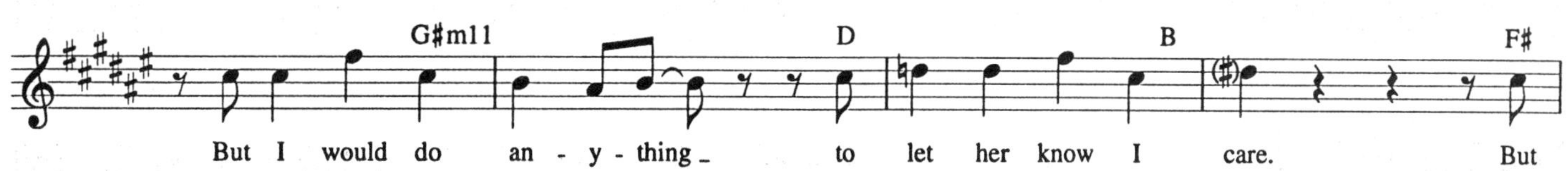
G#m11
D
B
F#
But I would do an - y - thing _ to let her know I care. But

G#m11
D
B
F#
I am on - ly talk - ing to _ my - self _ 'cause she _ is - n't _ there. _

w/Rhy. Fig. 1 *(Gtr. 1, 2 times)*

F♯5 A5 F♯5 E5 (C♯5)
F♯5 A5 F♯5 E5 (C♯5)
My sis - ter.

Verses 2 & 3:

w/Rhy. Figs. 2 *(Gtr. 1)* **& 2A** *(Gtr. 2), both 4 times.*

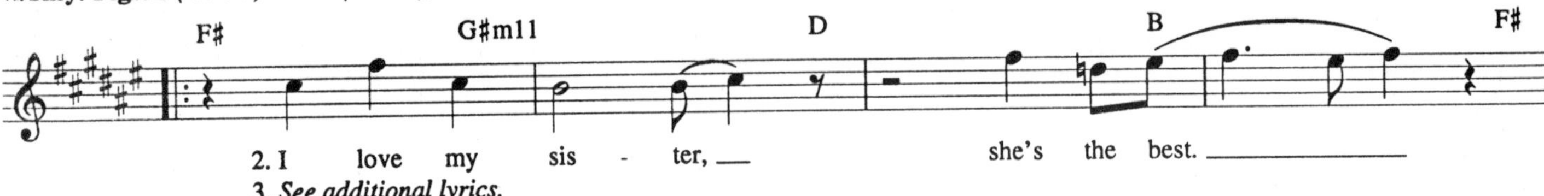
F♯ G♯m11 D B F♯
2. I love my sis - ter, she's the best.
3. See additional lyrics.

G♯m11 D B F♯
She's cool - er than an - y oth - er girl that I have ev - er met.

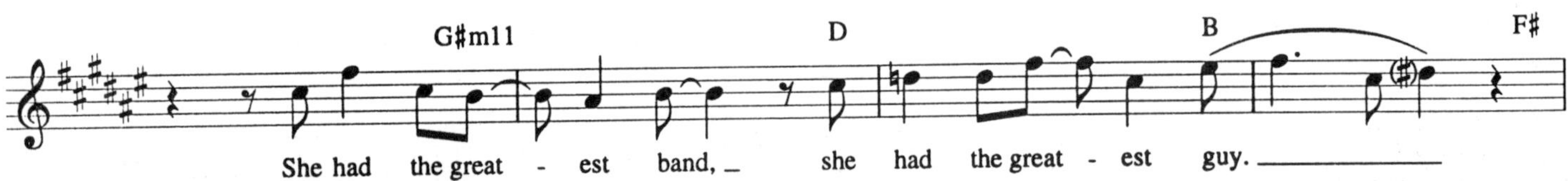
G♯m11 D B F♯
She had the great - est band, she had the great - est guy.

G♯m11 D B

She's good at ev - 'ry thing and does - n't e - ven try.

Interlude:

F♯ N.C. (F♯5) (E5) (F♯5) (E5)

Gtr. 3 **Riff A**

f 1/4 1/4

TAB: 4 4 | 2 4 4 /9 7 7 2 4 4 | 2 4 4 /9 7 7 2 4 4

Gtr. 4 **Riff A[1]**

f

TAB: 3 | 3 4 4 /6 5 5 6 3 | 3 4 4 /6 5 5 6 3

w/Riffs A *(Gtr. 3)* &A[1] *(Gtr. 4), both 6 times.*

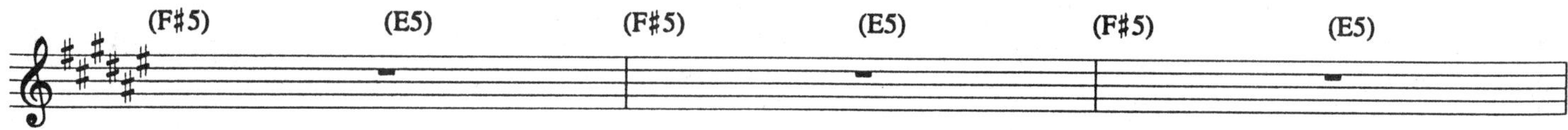

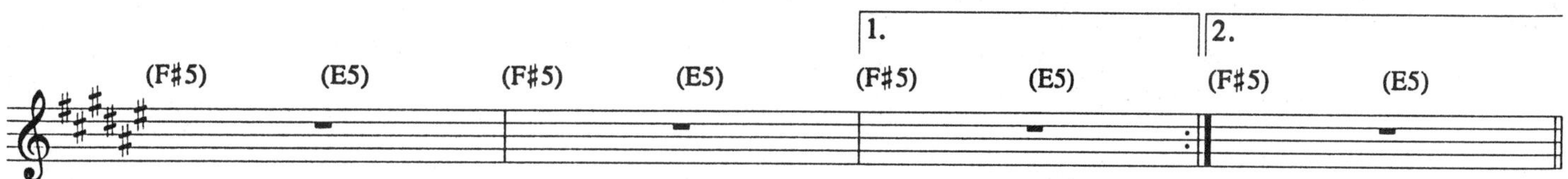

Verse 4:

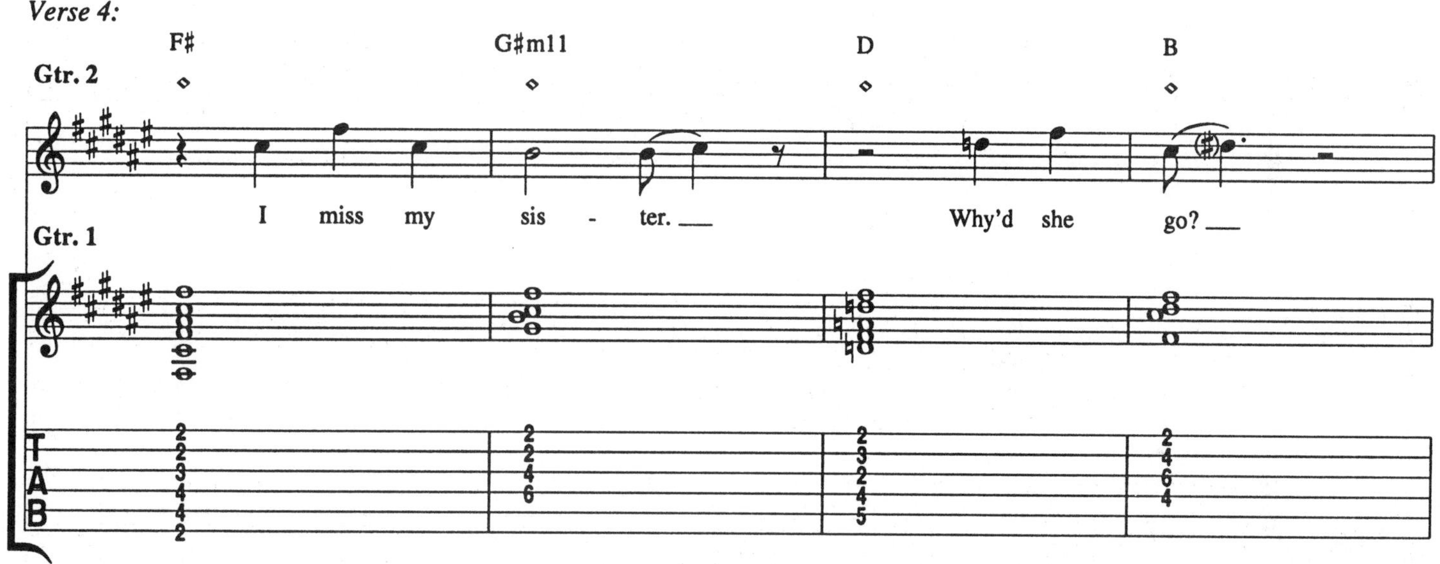

G♯m11
D
B
F♯
It was the Vi - 'lent Femmes _ and the Del - fue - gos. _ Be -
hold
hold
hold
hold

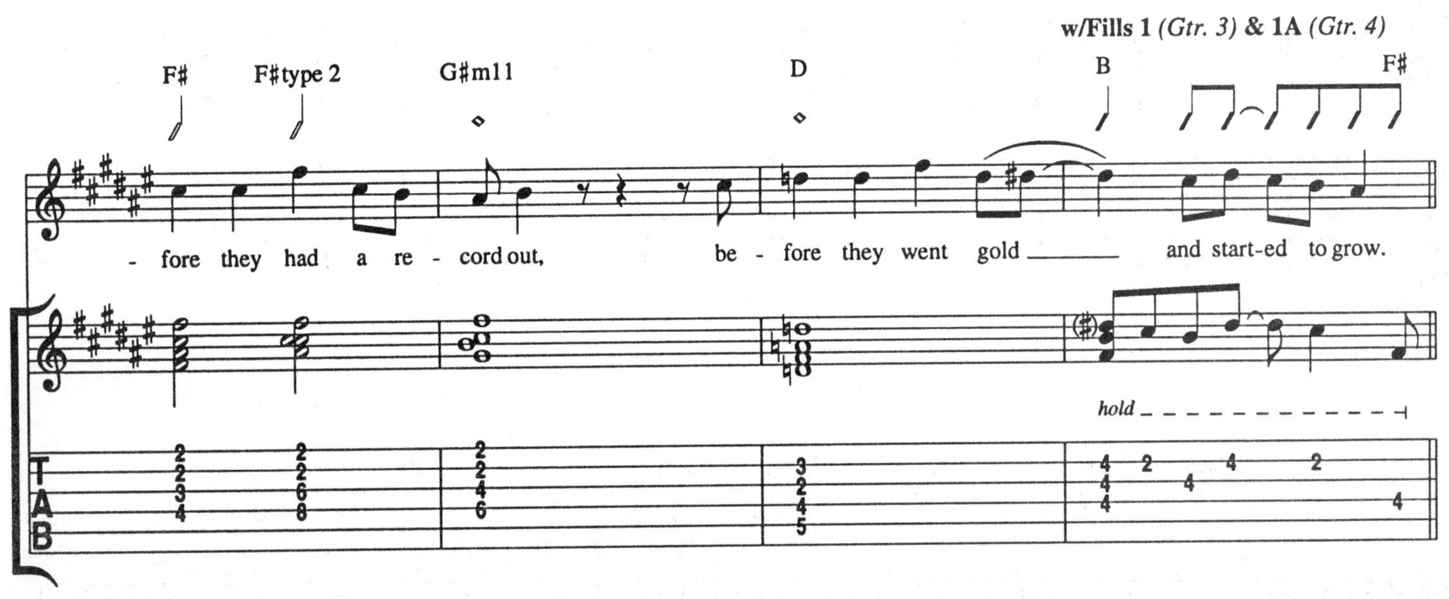
w/Fills 1 (Gtr. 3) & 1A (Gtr. 4)
F♯
F♯type 2
G♯m11
D
B
F♯
- fore they had a re - cord out, be - fore they went gold _____ and start-ed to grow.
hold

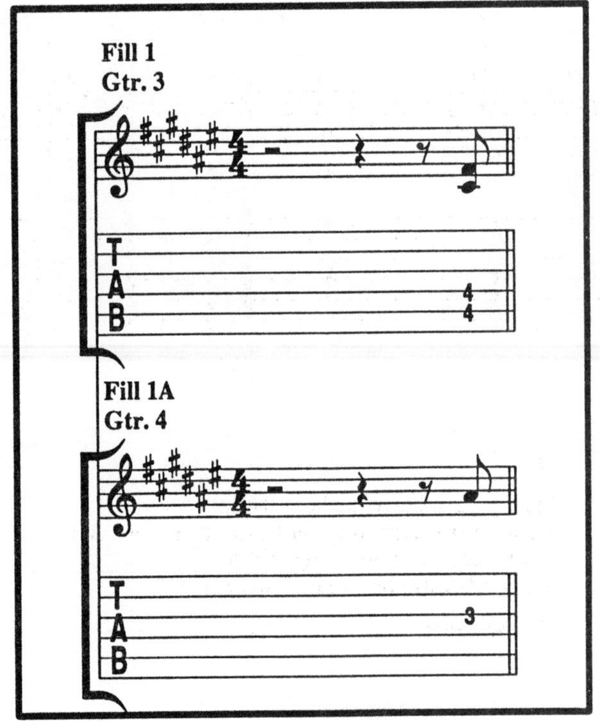
Fill 1
Gtr. 3
Fill 1A
Gtr. 4

Interlude:
w/Riffs A *(Gtr. 3)* **& A[1]** *(Gtr. 4), both 4 times.*

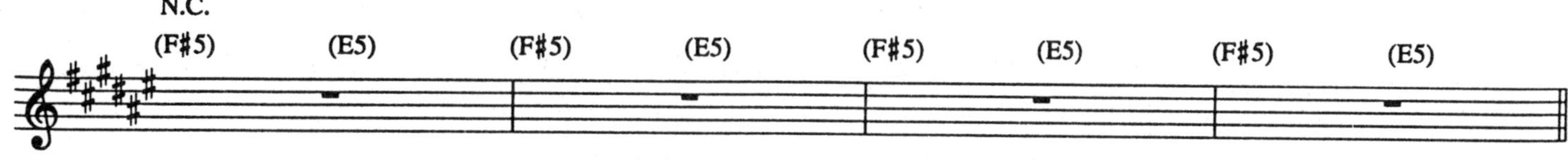

Outro:

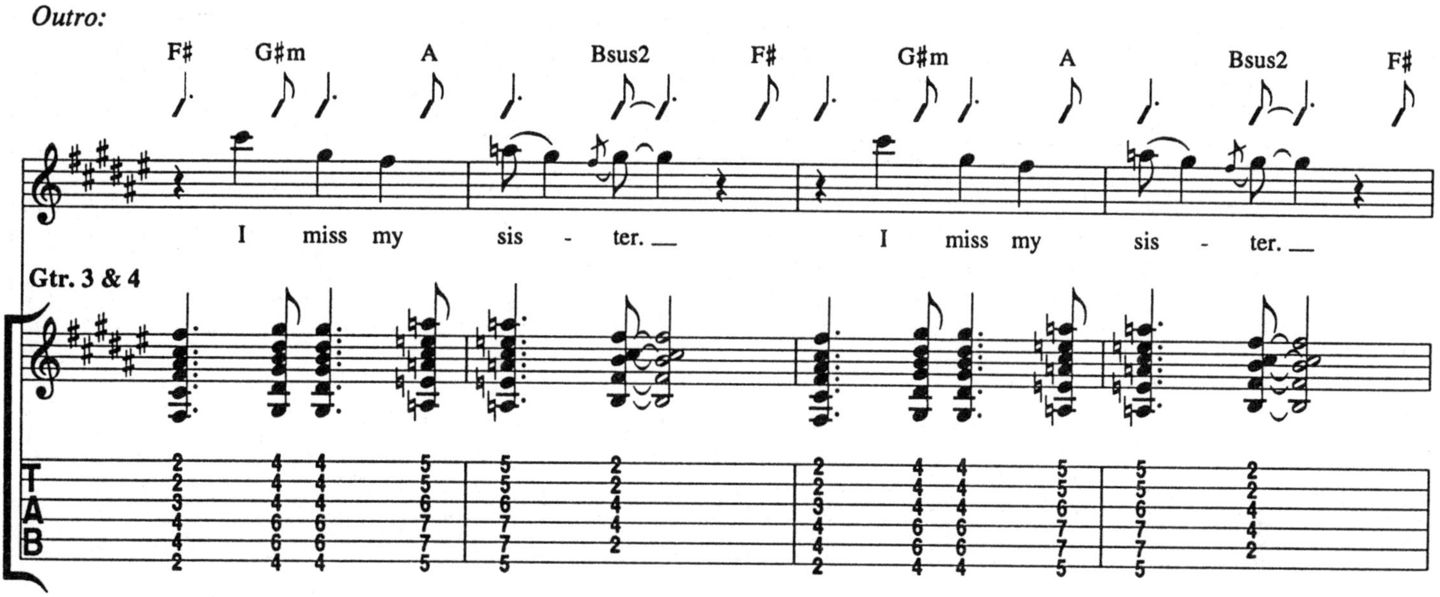

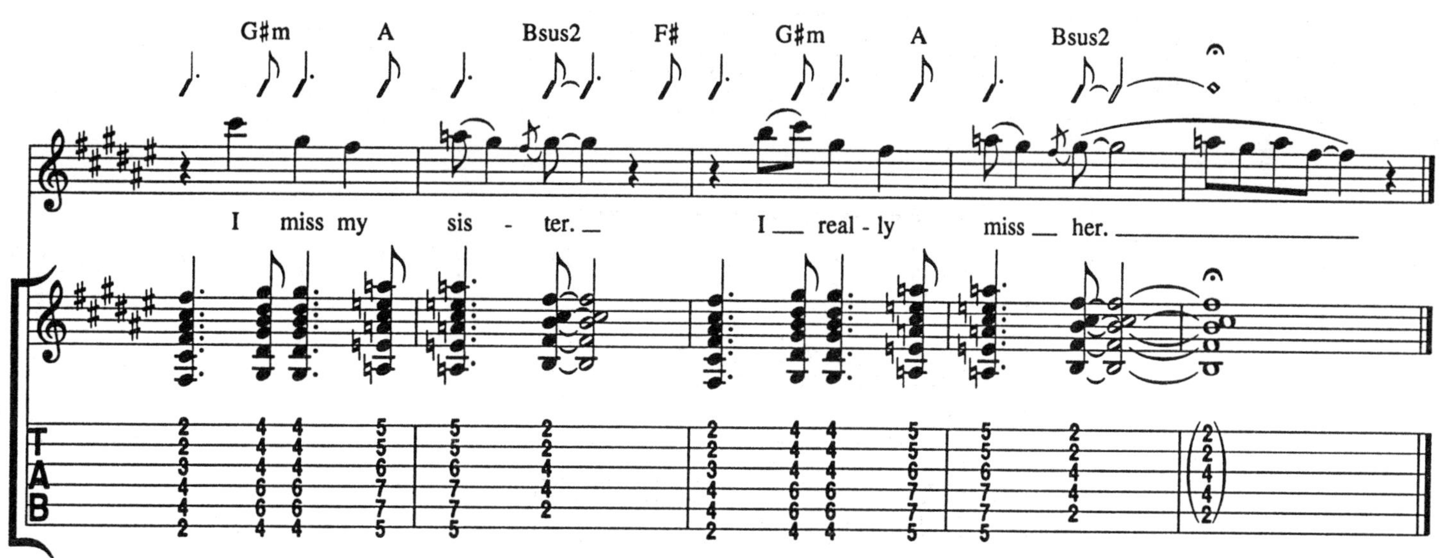

Verse 3:

She's got a wall around her nobody can climb.
She lets her ladder down for those who really shine.
I try to scale it but to me she's blind.
So I lit a firecracker, went off in my eye.

(To Interlude:)

PUSH IT

Words and Music by
DOUG ERIKSON, SHIRLEY MANSON,
STEVE MARKER and BUTCH VIG

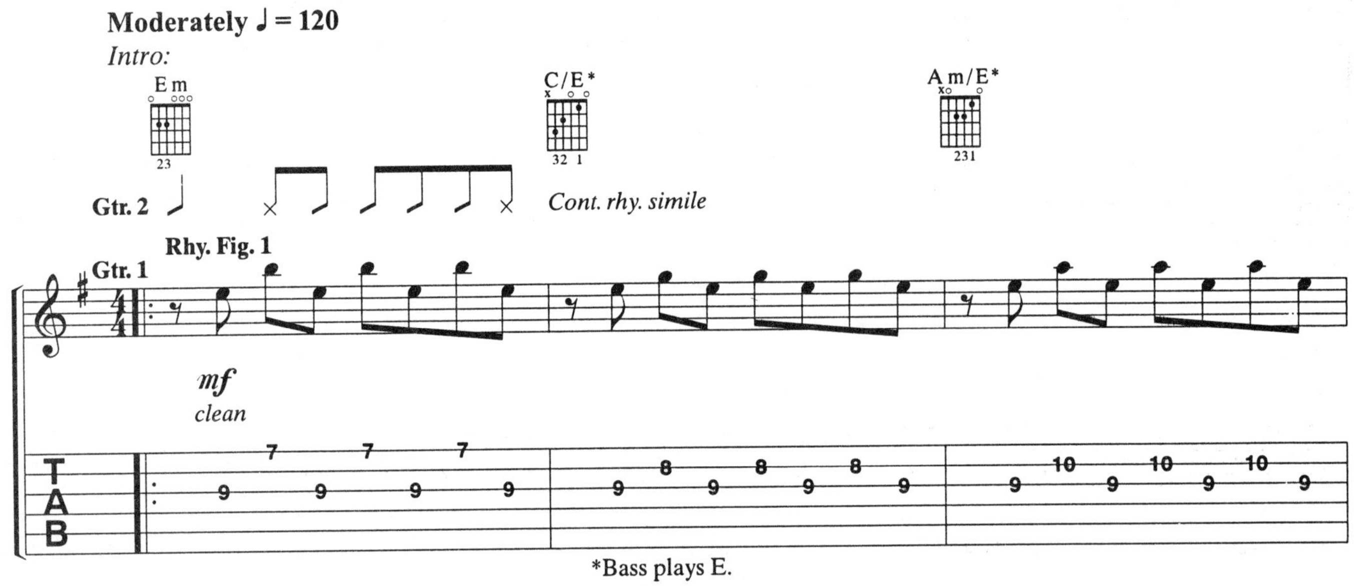

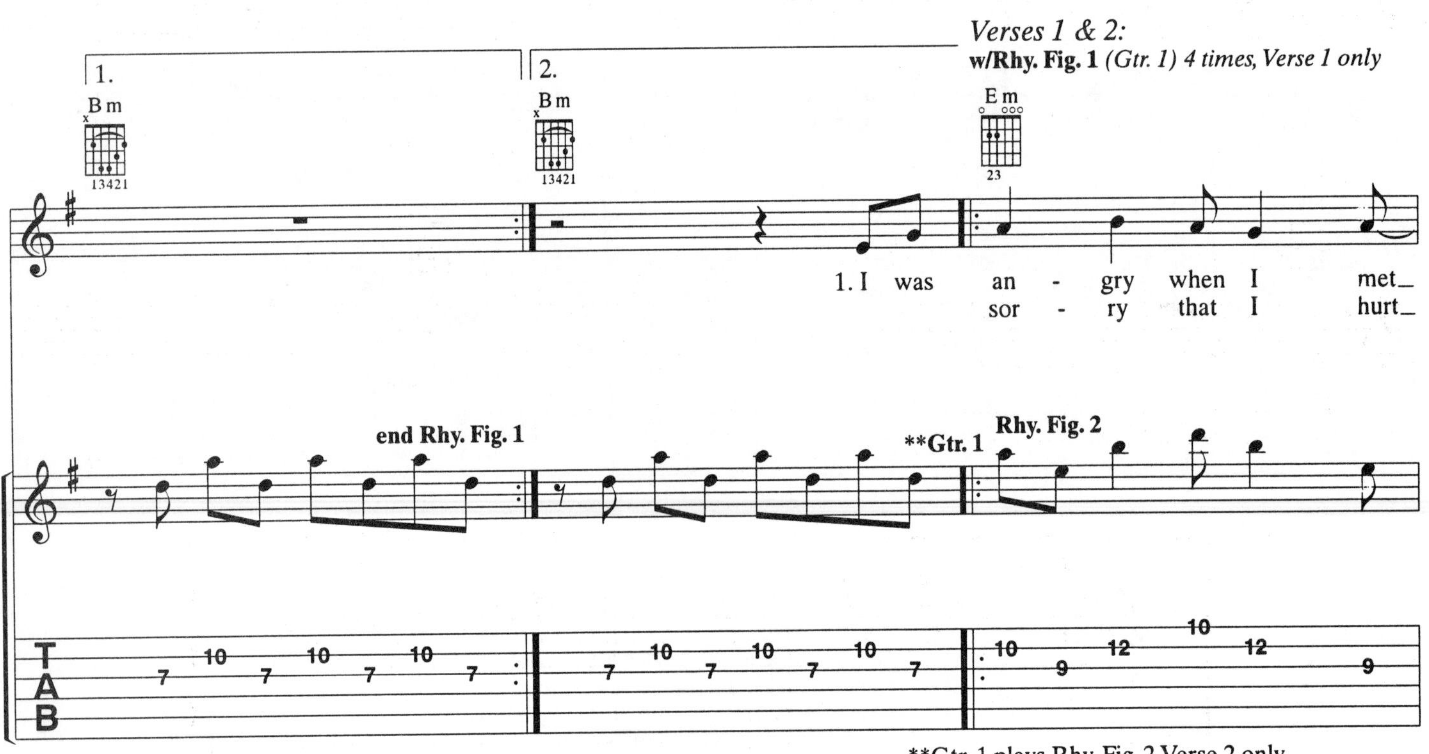

C/E*
Am/E*
Bm
you, I think I'm an - gry still. We can
you, please don't ask me why. I
end Rhy. Fig. 2
w/Rhy. Fig. 2 (Gtr. 1) 3 times, Verse 2 only
Em
try to talk it o - ver if you say you'll help me
want to see you hap - py, I want to see you
w/Fill 1 (Gtr. 3) 4 times
out. Don't wor - ry, ba - by, no
shine. Don't wor - ry, ba - by, don't
(Don't wor - ry, ba - by.)
need to fight. Don't wor - ry, ba - by,
be up - tight. Don't wor - ry, ba - by,
(Don't wor - ry,
Gtr. 3
Fill 1
mf w/dist.

C/E*
Am/E*
Bm
we'll be al - right.
we'll stay up all night.
ba - by.)
Pre-chorus:
A5
B5
C5
*Gtr. 4
Cont. rhy. simile
This is the noise that keeps me a - wake. My head ex - plodes and my
*Gtr. 4 w/wah wah.
Chorus:
D5
E5
C5
Gtr. 3
Cont. rhy. simile
Vocal Fig. 1
bod - y aches. (Whisper) Push it, make the beats go
Riff A
Gtr. 5
w/dist.
A5
D5
E5
end Vocal Fig. 1
fur - ther. Push it,
end Riff A

C5
A5
D5
5fr.
make the beats go fur - ther.

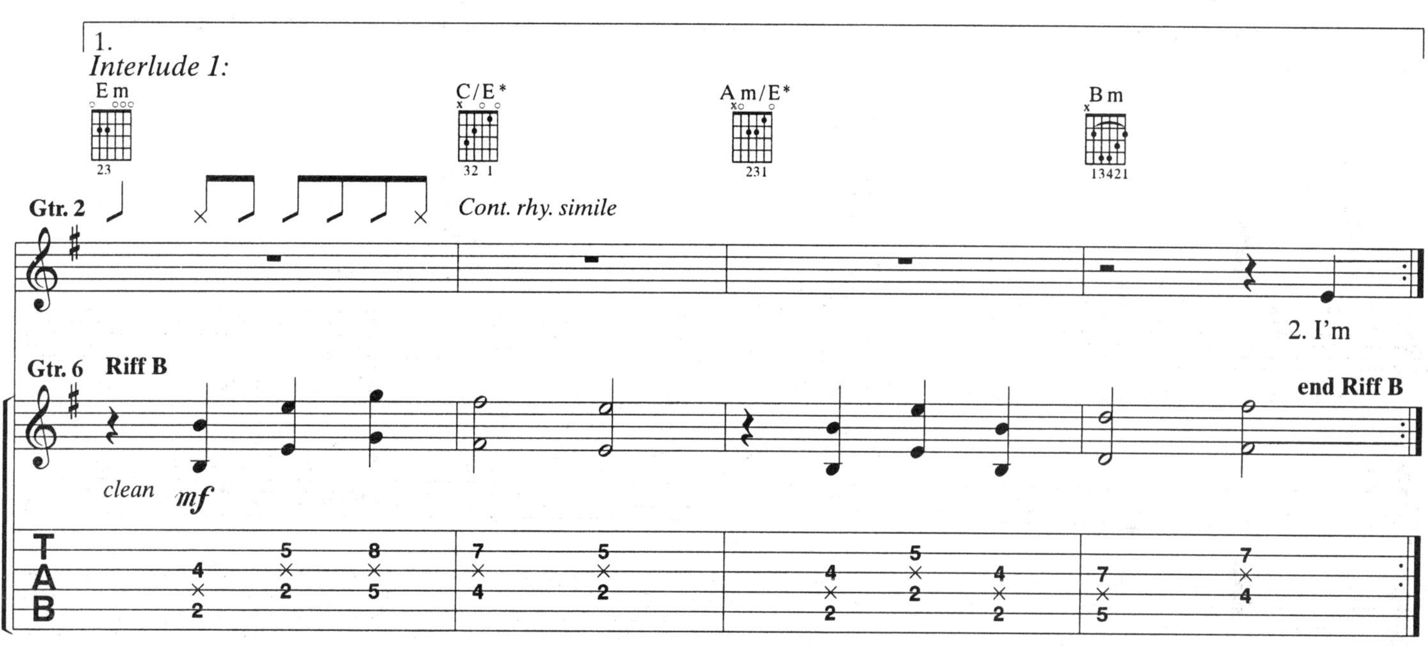
1.
Interlude 1:
Em
C/E*
Am/E*
Bm
Gtr. 2
Cont. rhy. simile
2. I'm
Gtr. 6
Riff B
end Riff B
clean
mf

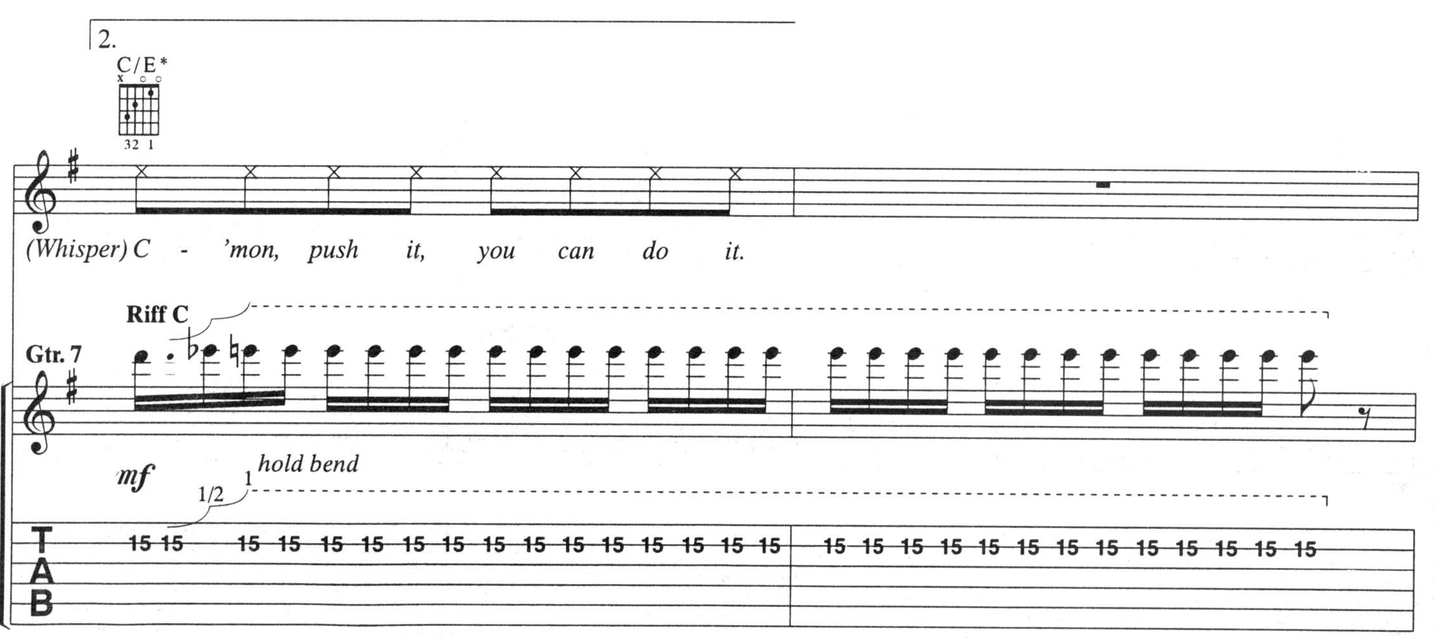
2.
C/E*
(Whisper) C - 'mon, push it, you can do it.
Riff C
Gtr. 7
mf
hold bend

Am/E*
Bm
C - 'mon, prove it, noth - ing to it.
end Riff C
hold bend
1/2
1
15 15 15 15 15 15 15 15 15 15 15 15 15 15
15 15 15 15 15 15 15 15 15 15 15 15 15
w/Riff C (Gtr. 7)
C/E*
Am/E*
C - 'mon, use it, let's get through it.
C - 'mon, push it, you can do it.
*Verse 3:
Bm
Em
C/E*
Don't wor - ry, ba - by,
(Don't wor - ry, ba - by.)
don't
*All gtrs. tacet.
Am/E*
Bm
Em
be up - tight.
Don't wor - ry, ba - by,
(Don't wor - ry,
C/E*
Am/E*
Bm
we'll stay up all night.
ba - by.)
Pre-chorus:
N.C.
This is the noise that keeps me a - wake.
My head ex - plodes and my

Chorus:
w/Riff A (Gtr. 5) & Vocal Fig. 1, Both 4 times
E5
C5
A5
Gtr. 3
Cont. rhy. simile
bod - y aches.
D5
5fr.
This is the noise that keeps me a - wake.
My head ex - plodes and my bod - y aches.
This is the noise that keeps
me a - wake. My head ex - plodes and my bod - y aches.
Interlude 2:
w/Riff B (Gtr. 6) 2 times
Em
C/E*
Am/E*
Gtr. 2
Cont. rhy. simile

Bm
13421
Em
23
C/E*
32 1
Don't wor - ry, ba - by,
it will
w/Riff B (Gtr. 6) 1st 3 meas. only
Am/E*
231
Bm
13421
Em
23
be al - right.
Don't wor - ry, ba - by,
C/E*
32 1
Am/E*
231
N.C.
we'll stay al - right.
Outro:
Play 4 times
E5
11
C5
133
E5
11
Gtr. 3
(Whisper) Push it.
Push it.
Gtr. 5
T
A
B
15
12
12
12
14
12
14
1
(14)
14

SEARCHING FOR AMERICA

Words and Music by
JANIS IAN

Dsus2
1. Where
T
A
B

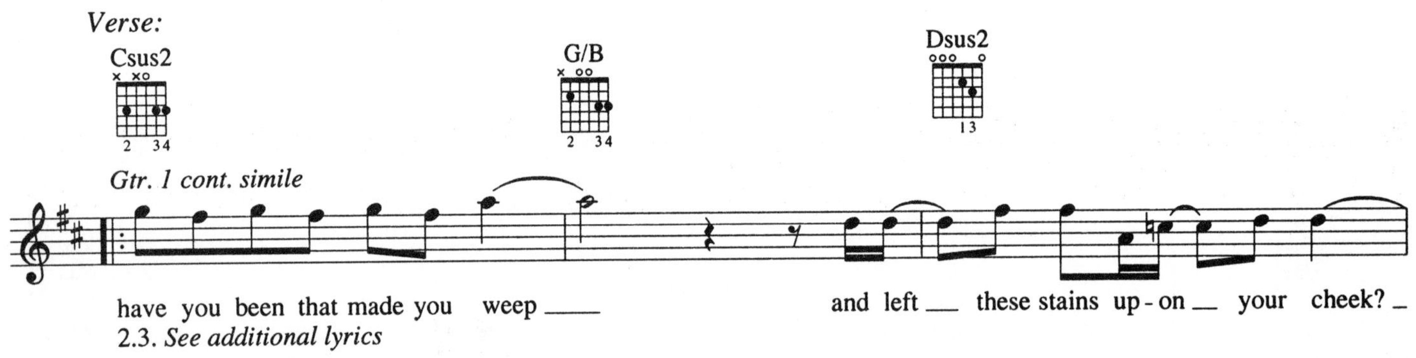
Verse:
Csus2
G/B
Dsus2
Gtr. 1 cont. simile
have you been that made you weep
and left these stains up-on your cheek?
2.3. See additional lyrics

Csus2
G/B
What did you see while you were gone
that haunts

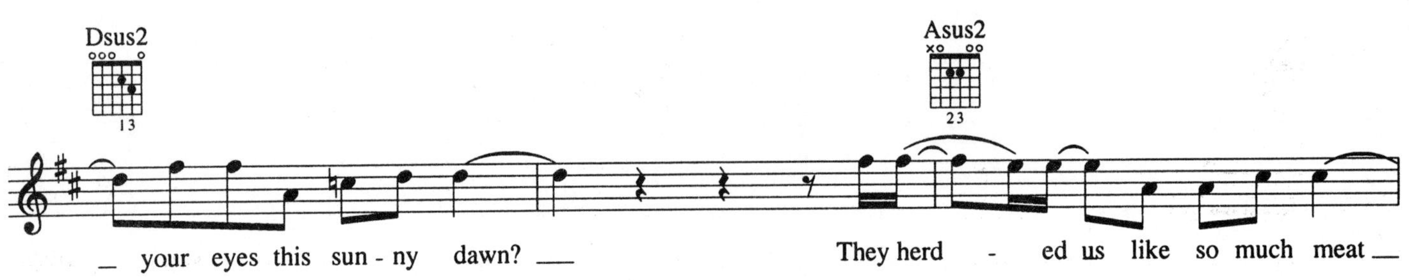
Dsus2
Asus2
your eyes this sun-ny dawn?
They herd - ed us like so much meat

A(9)/C♯
Dsus2
up from the sew - ers to the street
Where con-
Asus2
(A(9)/C♯)
Dsus2
- crete can-yons stretched their walls
so high it made us want to crawl
Asus2
A(9)/C♯
Past prov-erbs writ on sub-way cars
and
Dsus2
Asus2
in be-tween the win-dow bars
We walked un - til the pave-ment bled
(A(9)/C♯)
Dsus2
and not a curse was left un - said
In -
Csus2
G/B
to a place that knows no spring,
where on - ly steel and sil - ver sing
They

Csus2
G/B
made us dance un - til we dropped. And the mu - sic of the jack - ham - mers fi -
Dsus2
D5 Fmaj9(♯11)
D5 G(6)
nal - ly stopped I caught a cin - der
Dsus2
D5 Fmaj9(♯11)
in my eye search-ing for a patch of sky But the
D5 G(6)
Dsus2
sha - dows driz - zled down like in Pom - peii That's how I spent my yes - ter - day
Chorus:
Csus2
G/B
Search-ing for A - mer - i - ca in the riv - ets and the
Dsus2
Csus2
rust Search-ing for A - mer - i - ca

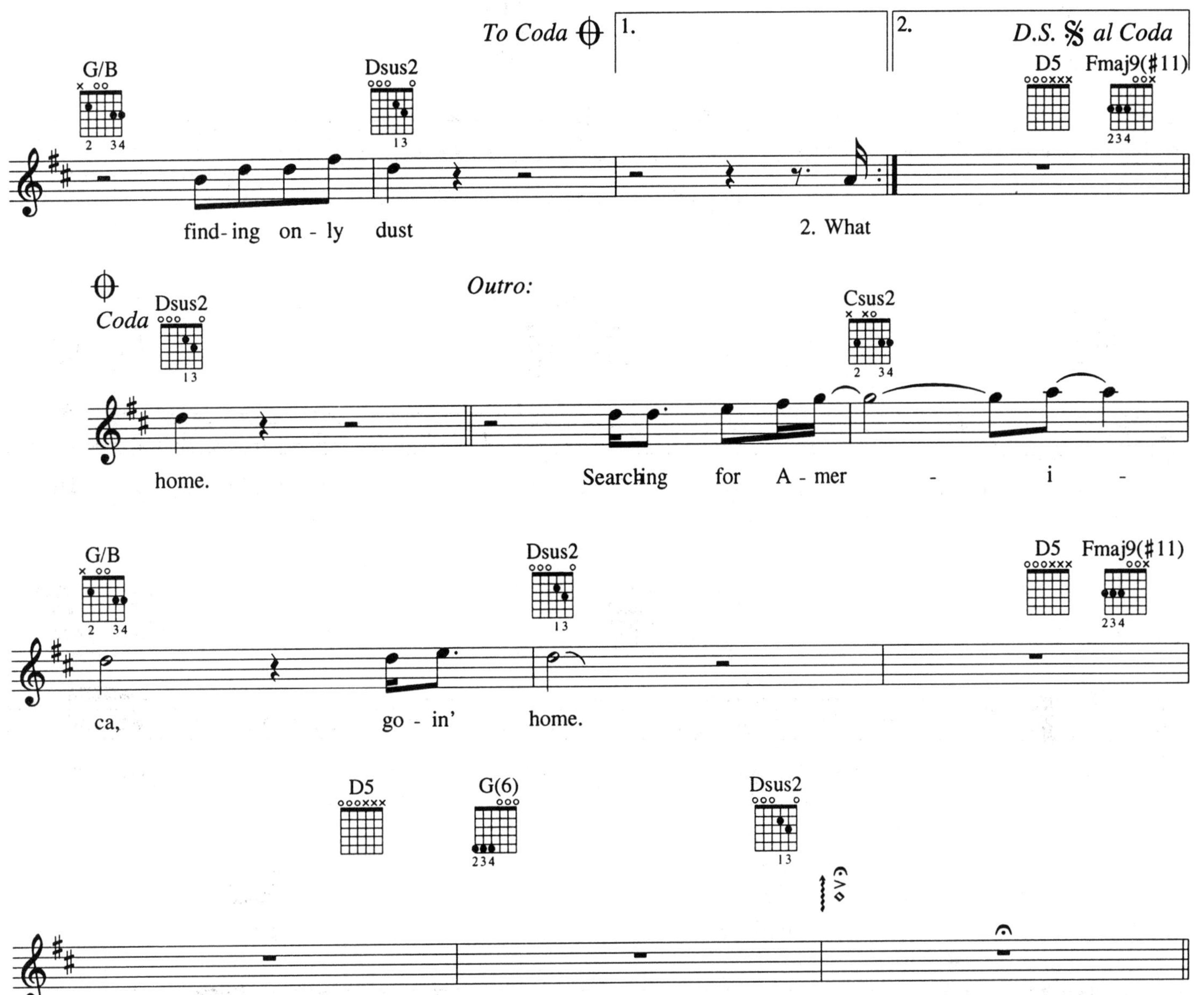

Verse 2:
What did you see that made you cry
And left these trackmarks on your eye?
What did you find while you were there
That sucks the light out of the morning air
They gave us each a cropper's shack
And land so hard it broke the back
Then fed us 'til our bellies burst
On promises that died at birth
So I lay the baby out each dawn
In between the tender corn
With sunrise for her bonnet
And flies her only blanket
We harvested until we bled
'Til every single root ran red
And when the work was finally done
They gave our names to immigration
I did not know how bad it hurt
Until I lay there eating dirt
And the cold seeped in between my bones
That's where I was when I left home

Chorus:
Searching for America
All her dreams and hopes
Searching for America
Finding only ghosts

Verse 3:
Who are these people you have seen
To dream this dark and distant dream?
To tell the stories you have told
To leave these bruises on your soul
They are the flesh, they are the bone
They are the very cornerstone
They leave their mansions and their shacks
To hide here in between the cracks
Their hope is tattooed on my lips
Bleeding from my fingertips
They are crawling toward the promised land
Hand over hand
To walk until they run no more
And wash up on some distant shore
Where truth is not the enemy
And whatever does not kill us, sets us free
Somewhere out there
Are millions just like me
Homesick for Eden
Heartsick at the memory

Chorus:
Searching for America
In every stick and stone
Searching for America
Going home
Seaching for America
Going home

QUEER

Words and Music by
DOUG ERIKSON, SHIRLEY MANSON,
STEVE MARKER and BUTCH VIG

I'll strip a - way your hard ve - neer
Do do do do do do.
end Riff B
1/2

w/Riff B (Gtr. 1)
and see what I can find;
Do do do do do do.
the queer- est of the queer.
Chorus:
w/Riff B (Gtr. 1) 4 times (first measure only on fourth time)
G5
E♭5
C5
F5
The strang- est of the strange, the cold- est of the cool, the lam- est of the lame, the numb- est of the dumb.
2. See additional lyrics

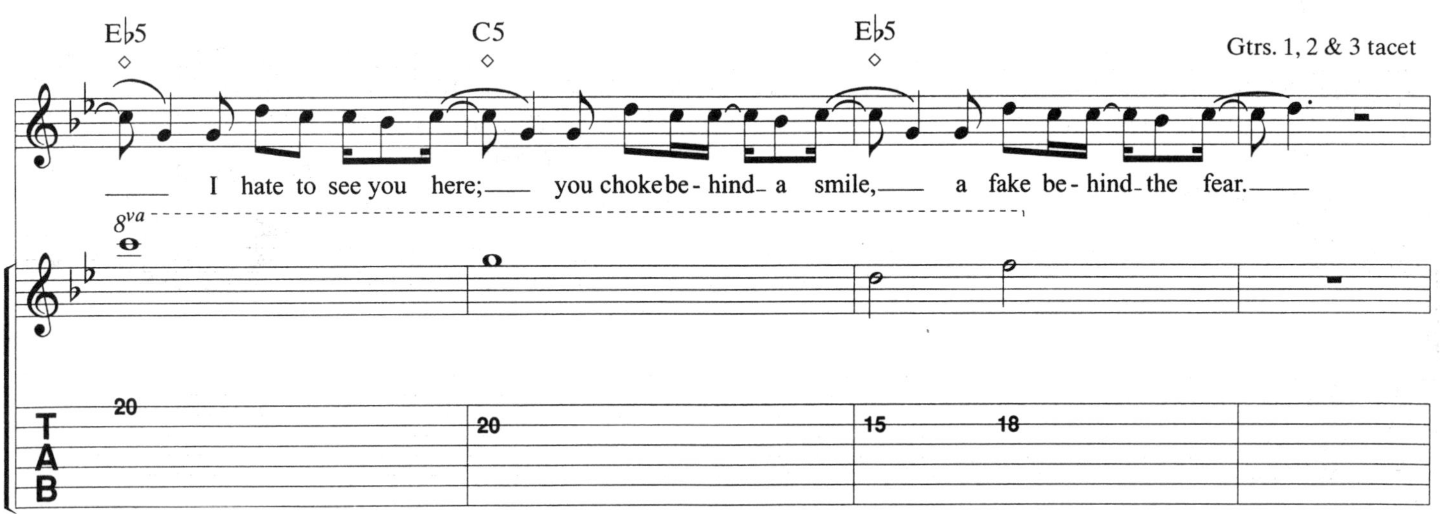
E♭5
C5
E♭5
Gtrs. 1, 2 & 3 tacet
I hate to see you here; you choke be- hind a smile, a fake be- hind the fear.

1. w/Riffs A (Gtr. 1) & A1 (Gtr. 2) 2 times
G5 E♭5 G5
the queer-est of the queer.
(Do do do do do do. Do do do do do do. Do do do do do do.
D5 G5 E♭5 G5 D5
Do do do do do do. Do do do do do do. Do do do do do do. Do do do do do do.)
2. B♭5 G♭5 B♭5 F5
Guitar Solo:
Gtr. 4
Rhy. Fig. 1
end Rhy. Fig. 1
Gtr. 5
8va
loco
trem. bar
w/Rhy. Fig. 1 (Gtr. 4) 2 times
B♭5 G♭5 B♭5 F5
Gtr. 5
8va
loco

Bridge:
B♭
G♭5
B♭5
I know what's good for you.
(You can touch me if you want.
I know you're dy-
(8)
F5
B♭
G♭5
ing to.
You can touch me if you want.
I know what's good for you:
You can touch me if you want.
Gtr. 5 out
Gtr. 4
Chorus:
w/Riff B (Gtr. 1) 7 1/2 times
w/Riff C (Gtr. 2) 7 times
B♭5
F5 N.C.
G5
Gtr. 3
But you can't stop.)
The queer-est of the queer,
the strang-est of the strange,
Gtr. 5
Riff D
Rhy. Fig. 2
Gtr. 4

Eb5
C5
F5
the cold-est of the cool, the lam-est of the lame, the numb-est of the dumb,
T
A
B
8
end Rhy. Fig. 2
w/Riff D (Gtr. 5) 3 times
w/Rhy. Fig. 2 (Gtr. 4) 3 times
G5
Eb5
C5
I hate to see you here; you choke be-hind a smile, a fake be-hind the fear,
D5
G5
Eb5
C5
the queer-est of the queer, the strang-est of the strange,
Bb5
Eb5
C5
the cold-est of the cool you're noth-ing spec-ial here;
Eb5
all Gtrs. tacet
a fake be-hind the fear, the queer-est of the queer,
Outro:
w/Riff A (Gtr. 1) & A1 (Gtr. 2) 6 1/2 times (till fade)
G5
Eb5
The queer-est of the queer,
Do do do do do do. Do do do do do do.

Verse 2:
This is what he pays me for.
I'll show you how it's done.
You learn to move the pain you feel
Like father, like son.

Chorus 2:
The queerest of the queer.
Hide inside your head.
The blindest of the blind.
The deadest of the dead.
You're hungry 'cause you starve.
While holding back the tears.
Choking on your smile.
A fake behind the fear.

SPIDERWEBS

Words and Music by
GWEN STEFANI and TONY KANAL

walk right through my ears, pre-sum-ing I like what I hear.
(8va)
Gtrs. 2 & 3
P.M. A.H. P.M.
A.H.
P.M.
A.H. pitch: D D
Pre-Chorus 1 & 2:
E♭5
F5
B♭
1. And now I'm stuck in the, the web you're
2. See additional lyrics
*Gtrs. 2 & 3
* Two gtrs. arr. for one at this point (throughout).
Gm
E♭
w/Fill 1 (Gtrs. 4 & 5)
F
spin - in'. You got me for your prey.
Fill 1
Gtr. 4 (Dist.)
Gtr. 4 out
mf w/slide steady gliss.
Gtr. 5 (Dist.)
Gtr. 5 out
mf w/slide steady gliss.

Chorus:

N.C.(B♭) (F) (Gm) (E♭)

Sor- ry, I'm not home right now. I'm walk-ing in- to spi- der-webs, so leave a mes- sage and I'll call you back.
(Yeah.)

Rhy. Fig. 2 (8va) A.H. **end Rhy. Fig. 2**

TAB: 1 1 1 1 1 1 1 0 | 1 1 1 1 1 1 1 1 | 3 3 3 3 3 3 3 0 | 1 1 0 0 3 3 1 0

A.H. pitch: D D B♭ B♭ F F A F E♭ C A A G D G G

w/Rhy. Fig. 2 *(Gtrs. 2 & 3) simile*

(B♭) (F) (Gm)

A like - ly sto - ry, *but* leave a mes - sage and I'll call
(Yeah.

1. (E♭) **w/Rhy. Fig. 1** *(Gtrs. 2 & 3) simile* (B♭) 2.3. (E♭)

you back. 2. You're in you back. And
)

Subst. w/Rhy. Fill 1 *(Gtr. 3)*

B♭ F Gm N.C.(E♭)

it's all your fault I screen my phone calls. No

Rhy. Fig. 3
Gtrs. 2 & 3 **end Rhy. Fig. 3**

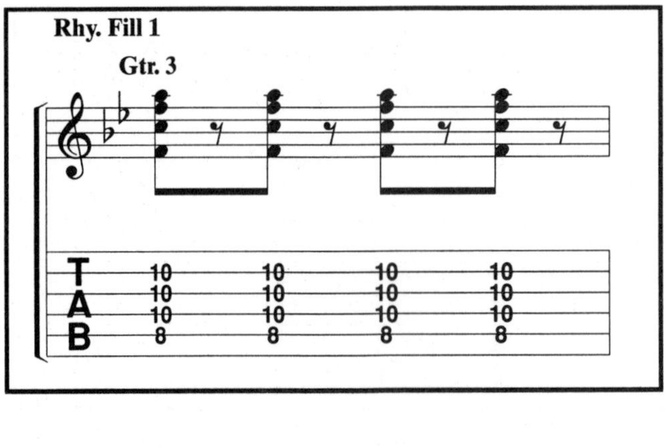

TAB: 3 3 3 1 (×4) | 3 3 1 (×4) | 3 5 5 3 (×4) | 1 1 0 0 3 3 1 0

Rhy. Fill 1
Gtr. 3

TAB: 10 10 10 8 (×4)

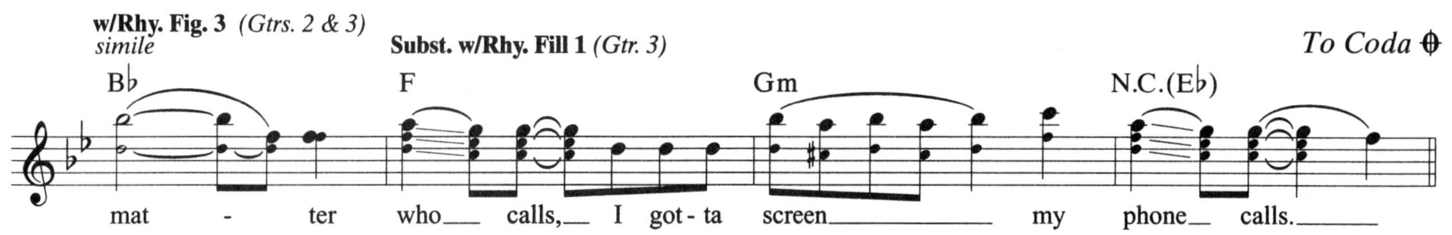

Guitar Solo:

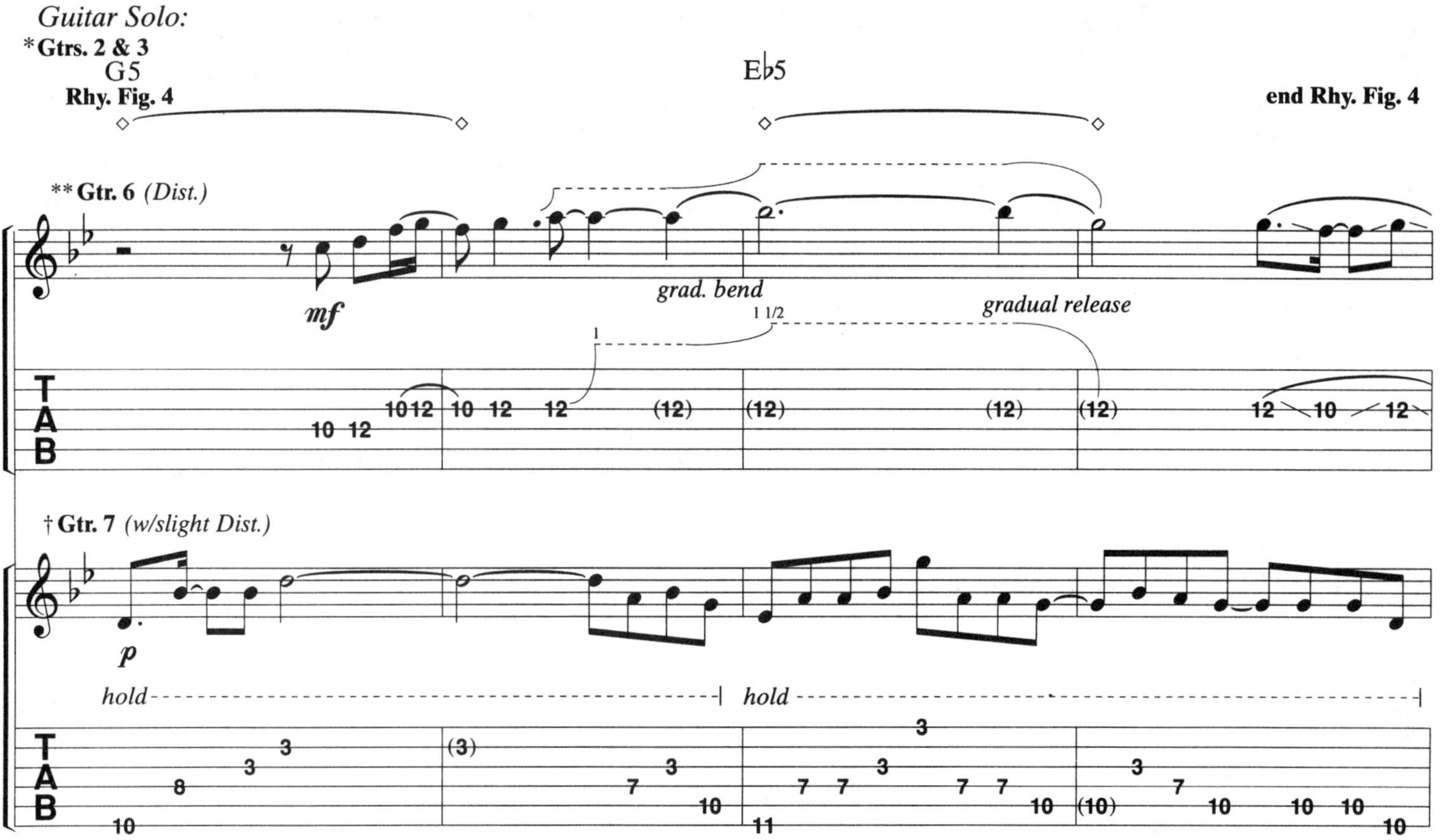

* w/tremolo effect (8th note pulse).
**Backwards gtr.
†w/chorus, Capo at 3rd fret (open strings denoted by 3).

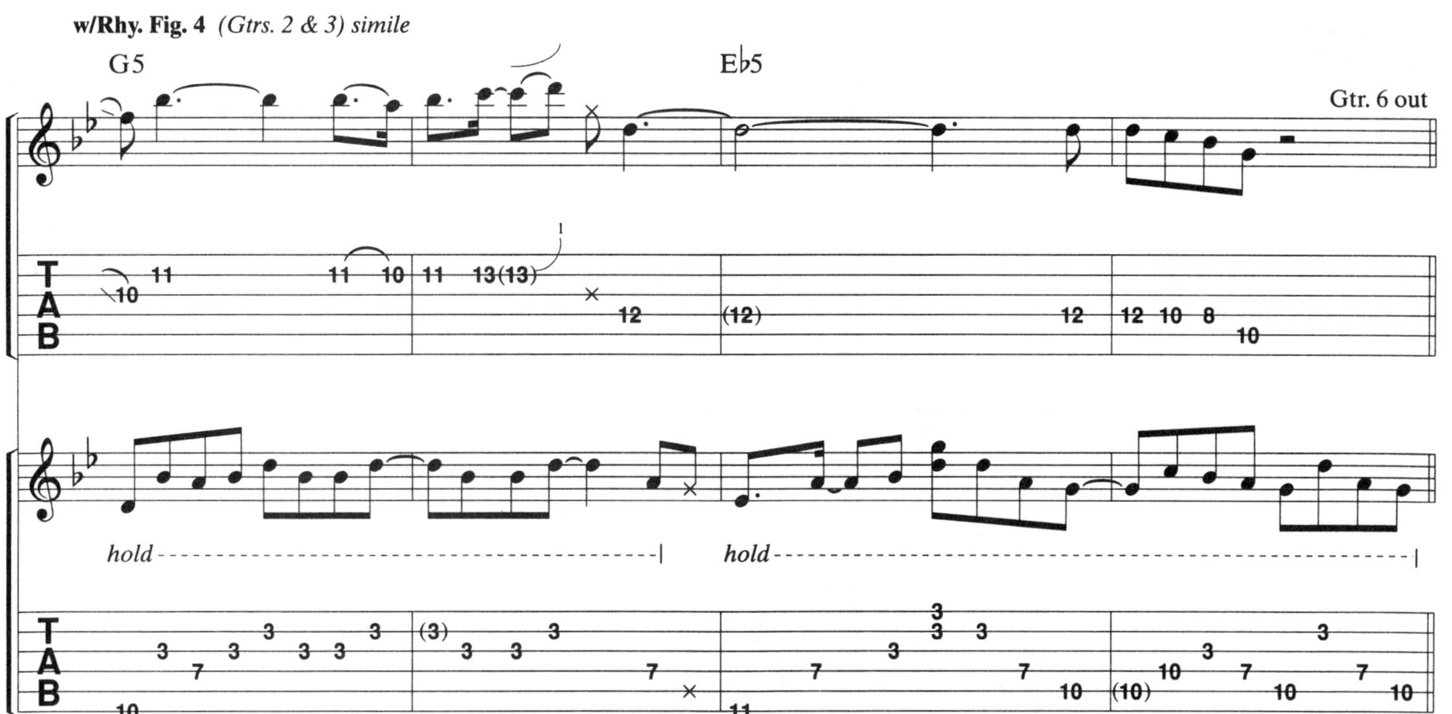

Bridge:
w/Rhy. Fig. 4 (Gtrs. 2 & 3) 3 times, simile
G5
E♭5
Now it's gone too deep.
(Now it's gone too. . .)
You
Gtr. 7
hold
hold
wake me in my sleep.
(Wake me in my
My
dreams be - come night - mares,
sleep.)
(Dreams be - come.)
'cause you're
Gtr. 7 out

D.S. 𝄋 al Coda
G5
N.C. (E♭)
ring - ing in my ears.
(Ring - in' in my)
Gtr. 2
Gtrs. 2 & 3
Coda B♭5
F5
Ooh, the spi - der - webs.
Gtrs. 2 & 3
(8va)
A.H.
A.H. pitch: A F
G5
N.C. (E♭)
B♭5
Leave a mes - sage and I'll call you back.
I'm walk - ing in - to
Rhy. Fig. 5
(8va)
A.H.
A.H. pitch: E♭ C A♭ F

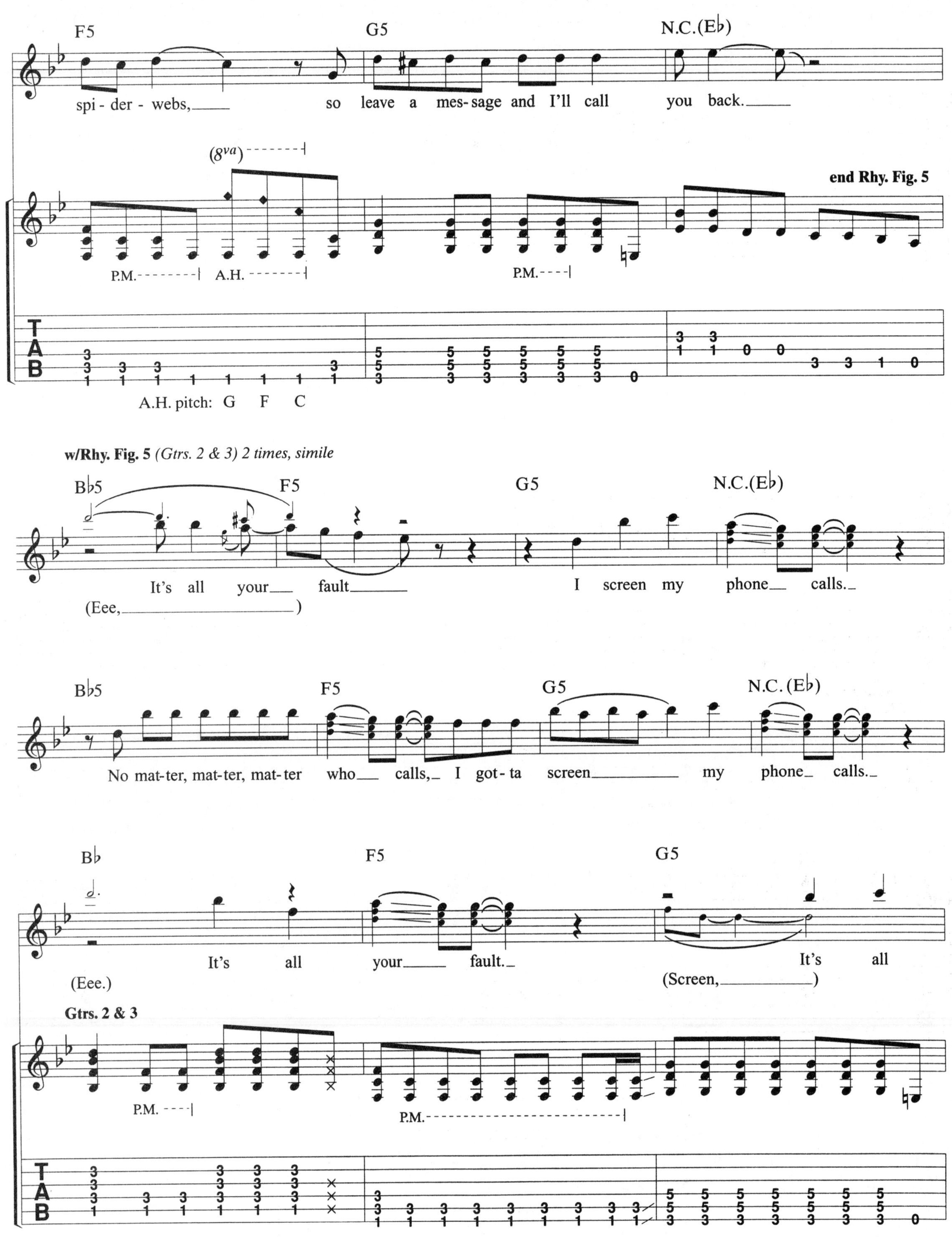
F5
G5
N.C.(E♭)
spi - der - webs, so leave a mes- sage and I'll call you back.
(8va)
end Rhy. Fig. 5
P.M.
A.H.
P.M.
T
A
B
A.H. pitch: G F C
w/Rhy. Fig. 5 (Gtrs. 2 & 3) 2 times, simile
B♭5
F5
G5
N.C.(E♭)
It's all your fault I screen my phone calls.
(Eee,)
B♭5
F5
G5
N.C. (E♭)
No mat-ter, mat-ter, mat-ter who calls, I got- ta screen my phone calls.
B♭
F5
G5
It's all your fault. It's all
(Eee.)
(Screen,)
Gtrs. 2 & 3
P.M.
P.M.
T
A
B

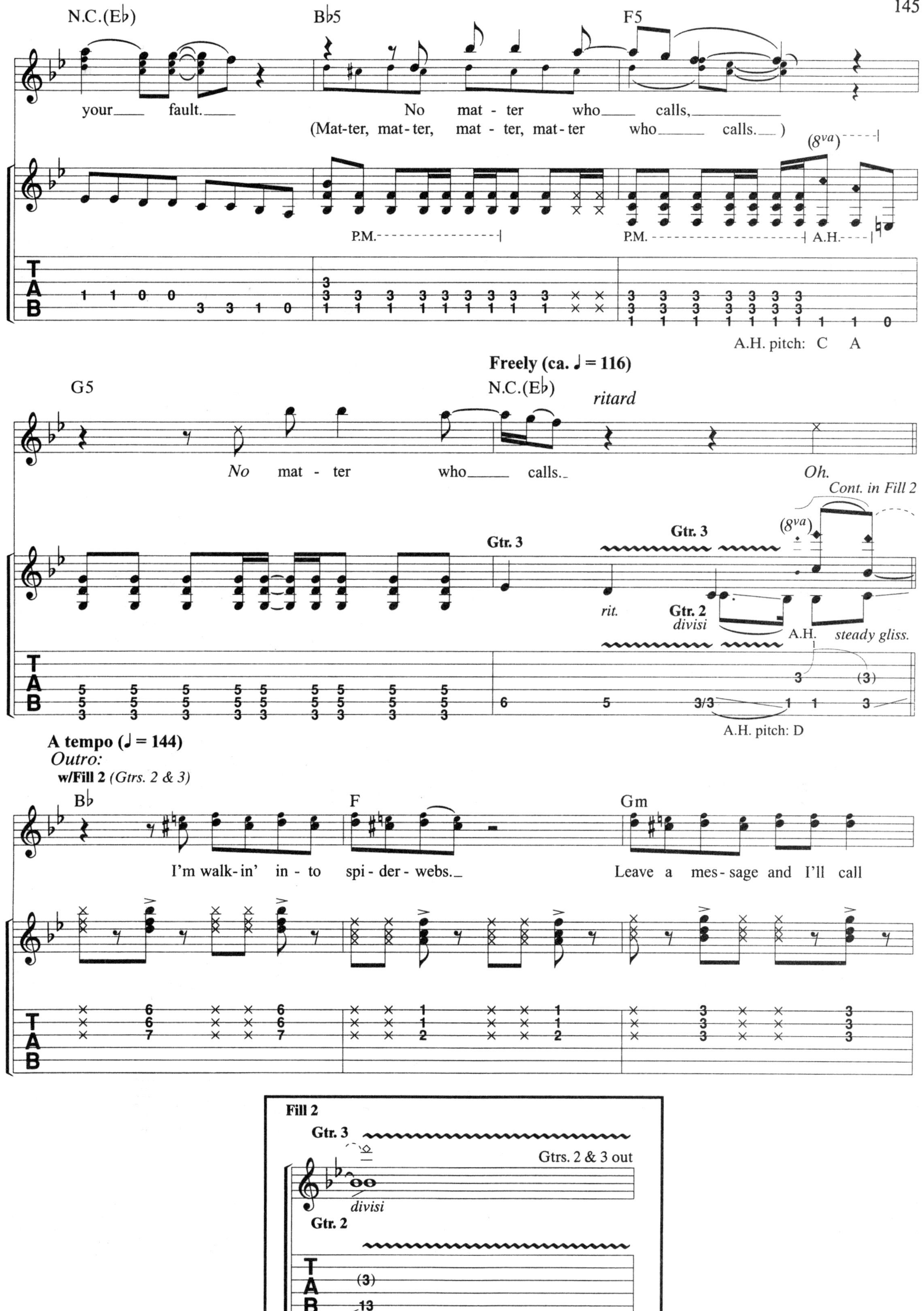

N.C.(E♭)
B♭5
F5
your___ fault.___
No mat - ter who___ calls,___
(Mat-ter, mat-ter, mat - ter, mat-ter who___ calls.__)
(8va)
P.M.
P.M.
A.H.
A.H. pitch: C A
G5
Freely (ca. ♩ = 116)
N.C.(E♭)
ritard
No mat - ter who___ calls._
Oh.
Cont. in Fill 2
Gtr. 3
Gtr. 3
(8va)
rit.
Gtr. 2
divisi
A.H.
steady gliss.
A.H. pitch: D
A tempo (♩ = 144)
Outro:
w/Fill 2 (Gtrs. 2 & 3)
B♭
F
Gm
I'm walk-in' in - to spi - der - webs._
Leave a mes - sage and I'll call
Fill 2
Gtr. 3
Gtrs. 2 & 3 out
divisi
Gtr. 2

Repeat and fade
(w/ad lib vocal)

Verse 2:
You're intruding on what's mine
And you're taking up my time.
Don't have the courage inside me
To tell you please let me be.

Pre-Chorus 2:
Communication, a telephonic invasion.
I'm planning my escape.
(To Chorus:)

STRONG ENOUGH

Words and Music by
SHERYL CROW, KEVIN GILBERT, BRIAN MacLEOD,
DAVID RICKETTS, BILL BOTTRELL and DAVID BAERWALD

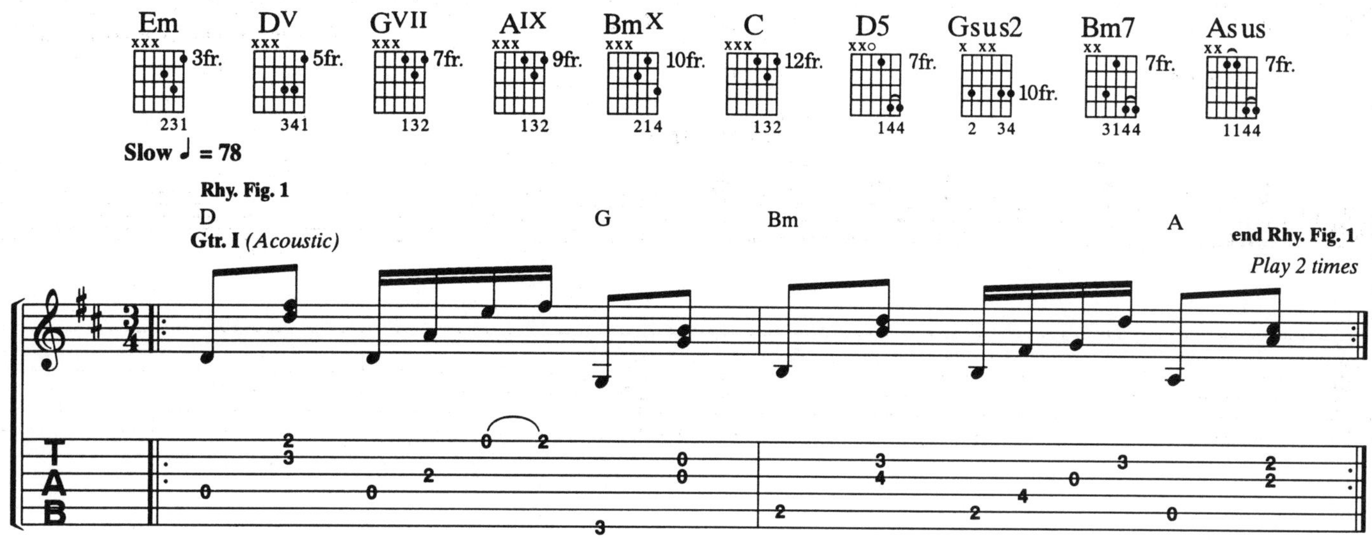

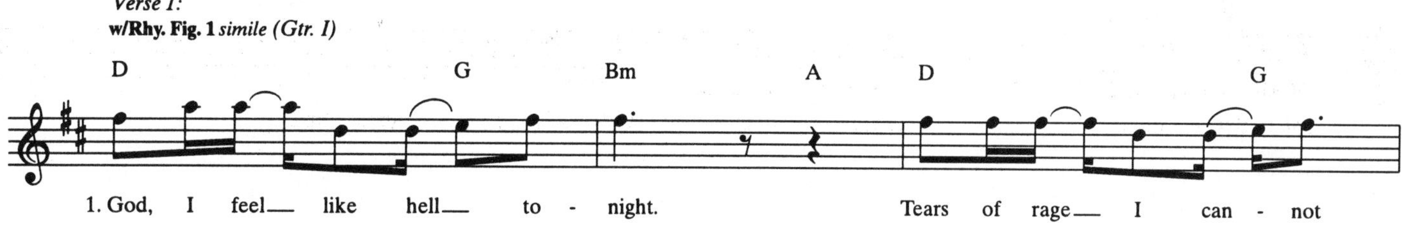

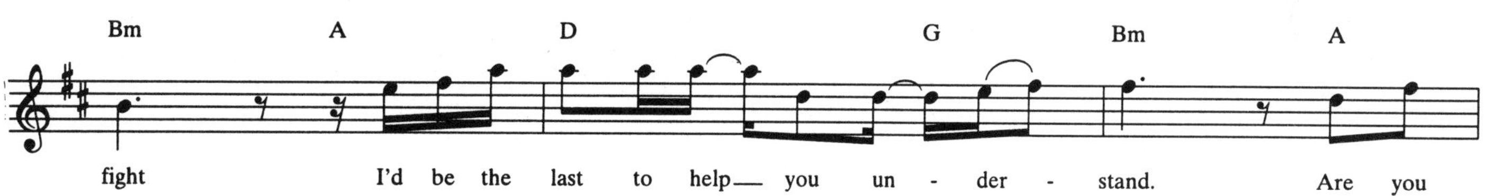

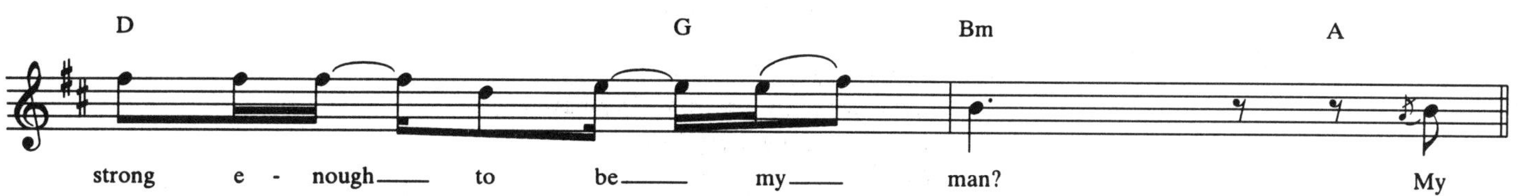

Interlude 1:
w/Rhy. Fig 1 simile (Gtr.I)
w/Gtr. II (12 string Acoustic), simile
D G Bm A D G Bm A
man.
D G Bm A D G Bm A
Verses 2, 3 & 4:
w/Rhy. Fig. 1 (Gtrs. I & II)
D G Bm A D G
1. Noth - ing's true and noth - ing's right. So let me be a - lone to -
2.3.See additional lyrics
Bm A D G Bm A
night. 'Cause you can't change the way I am. Are you
To Coda I
D G Bm A
strong e - nought to be my man?
Chorus:
Rhy. Fig. 2
Em D II G II A II
Gtr. II
Lie to me. I
Rhy. Fig. 3
Gtr. I
Bm II C G II A II
end Rhy. Fig. 2
prom - ise, I'll be - lieve.
end Rhy. Fig. 3

Verse 3:
I have a face I cannot show.
I make the rules up as I go.
It's try and love me if you can.
Are you strong enough to be my man?
My man.

Verse 4:
When I've shown you that I just don't care,
When I'm throwing punches in the air,
When I'm broken down and I can't stand,
Will you be man enough to be my man?

STAY (I MISSED YOU)

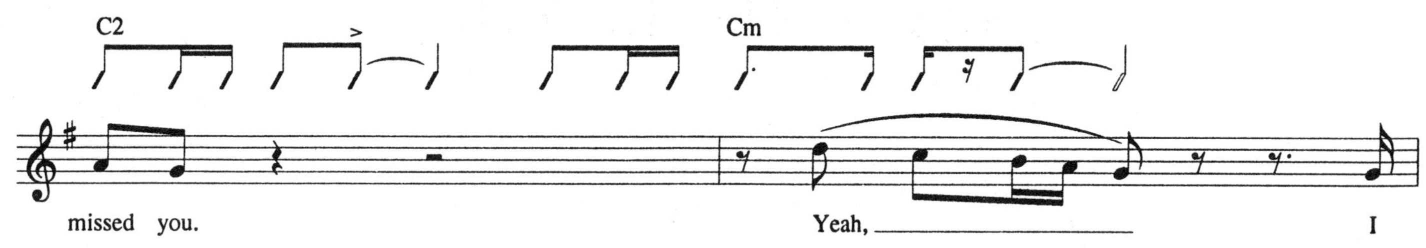
C2
Cm
missed you.
Yeah, I

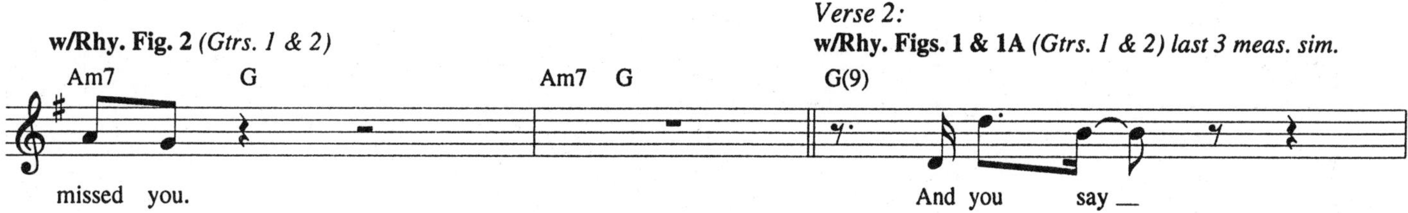
w/Rhy. Fig. 2 (Gtrs. 1 & 2)
Verse 2:
w/Rhy. Figs. 1 & 1A (Gtrs. 1 & 2) last 3 meas. sim.
Am7 G
Am7 G
G(9)
missed you.
And you say

Em7
Am7(♭9)
G/B
I on-ly hear what I want to: I don't lis-ten hard, I don't pay at-ten-tion to the

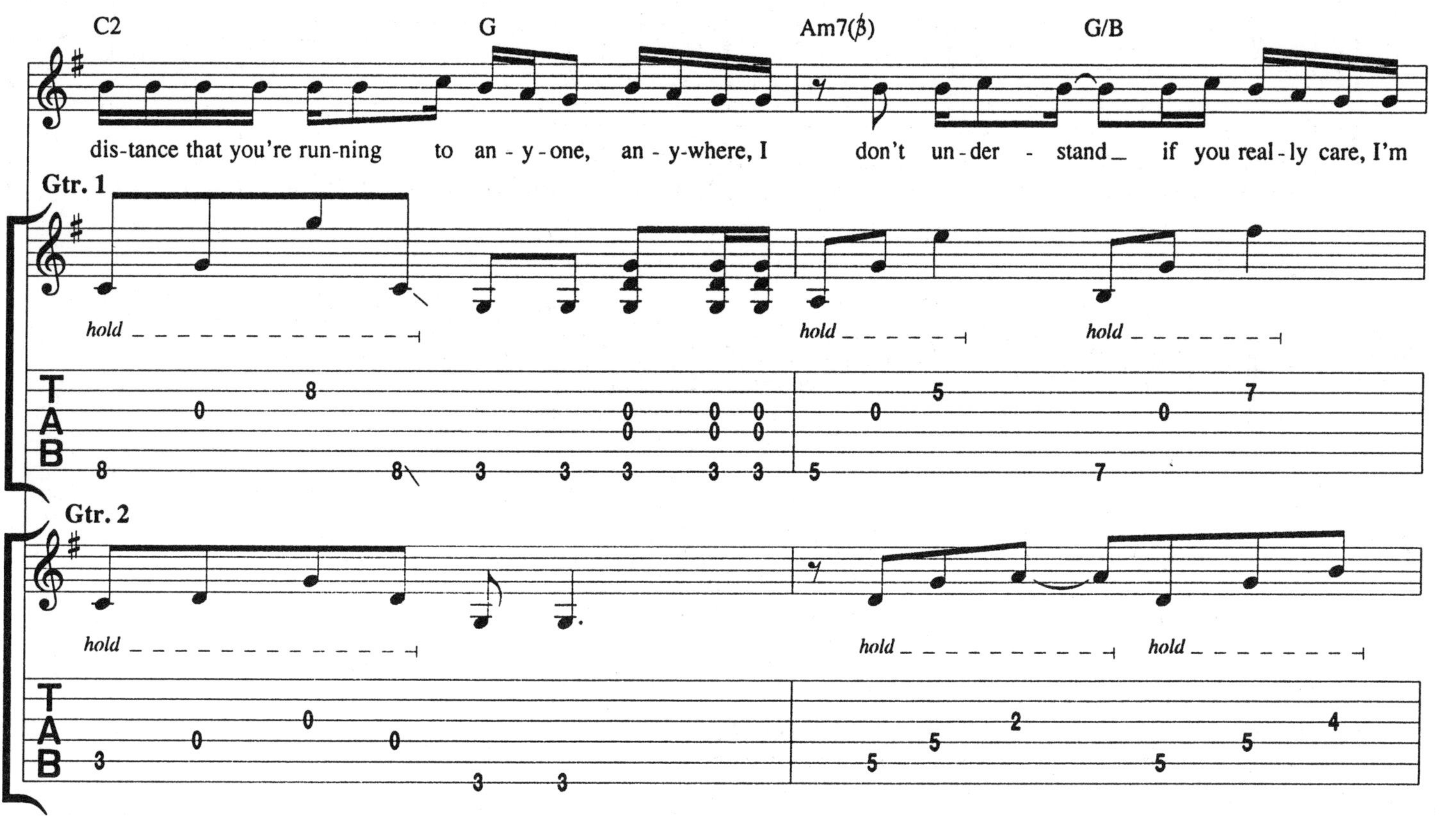
C2
G
Am7(♭9)
G/B
dis-tance that you're run-ning to an-y-one, an-y-where, I don't un-der-stand if you real-ly care, I'm
Gtr. 1
hold
hold
hold
Gtr. 2
hold
hold
hold

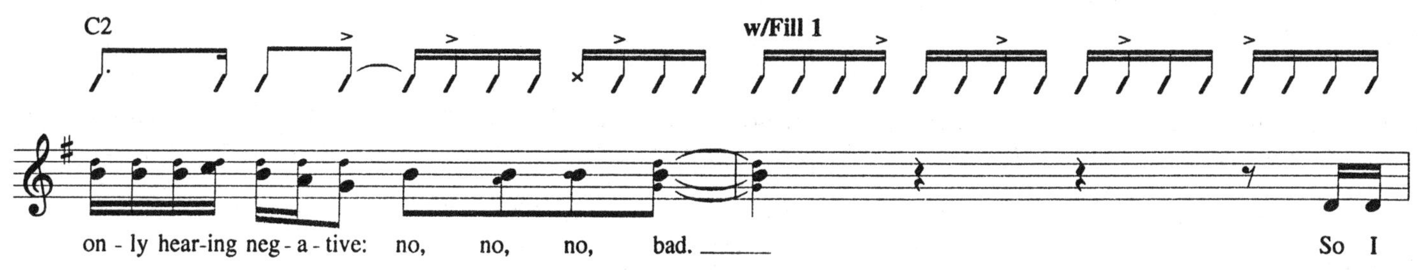
C2
w/Fill 1
on-ly hear-ing neg-a-tive: no, no, no, bad.
So I

w/Rhy. Fig. 2 (Gtrs. 1 & 2) 8 times sim.
Am7 G5 Am7 G5
I turned the ra - di - o on, I turned the ra - di - o up, and this wom-an was sing-ing my song: The
I turned the ra - di - o on, turned the ra - di - o up
Am7 G5 Am7 G5
lov-er's in love, and the oth-er's run a - way. (The) lov - er is cry - in' 'cause the oth - er won't stay.
Am7 G5 Am7 G5
some of us hov - er when we weep for the oth - er who was dy - in' since the day they were born, well,
(some)
Am7 G5 Am7 G5
this is not that: I think that I'm throw-ing, but I'm thrown. And I
Bridge:
Am
thought I'd live for - ev - er, but now I'm not so sure. You try to
C2
sim.
tell me that I'm clev - er, but that won't take me an - y - how,
Am7(♭) G/B C2
or an - y-where with you.
an - y - where

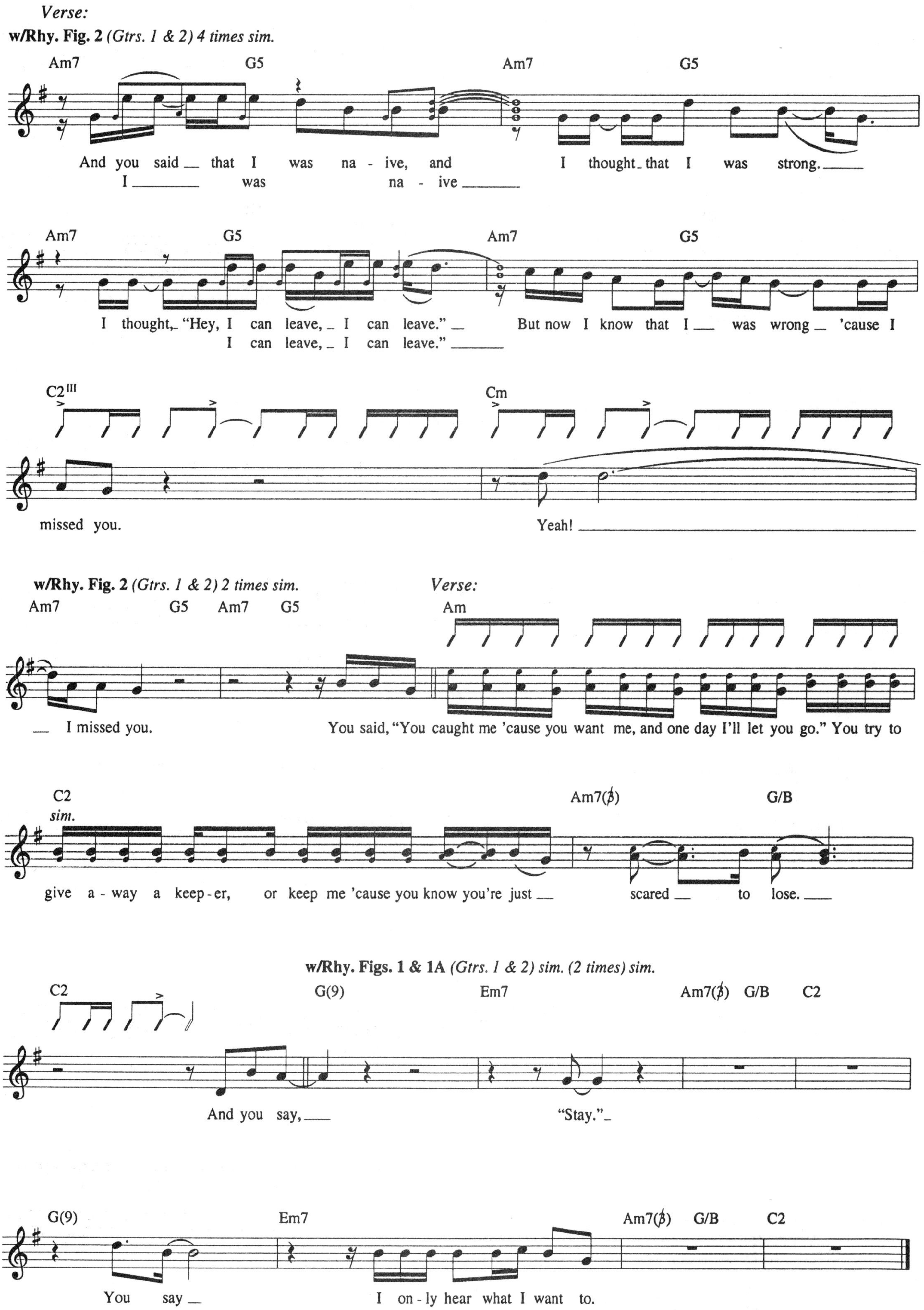

Verse:

w/Rhy. Fig. 2 *(Gtrs. 1 & 2) 4 times sim.*

Am7 G5 Am7 G5

And you said __ that I was na - ive, and I thought_ that I was strong. ____

I ______ was na - ive ______

Am7 G5 Am7 G5

I thought,_ "Hey, I can leave, _ I can leave." _ But now I know that I __ was wrong _ 'cause I

I can leave, _ I can leave." ______

C2III Cm

missed you. Yeah! ______

w/Rhy. Fig. 2 *(Gtrs. 1 & 2) 2 times sim.*

Am7 G5 Am7 G5

_ I missed you.

Verse:

Am

You said, "You caught me 'cause you want me, and one day I'll let you go." You try to

C2 *sim.* Am7(♭) G/B

give a - way a keep - er, or keep me 'cause you know you're just __ scared __ to lose. ___

w/Rhy. Figs. 1 & 1A *(Gtrs. 1 & 2) sim. (2 times) sim.*

C2 G(9) Em7 Am7(♭) G/B C2

And you say, ___ "Stay."_

G(9) Em7 Am7(♭) G/B C2

You say __ I on - ly hear what I want to.

STEADY ON

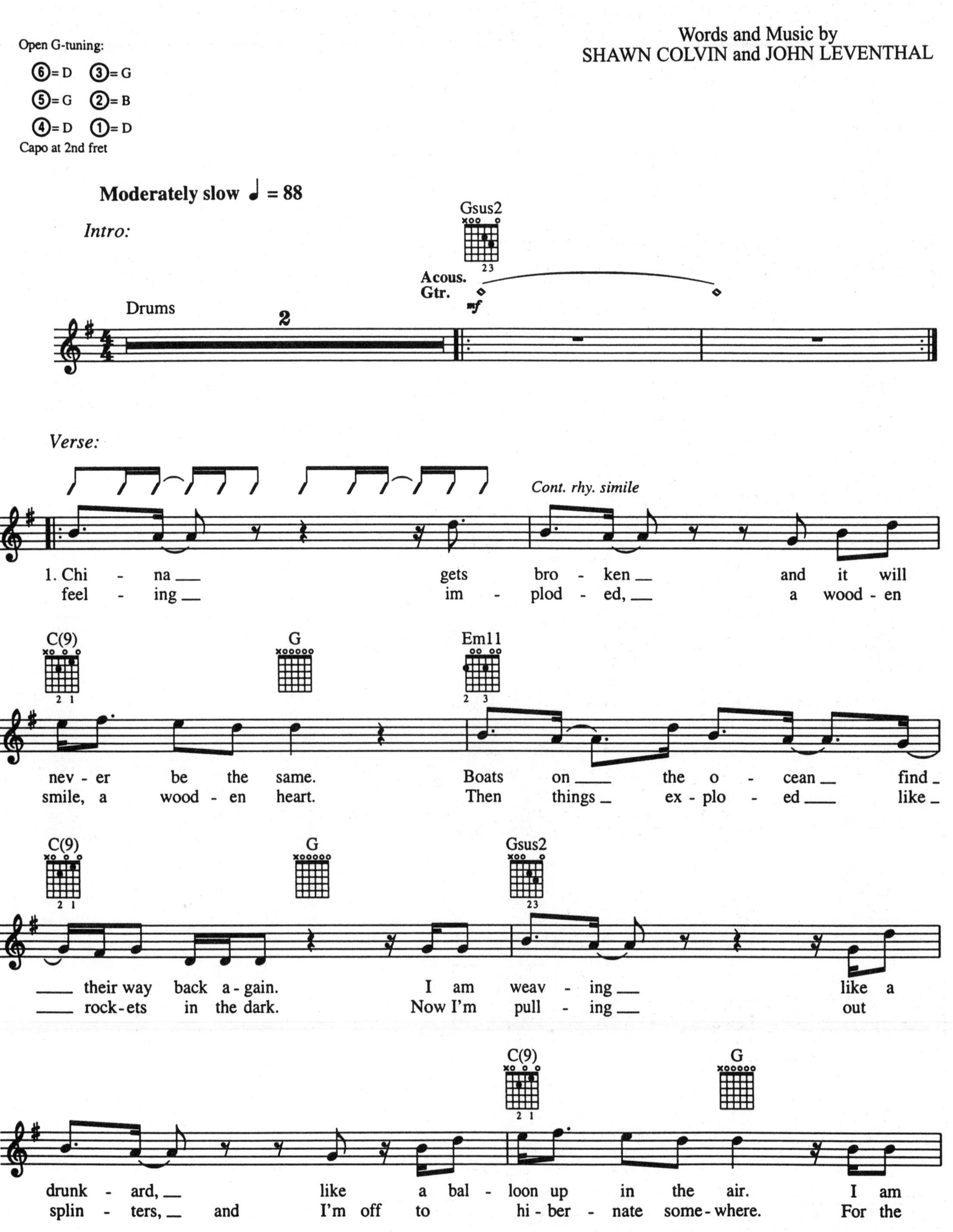

Steady On - 4 - 1

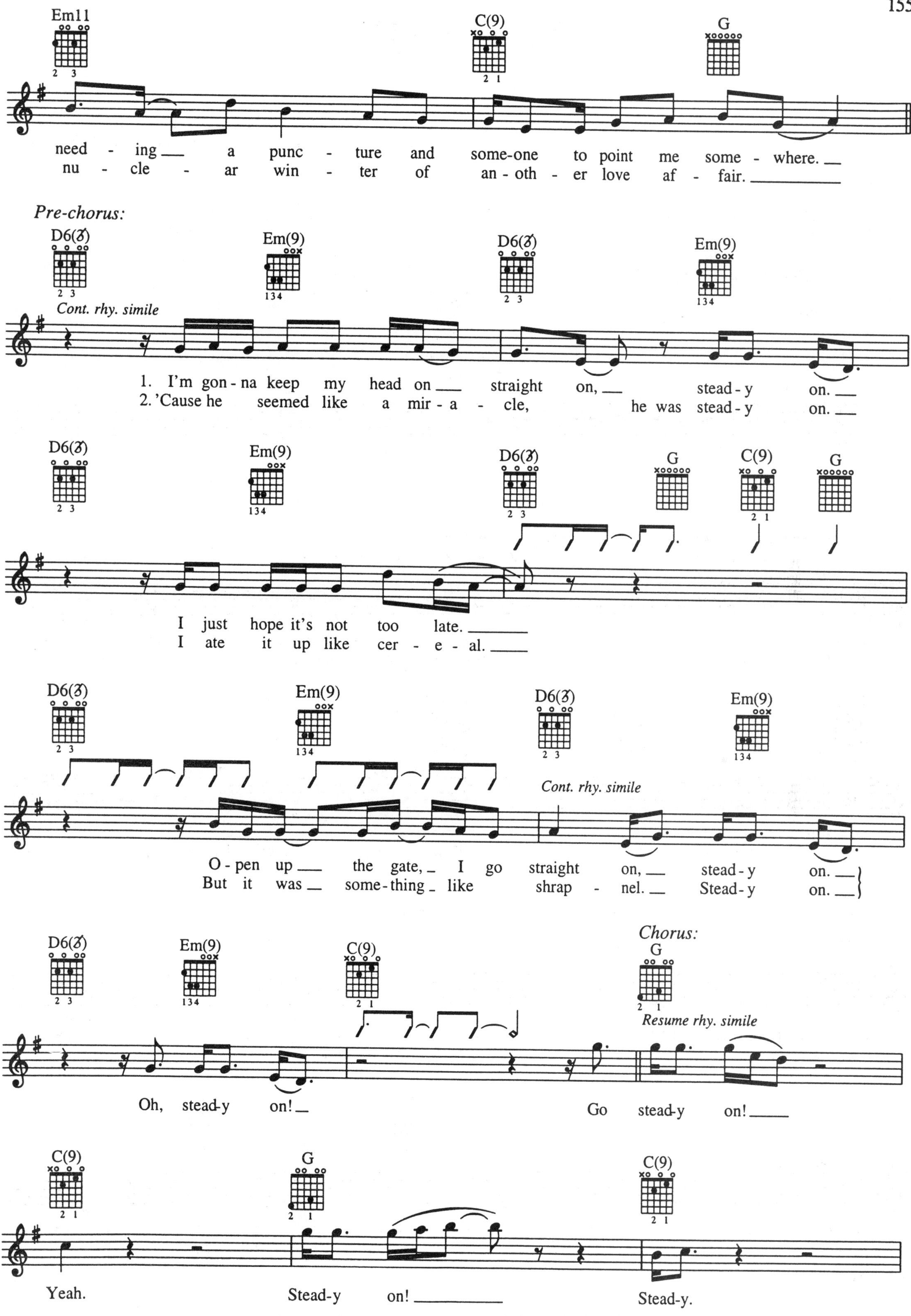
Em11
C(9)
G
need - ing a punc - ture and some-one to point me some - where.
nu - cle - ar win - ter of an - oth - er love af - fair.
Pre-chorus:
D6(3)
Em(9)
Cont. rhy. simile
1. I'm gon - na keep my head on straight on, stead - y on.
2. 'Cause he seemed like a mir - a - cle, he was stead - y on.
I just hope it's not too late.
I ate it up like cer - e - al.
O - pen up the gate, I go straight on, stead - y on.
But it was some - thing like shrap - nel. Stead - y on.
Chorus:
Resume rhy. simile
Oh, stead-y on!
Go stead-y on!
Yeah.
Stead-y on!
Stead-y.

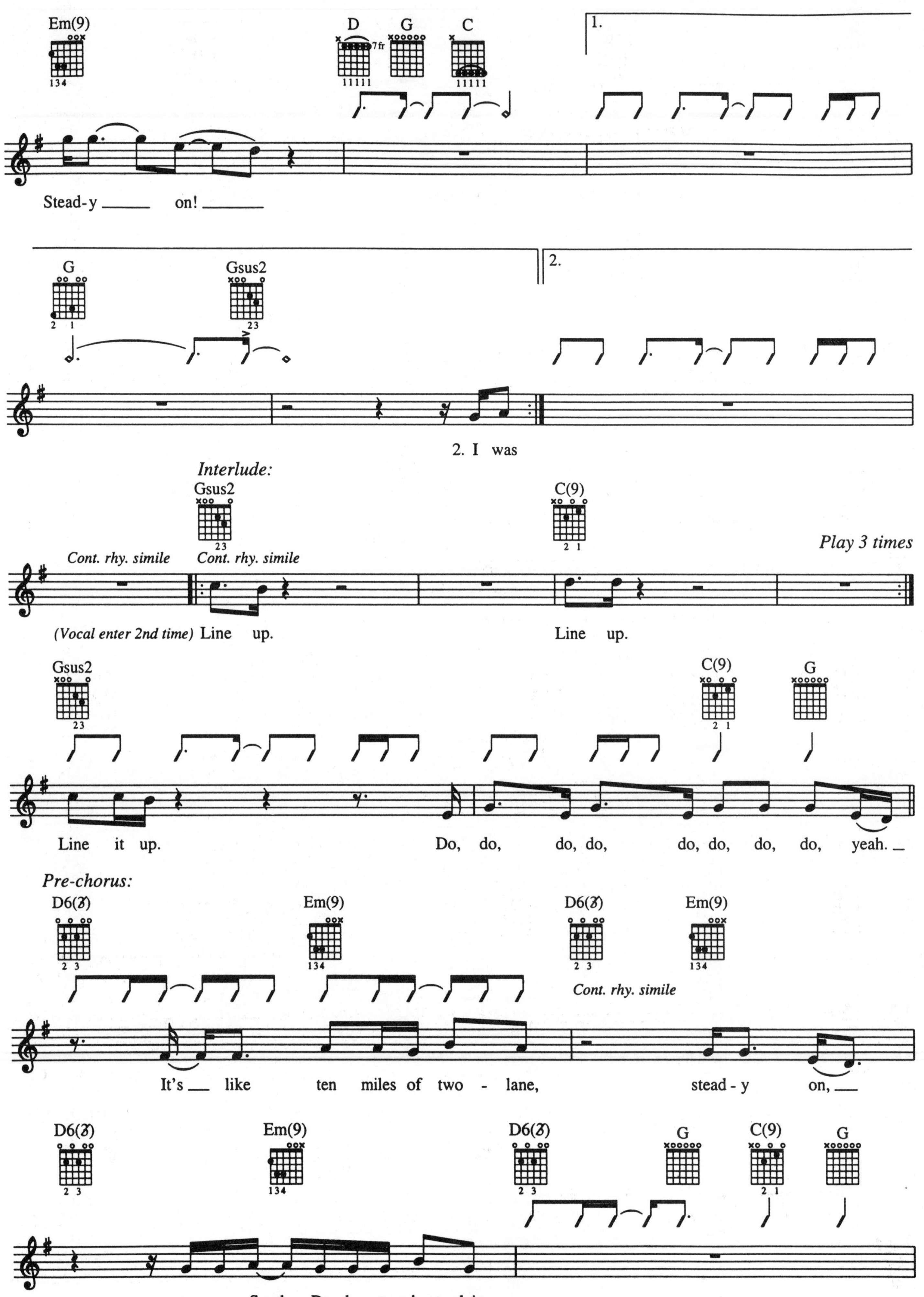
Em(9)
D
G
C
1.
Stead-y on!
G
Gsus2
2.
2. I was
Interlude:
Gsus2
C(9)
Cont. rhy. simile
Cont. rhy. simile
Play 3 times
(Vocal enter 2nd time) Line up.
Line up.
Gsus2
C(9)
G
Line it up.
Do, do, do, do, do, do, do, do, yeah.
Pre-chorus:
D6(3)
Em(9)
D6(3)
Em(9)
Cont. rhy. simile
It's like ten miles of two - lane, stead - y on,
D6(3)
Em(9)
D6(3)
G
C(9)
G
on a South Da - ko - ta wheat plain.

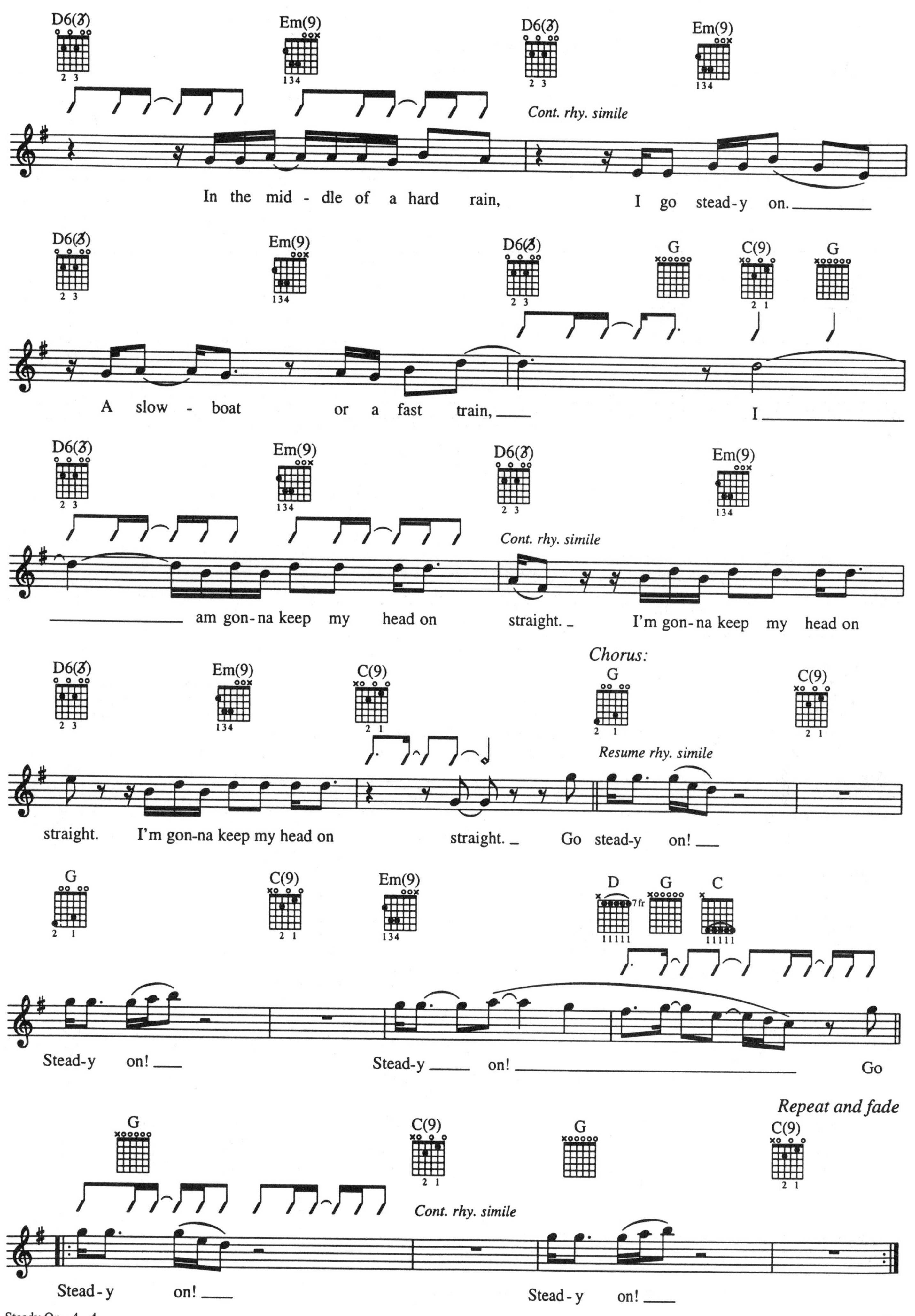
D6(3)
Em(9)
G
C(9)
D
C
Cont. rhy. simile
Resume rhy. simile
Chorus:
Repeat and fade
In the mid - dle of a hard rain, I go stead-y on.
A slow - boat or a fast train, I
am gon-na keep my head on straight. I'm gon-na keep my head on
straight. I'm gon-na keep my head on straight. Go stead-y on!
Stead-y on! Stead-y on! Go
Stead - y on! Stead - y on!

SUNNY CAME HOME

Words and Music by
SHAWN COLVIN and JOHN LEVENTHAL

w/Fill 1 (Gtr. 4)
C
G5
F♯m7(♭5)
G
F
Em
F
G5
w/Fill 2 (Gtr. 4)
A5
Fill 1
Gtr. 4
hold
Fill 2
Gtr. 4

Verse 1:
Am
G
F
Em
Am
G
1. Sun-ny came home to her fa - v'rite room.
A-sun-ny set down in the
Gtrs. 1 & 3
P.M.
P.M.
simile
C
G5
Am/F♯
G5
kitch - en.
She o-pened a book and a
Dm
Am
F
Gtr. 1
F
Em
box of tools.
Sun-ny came home with a mis-sion.
She says, "Days
Gtr. 3

Chorus:
C
G
Dm
Fsus2
Rhy. Fig. 2
go by I'm hyp - no - tized. I'm walk -
Gtr. 4
*Rhy. Fig. 2A
f hold throughout section
*Includes Gtr. 4 only.
C
G
Dm
ing on a wire. I close
C
G
Dm
Am
end Rhy. Fig. 2
my eyes and fly out of my mind,

w/Rhy. Fill 1 (Gtr. 1)
D/F♯
G
Fmaj7
G
in - to the fire.
Gtr. 4
end Rhy. Fig. 2A
Gtr. 2
A5
Am
G5
G
F5
F
E5
Em
Gtr. 1
Hmm hmm hmm hmm hmm.
1/2
A5
Am
G5
G
C
G5
G
Rhy. Fill 1
Gtr. 1

Verse 2:
w/Fill 3 (Gtrs. 2 & 4)
Am G C G5 Am Gsus2
2. Sun - ny came home with a list of names. She did - 'nt be - lieve in tran -
Gtrs. 1 & 3
P.M. P.M.
simile
C Em F G Am7 G
scend - ence. "And it's time for a few small re - pairs," she said.
Dm Am
Gtr. 1
w/Fill 4 (Gtr. 4)
F
A - sun - ny come home with a ven - gence. She says, "Days
Gtr. 3
Fill 3
Gtr. 4
Gtr. 2
trem. bar
Fill 4
Gtr. 4

Chorus:
w/Rhy. Figs. 2 (Gtr. 3) & 2A (Gtr. 4)
C G Dm Fsus2
go by, I don't know why. I'm walk -
C G Dm C G
ing on a wire. I close my eyes and fly
w/Rhy. Fill 1 (Gtr. 1)
Dm Am D/F♯ G
out of my mind, in - to the fire. Get
Bridge:
G/B Em7 F G/B Em7
the kids and bring a sweat - er. Dry is good and wind
F G/F G/B Em7 F G
is bet - ter. Count the years, you al - ways knew it. Strike
G/B Em7 F G
a match, go on and do it. Oh, days
it. Days
Chorus:
C G Dm Fsus2 C G
Rhy. Fig. 5
f
go by I'm hyp - no - tized. I'm walk - ing on a wire.
Gtr. 4
T
A
B

end Rhy. Fig. 5
w/Rhy. Fig. 5 (Gtr. 1)
C G Dm Fsus2
I close my eyes and fly out of my mind,
hold
C G Dm
in - to the fire.
w/Rhy. Fig. 2 (Gtr. 1)
C G
Oh, light the sky and hold
P.M.
Dm Fsus2 C G Dm Dm/F
on tight. The world is burn - ing down.
She's out
C G Dm Am D/F♯ G
there on her own and she's al - right.
Sun-ny came

Fmaj7
G
D/F♯
Am
D(9)/F♯
home.
Sun-ny came
trem. bar
Outro:
w/Rhy. Fig. 1 (Gtr. 1) 3½ times, simile
Am
G(11)
F
G(11)
Am
G(11)
*Gtr. 3
Cont. rhy. simile
home.
I'm
home.
*Keybds. & bass gtr. arr. for gtr.
F
G(11)
Am
G(11)
F
G(11)
Dsus2
I'm
home.
F
Am
Esus
E
G
Gtr. 4
hold
hold
D
Fmaj7
Am
*Gtr. 1
*Mandolin arr. for gtr.

TAKE NO PRISONERS

Words and Music by
JANIS IAN

Verse:
Dm7
Gtr. 1 cont. simile
Dm6
1. The writ - er wrote The sing - er sung
2. See additional lyrics
Dm7
Dm6
The rec - ord broke The au - di - ence was stunned
Dm7
Dm6
Some they begged for mer - cy Oth - ers e - ven cried
A7sus
Dm7
N.C.
Some they fled, left for dead, some said it changed their lives
1. And the
2. See additional lyrics
Gtr. 1
mp
Pre-Chorus:
Gm7
Am7
writ - er said "I wish you'd known me when
3. lov - er said "Why don't you touch me?
B♭6
Csus2
I still be - lieved in the truth Now it's
Reach out your hand just like this You can

Gm7
C(9)
all I ___ have left, a long with _ my debts and lack of
cap - ture _ my soul, you can take _ hold and
D5
youth."
kill me with a kiss." ___
He ___ said _
She ___ said _
Chorus:
Dm7
Dm6
Take ___ no pris - on - ers
Tell ___ no lies.
Gr. 1
mf
Dm6
Dm7
Fmaj9/D
Em7
No pret - ty songs ___ of com - pro - mise

Dm7
Dm6
Take no pris - on - ers
Tell no lies
A
B♭/A
B/A
Am7
A7
To Coda
It's a good day to
1. w/Rhy. Fig. 1 (Gtr. 1) 3 times, simile
w/Rhy. Fig. 2 (Gtr. 1) simile
2.
Dm9
Gtr. 1 tacet
Piano ad lib.
die."
die."
Interlude:
N.C. (Dm)
Gtr. 1
mf
harm.

Verse 2:
God spoke
The people laughed
The tablets broke
While they were pissing on the golden calf.
Some they found their heaven
Others found their hell
Some they ran to Canaan Land
Some just lay where they fell.

Pre-Chorus 2:
And God said "Hey I wish you'd known me
When I still believed you'd be true
Now for the rest of your days
When you call out my name
I'll be Mister God to you."
(To Chorus:)

UNINVITED

Music and Lyrics by
ALANIS MORISSETTE

Slowly ♩ = 64

Verse 1:
D+
2
Like an - y - one would be, I am flat - tered

Gm
D+
by your fas - ci - na - tion with me. Like an - y hot - blood - ed wom-

Gm
D+
- an, I have sim - ply want - ed an ob - ject to crave. But

D7
G
D
you, you're not al - lowed; you're un - in - vit - ed: an un - for - tu -

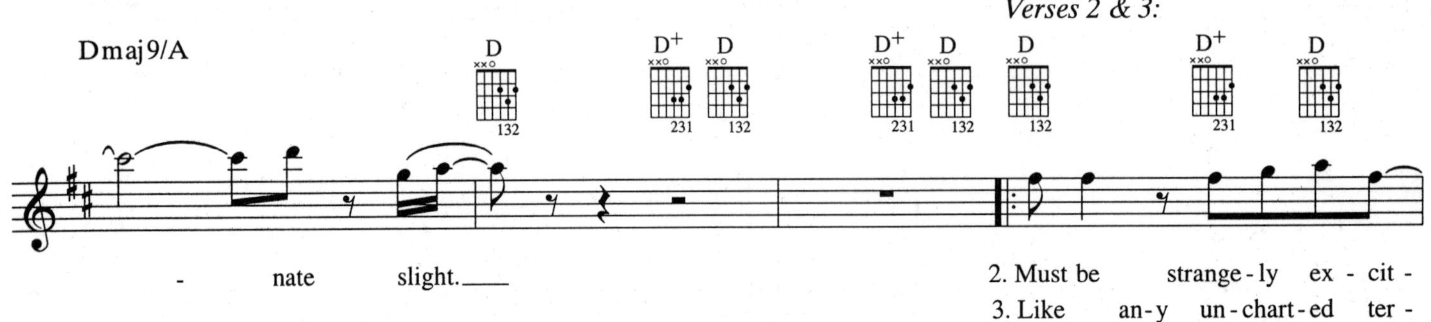
Dmaj9/A
D
D+
Verses 2 & 3:
- nate slight.
2. Must be strange - ly ex - cit -
3. Like an - y un - chart - ed ter -

D+
D
Gm
D
D+
D
- ing to___ watch the sto - ic squirm.___
- ri - tor - y, I must___ seem great - ly in - trigu - ing.
D+
D
D+
D
Gm
Must be some - what heart - en - ing to___ watch shep - herd___ meet shep - herd._
You speak of my love___ like you___ have ex - per - i - enced love like mine be -
D
D+
D
D7
G
___ But you, you're not___ al - lowed; you're un - in - vit -
fore. But this is not___ al - lowed; you're un - in - vit -
D
Dmaj9/A
D
D+
D
D+
D
- ed: an un - for - tu - nate slight.___
- ed: an un - for - tu - nate slight.___
Outro:
D+
D
D+
D
D+
2
I don't think you un - wor - thy, I need a mo -
Play 4 times
Gm
D
D
D+
D
D+
D
Dmaj9/A
- ment to de - lib - er - ate.___

UNIVERSAL HEART-BEAT

Words and Music by
JULIANA HATFIELD

Chorus:
Vcl. Fig. 1
G5 E5 A5 C5
heart, a heart that hurts is a
Rhy. Fig. 3
end Rhy. Fig 3
w/ Rhy. Fig. 3 (Gtr. 1, 3 times) simile
G5 E5 A5 C5 G5 E5
heart, a heart that works. A heart, a
A5 C5 G5 E5 A5 C5
To Coda
end Vcl. Fig. 1
heart that hurts is a heart, a heart that works.
Gtr. 1: w/Rhy. Fig. 1 (Gtr. 1, 4 times) simile
Gtr. 2 (Electric)
G7 E A7 G7 E A7
mf
w/dist.
Verse 2:
G7 E A7 G7 E A7
2. Sweet, sweet pain comes with the sun. Lie down and soak it up.
G7 E A7 G7 E A7
Burn off lay - ers in - su - la - tors. Ex -
G7 E A7 G7 E A7
posed, nose to the cold. I'm

w/Rhy. Fig. 2 (Gtr. 1) simile
G
E
A(5)
G
E
bleed - ing pret - ty col - ors,
A(5)
G
E
A(5)
yeah, all o - ver my - self. A
Chorus:
w/Rhy. Fig. 3 (Gtr. 1,3 1/2 times)
w/Vcl. Fig. 1
A5
C7
heart that works,
D♯9
C7
works.
D7
C♯7
steady gliss.
D.C. al Coda
Hey!

Verse 3:
Black wave comes to take me away.
I ride it almost to the grave,
Landing on a crowded shore, high-fivin'.
What a trip, I'm better for it.
I feel a live sensation.

WHO WILL SAVE YOUR SOUL

Words and Music by
JEWEL KILCHER

Chorus:
w/Rhy. Fig. 1 (Gtr. 1) 4 times, simile
Am C(9) G Dsus D
who_ will save_ your soul,_ when it comes_ to the flow-ers, now?_
Am C(9) G Dsus D
Oh,_ who_ will save_ your soul_ af-ter all those lies_ that you told,_ boy?_
Am C(9) G Dsus D
And who will save_ your souls_ if you won't_ save your own?_
To Coda I
Am C(9) G Dsus D
La da da da_ di da da la da da ya_ die._
Verses 2 & 3:
Am C(9) G
1. We try to hus - tle them, try to bus - tle them, try to cuss_ them. The cops want_ some-one to bust down on Or-
2. See additional lyrics
Rhy. Fig. 2
T
A
B
Dsus D Am C(9)
- leans_ Av - e - nue._ An - oth - er day, an - oth - er dol-lar, an-oth - er war, an - oth - er

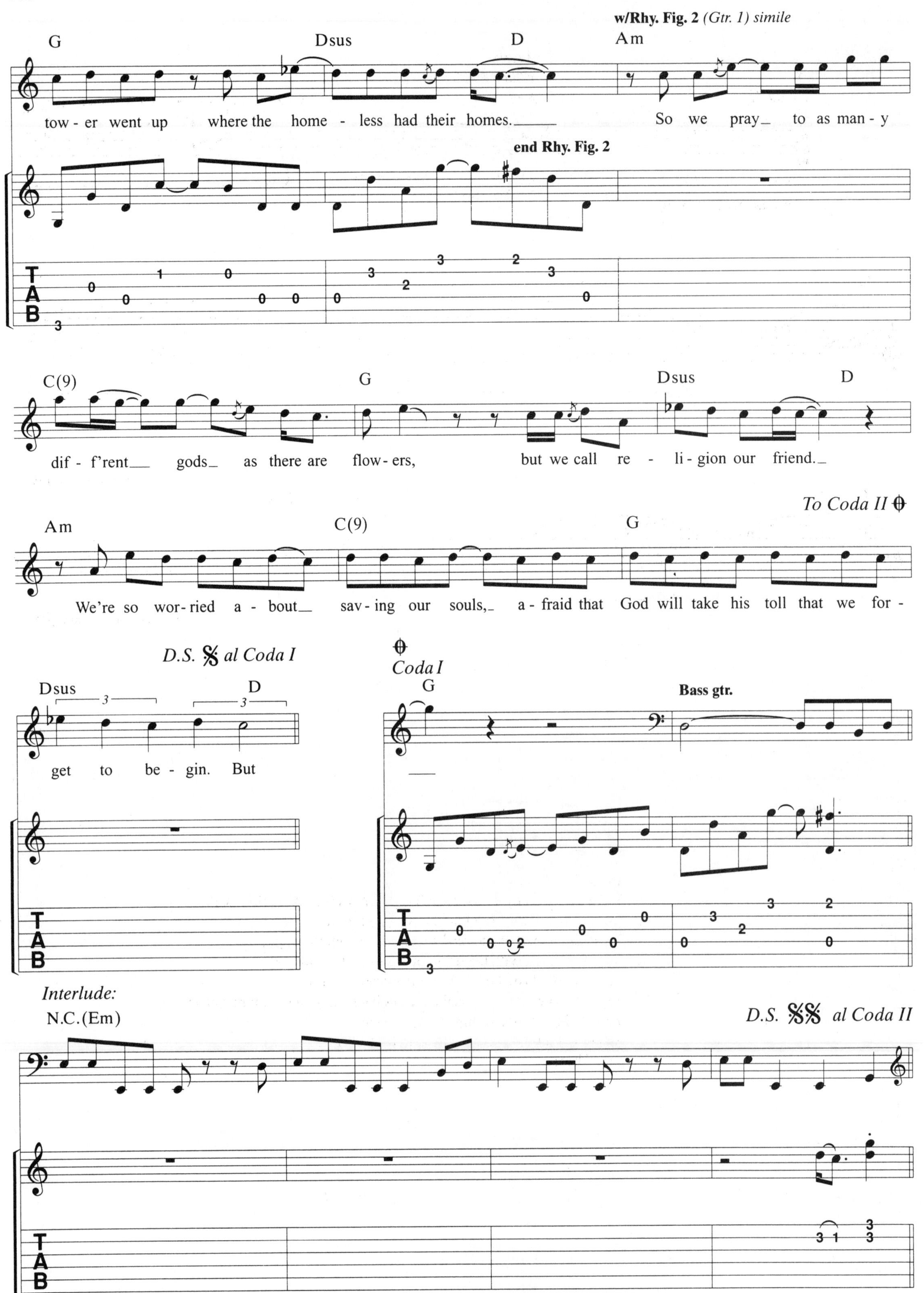
w/Rhy. Fig. 2 (Gtr. 1) simile
G
Dsus
D
Am
tow - er went up where the home - less had their homes.
So we pray to as man - y
end Rhy. Fig. 2
C(9)
G
Dsus
D
dif - f'rent gods as there are flow - ers, but we call re - li - gion our friend.
To Coda II
Am
C(9)
G
We're so wor - ried a - bout sav - ing our souls, a - fraid that God will take his toll that we for -
D.S. al Coda I
Dsus
D
get to be - gin. But
Coda I
G
Bass gtr.
Interlude:
N.C.(Em)
D.S. al Coda II

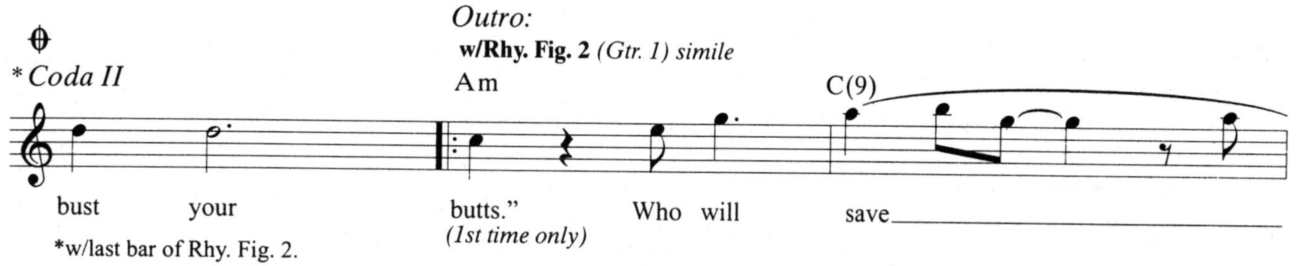

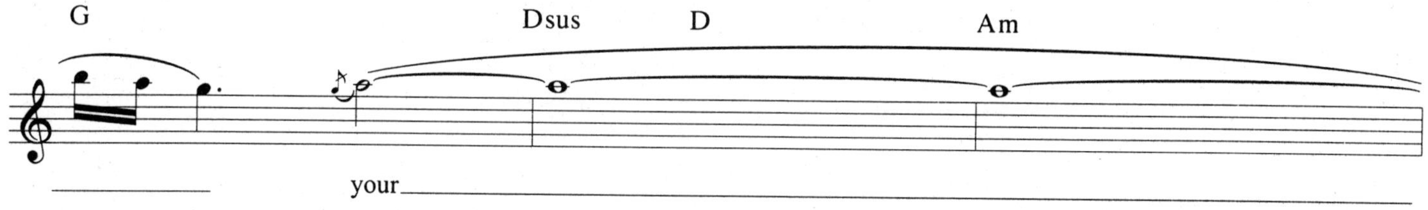

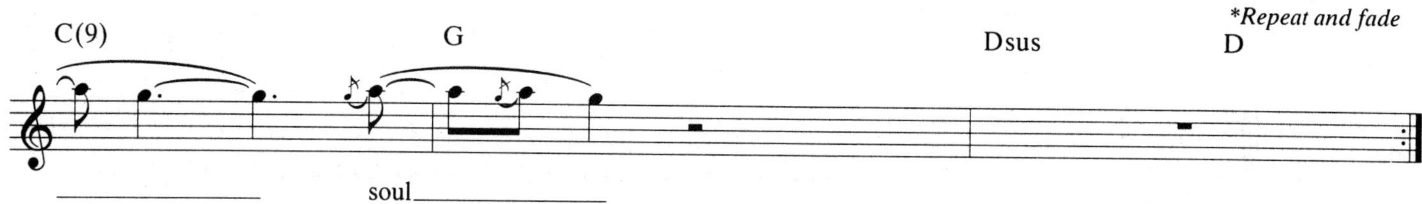

Verse 3:
Some are walking, some are talking, some are stalking their kill.
Got social security, but that don't pay your bills.
There are addictions to feed and there are mouths to pay,
So you bargain with the devil, but you're O. K. for today.
Say that you love them, take their money and run.
Say, "It's been swell, sweetheart, but it was just one of those things,
Those flings, those strings you got to cut,
So get out on the streets, girls, and bust your butts."
(To Chorus:)

YOU LEARN

Lyrics by
ALANIS MORISSETTE

Music by
ALANIS MORISSETTE and GLEN BALLARD

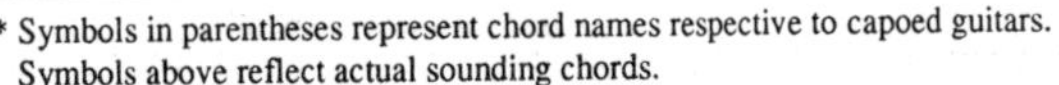
* Symbols in parentheses represent chord names respective to capoed guitars.
Symbols above reflect actual sounding chords.

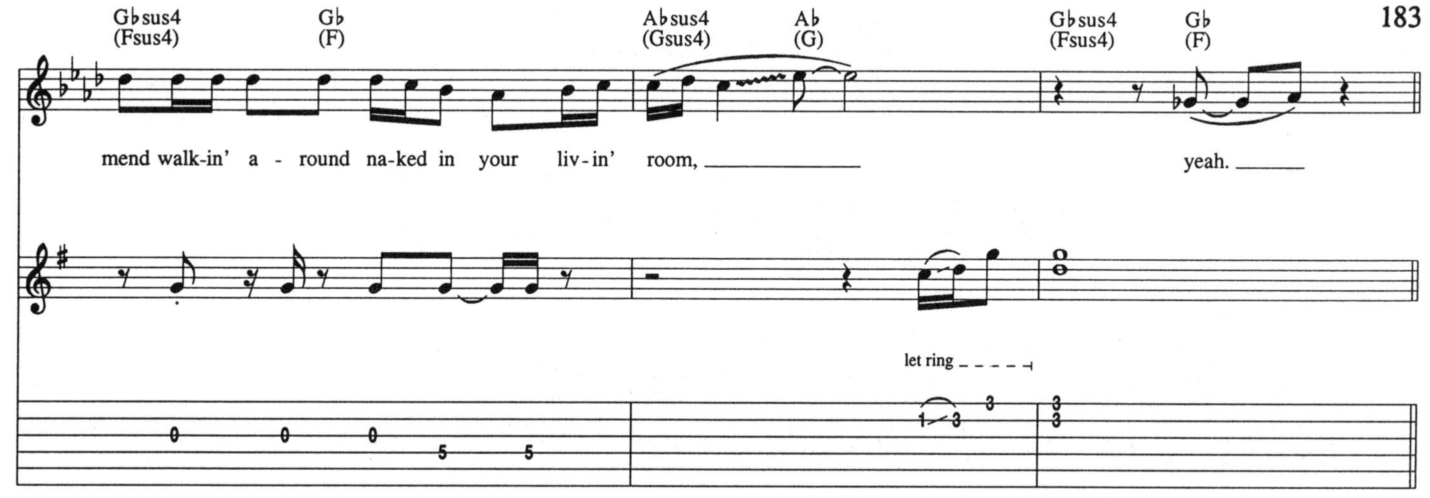

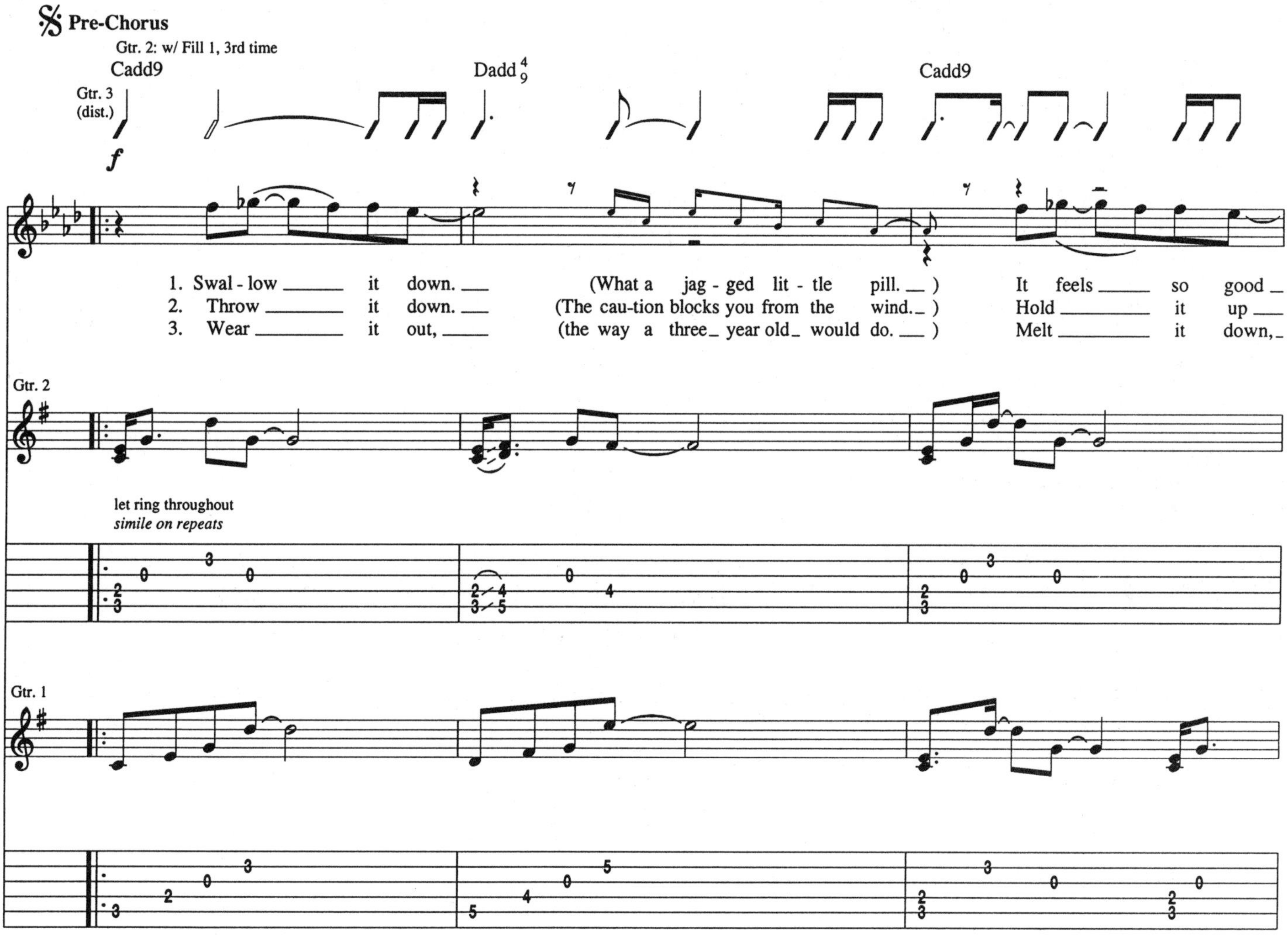

𝄋 Pre-Chorus

Gtr. 2: w/ Fill 1, 3rd time

Cadd9 Dadd 4/9 Cadd9

Gtr. 3 (dist.)

f

1. Swal - low it down. (What a jag - ged lit - tle pill.) It feels so good
2. Throw it down. (The cau-tion blocks you from the wind.) Hold it up
3. Wear it out, (the way a three year old would do.) Melt it down,

Gtr. 2

let ring throughout
simile on repeats

Gtr. 1

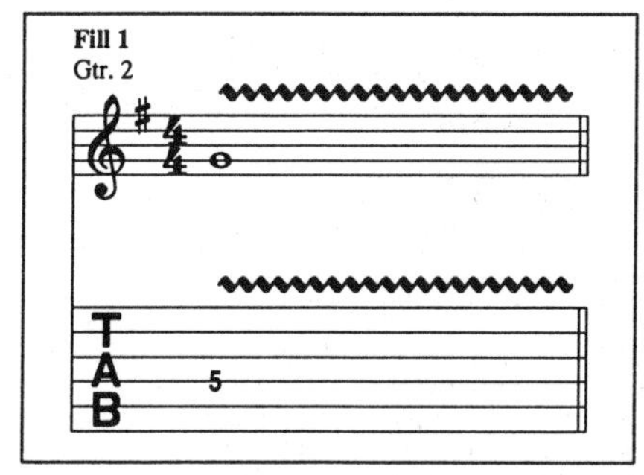

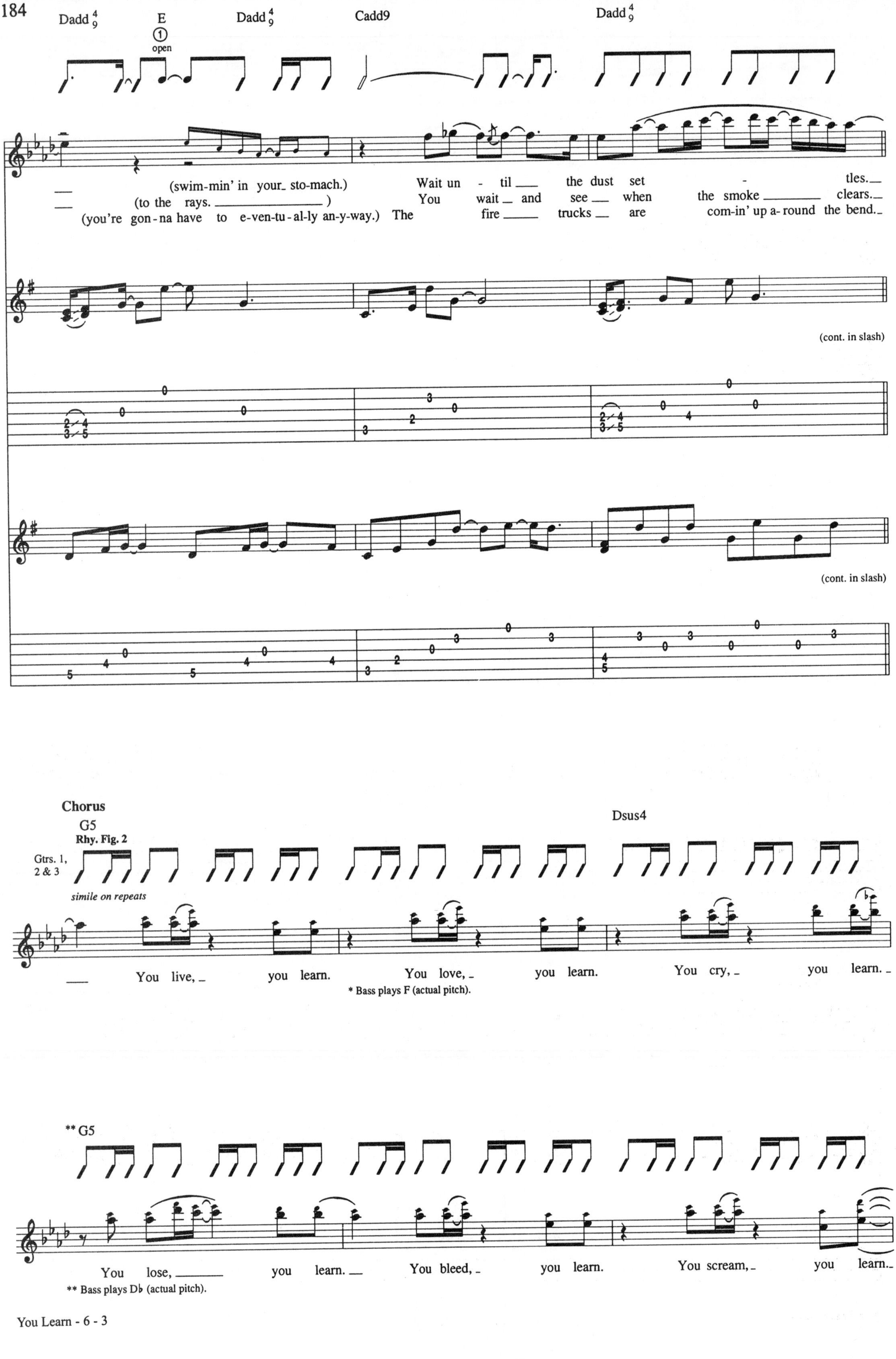

Dadd $^{4}_{9}$ E ① open Dadd $^{4}_{9}$ Cadd9 Dadd $^{4}_{9}$

(swim-min' in your_ sto-mach.) Wait un - til ___ the dust set - tles.___

(to the rays. _______________) You wait ___ and see ___ when the smoke _________ clears.___

(you're gon-na have to e-ven-tu-al-ly an-y-way.) The fire _____ trucks ___ are com-in' up a-round the bend.__

(cont. in slash)

(cont. in slash)

Chorus
G5
Rhy. Fig. 2
Gtrs. 1, 2 & 3
simile on repeats
Dsus4
___ You live, _ you learn. You love, _ you learn. You cry, _ you learn. _
* Bass plays F (actual pitch).

** G5
You lose, _______ you learn. ___ You bleed, _ you learn. You scream, _ you learn._
** Bass plays D♭ (actual pitch).

1.

To Coda

Verse

Gtr. 3 tacet
Gtr. 1: w/ Rhy. Fig. 1, 2 times, simile

Dsus4 End Rhy. Fig. 2 G5 Absus4 (Gsus4) Ab (G)

*(Gtr. 2 cont. in notation)

2. Oh, oh. I rec-om-

Gtr. 2

*1st time

Gbsus4 (Fsus4) Gb (F) Absus4 (Gsus4) Ab (G) Gbsus4 (Fsus4) Gb (F)

mend bit-ing off more than you can chew to an-y-one. I cer-tain-ly do, oh.

Absus4 (Gsus4) Ab (G) Gbsus4 (Fsus4) Gb (F) Absus4 (Gsus4) Ab (G)

I rec-om-mend stick-in' your foot in your mouth at an-y-time.

2.
Interlude
Gtr. 1 tacet
Gb sus4 Gb
(Fsus4) (F)
G5
Gtrs. 1 & 2
Gtr. 2
Bkgd. Voc. Fig. 1
End Bkgd. Voc. Fig. 1
Feel free.
Oh, oh.
Hey, hey!
(Ya, la!)
Gtr. 3
Rhy. Fig. 3
w/ amplifier vibrato
w/ Bkgd. Voc. Fig. 1, 2 times
Gtr. 3: w/ Rhy. Fig. 3, 2 1/2 times, simile
(cont. in notation)
Hey, ah!
Oh.
(Yeah, yeah, hey.)
End Rhy. Fig. 3
Gtr. 2
w/ Bkgd. Voc. Fig. 1
w/ pick & fingers
1/4
D.S. al Coda
Gtr. 2
Gtr. 3

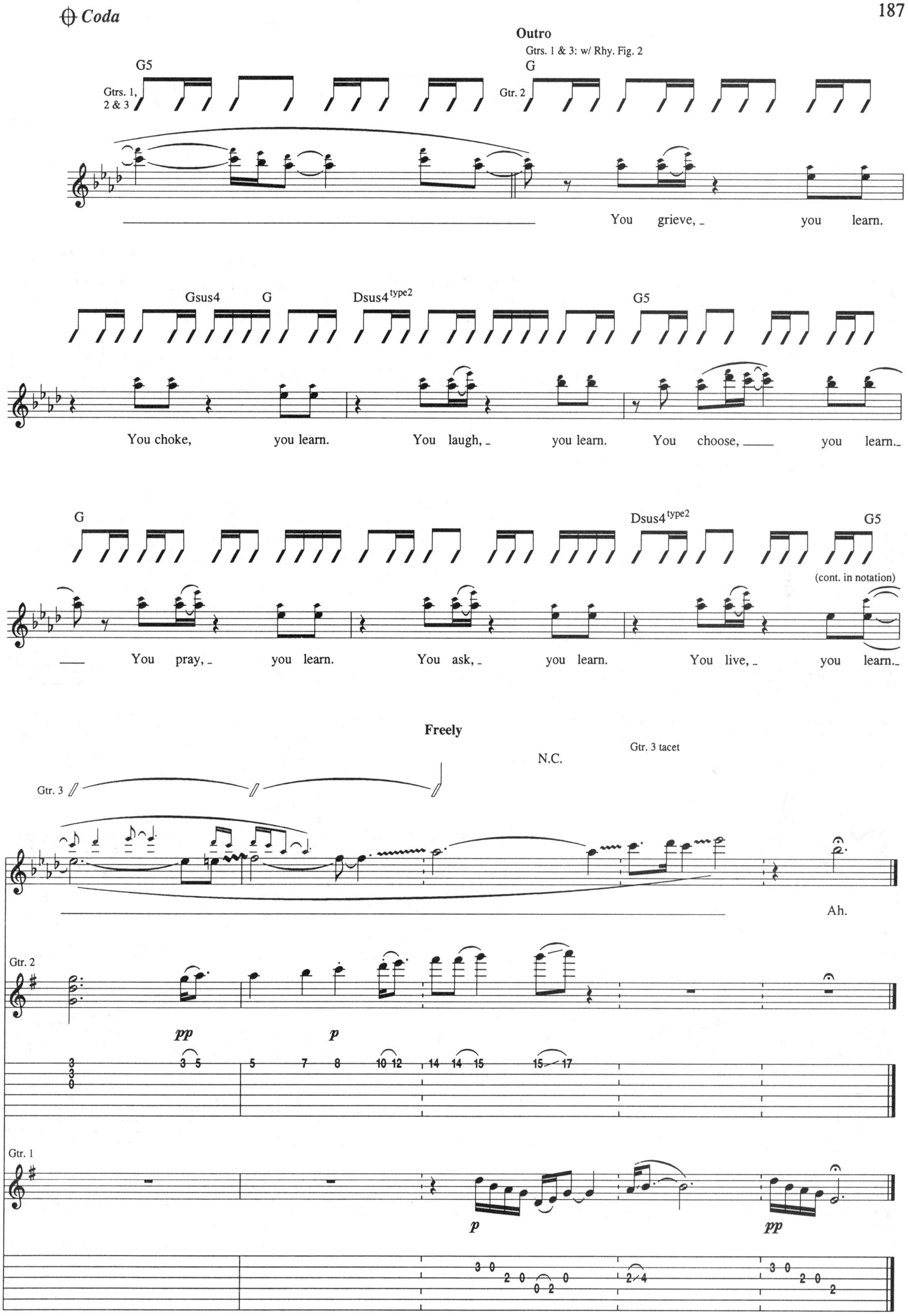

Coda

Outro
Gtrs. 1 & 3: w/ Rhy. Fig. 2
G5
G
Gtrs. 1, 2 & 3
Gtr. 2
You grieve, you learn.

Gsus4 G
Dsus4 type2
G5
You choke, you learn. You laugh, you learn. You choose, you learn.

G
Dsus4 type2
G5
(cont. in notation)
You pray, you learn. You ask, you learn. You live, you learn.

Freely

N.C.

Gtr. 3 tacet

Gtr. 3

Ah.

Gtr. 2

pp *p*

Gtr. 1

p *pp*

YOU WERE MEANT FOR ME

All gtrs. tune down 1/2 step:
⑥ = E♭ ③ = G♭
⑤ = A♭ ② = B♭
④ = D♭ ① = E♭

Words and Music by
JEWEL KILCHER and STEVE POLTZ

Moderately ♩ = 132 (♫ = ♩♪ triplet)

Intro:

C(9) G6/B C Em

Gtr. 1 *(Acoustic)*

mf
hold throughout

Verse:

C(9) G6/B C Em

1. I hear the clock, it's six A.__ M.,___ I feel so far__ from where I've__ been.__
2.3. *See additional lyrics*
Rhy. Fig. 1

C(9) G6/B C D
I got my eggs, I got my pan-cakes, too.___ *I got my ma-ple syr-up,* ev-'ry-thing but__ you.__
end Rhy. Fig. 1

w/Rhy. Fig. 1 *(Gtr. 1)*

C(9) G6/B
I break the yokes and make a smile - y___ face,___

C
Em
C(9)
I kind of like it in my brand-new place. Wipe the spots a-bove the mir-ror, don't leave my
G6/B
C
D
keys in the door. I nev-er put wet tow-els on the floor an-y-more, 'cause
Chorus:
C
D
G
G5/F♯
Em
dreams last so long, e-ven af-ter you're gone.
C
D
G
G/F♯
Em
I know that you love me and soon you will see you were
C
D
To Coda
1.
Em
(D6)
meant for me, and I was meant for you.
8va
harm.

2.
Bridge:
Em
Am7
D
you.
I
go a- bout my bus- 'ness, I'm
do- ing fine. Be- sides, a-
Bm
D
C
G/B
Am7
what would I say
if I had
you on the line?
Same old sto - ry not
D
Bm
E5
D.C. al Coda
much to say,
hearts are bro - ken ev - 'ry - day.
Coda
Em
C
you.
Yeah,
you were meant for me
and

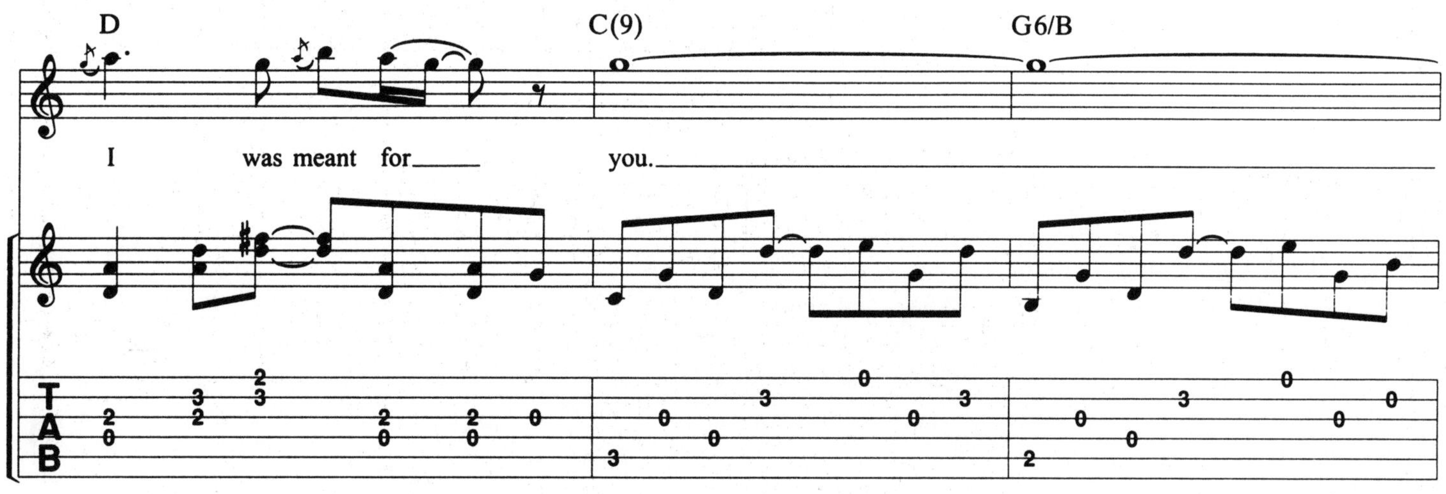

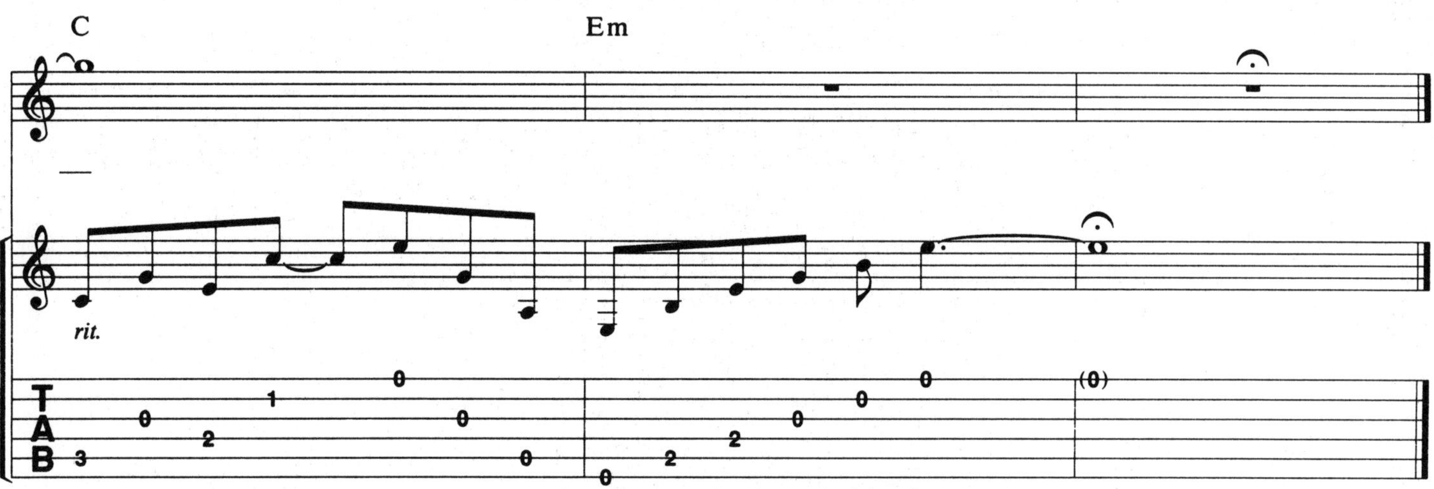

Verse 2:
I called my mama, she was out for a walk.
Consoled a cup of coffee, but it didn't wanna talk.
So I picked up a paper, it was more bad news.
More hearts being broken or people being used.
Put on my coat in the pouring rain.
I saw a movie, it just wasn't the same.
'Cause it was happy and I was sad
And it made me miss you, oh, so bad.
(To Chorus:)

Verse 3:
I brush my teeth and put the cap back on.
I know you hate it when I leave the light on.
I pick a book up and then I turn the sheets down,
And then I take a deep breath and a good look around.
Put on my pj's and hop into bed.
I'm half alive, but I feel mostly dead.
I try and tell myself it'll be all right,
I just shouldn't think anymore tonight.
(To Chorus:)

WHAT I AM

Words and Music by EDIE BRICKELL,
KENNETH WITHROW, JOHN HOUSER,
JOHN BUSH and ALAN ALY

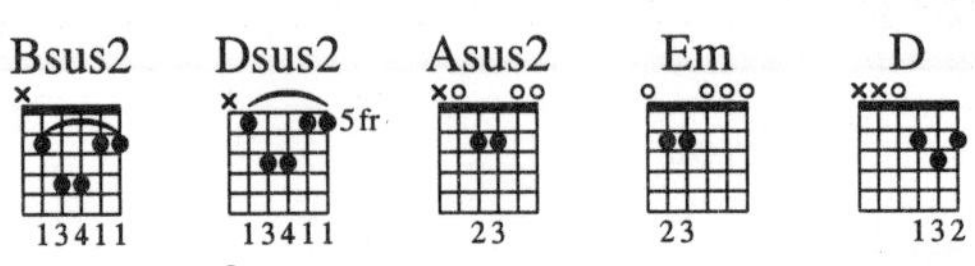

Moderately ♩ = 90

Intro:

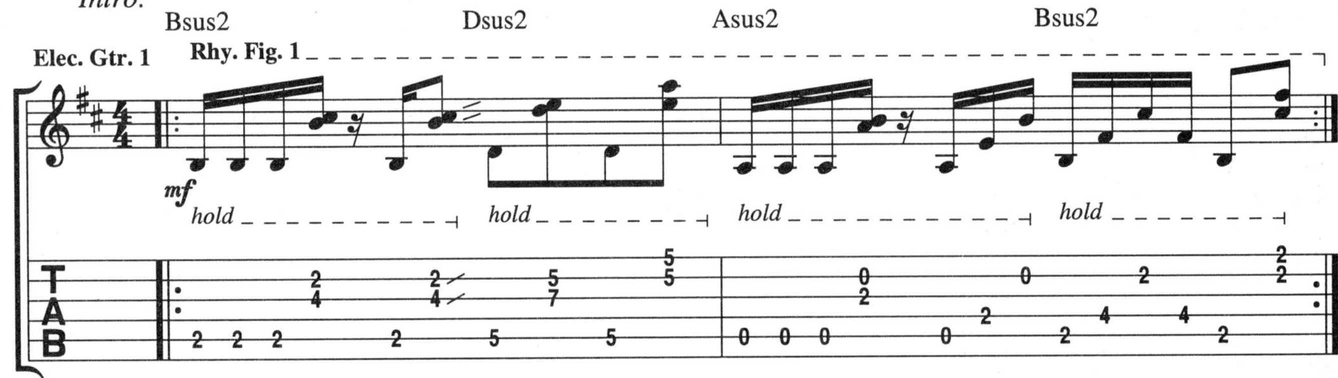

Verse:

w/Rhy. Fig. 1 *(Elec. Gtr. 1) 8 times, simile*

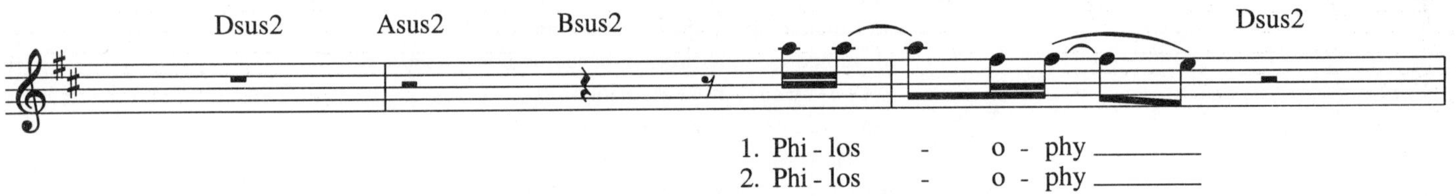

To Coda
Asus2
Bsus2
Dsus2
Asus2
Bsus2
know what I know, _ if you know what I mean.
Do, do yeah. _

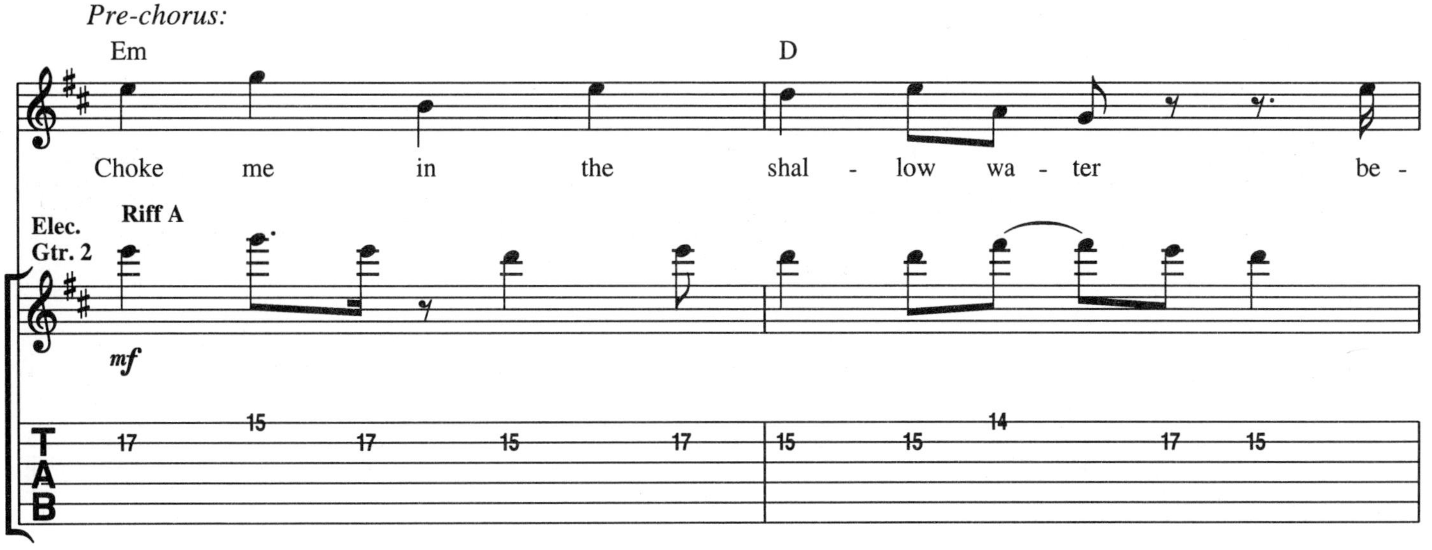
Pre-chorus:
Em
D
Choke me in the shal - low wa - ter be -
Elec. Gtr. 2
Riff A
mf
T
A
B
17 15 17 15 17 15 15 14 17 15

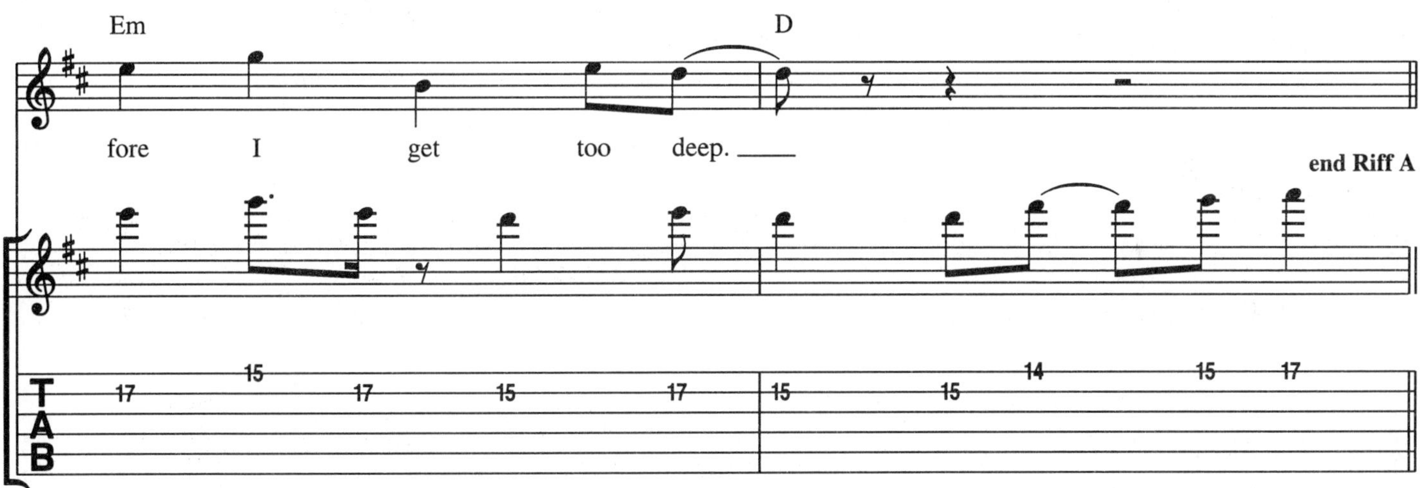
Em
D
fore I get too deep. ____
end Riff A
T
A
B
17 15 17 15 17 15 15 14 15 17

Chorus:
w/Rhy. Fig. 1 (Elec. Gtr. 1) 2 times, simile
Bsus2
Dsus2
Asus2
Bsus2
What I am __ is what I am. __ Are you what you are __ or what? __

D.S. al Coda
Dsus2
Asus2
Bsus2
What I am __ is what I am. __ Are you what you are __ or? Oh,

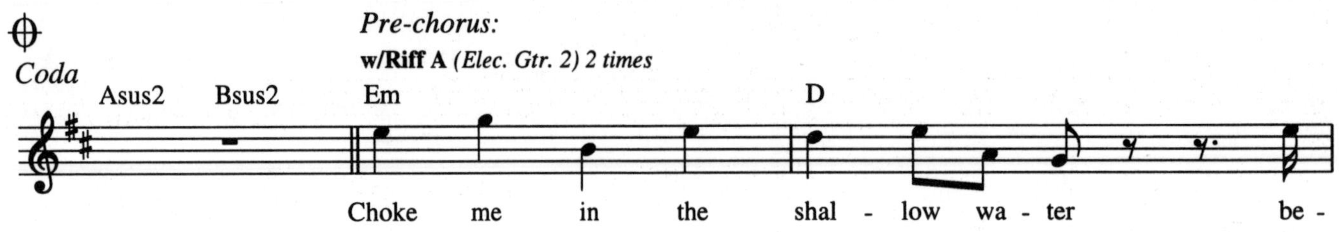
Coda
Pre-chorus:
w/Riff A (Elec. Gtr. 2) 2 times
Asus2 Bsus2 Em D
Choke me in the shal - low wa - ter be -

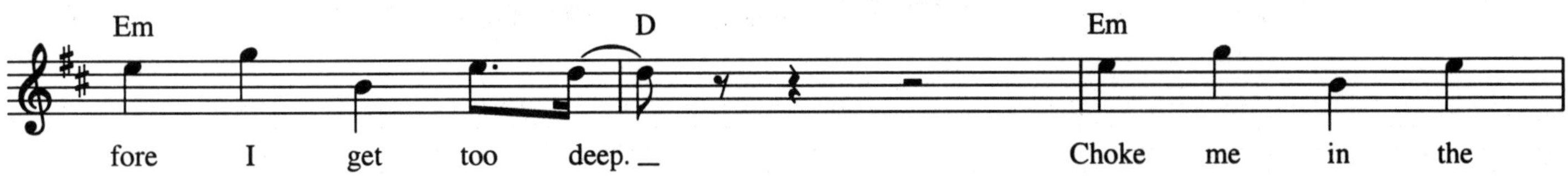
Em D Em
fore I get too deep. Choke me in the

D Em D
shal - low wa - ter be - fore I get too deep,

Chorus:
w/Rhy. Fig. 1 (Elec. Gtr. 1) 4 times, simile
Bsus2 Dsus2 Asus2 Bsus2
What I am is what I am. Are you what you are or what?

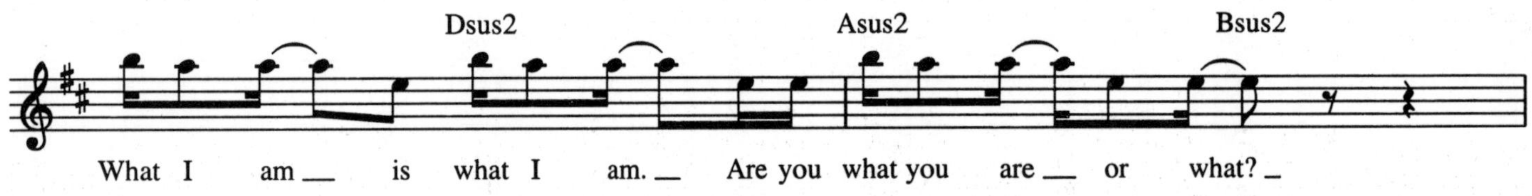
Dsus2 Asus2 Bsus2
What I am is what I am. Are you what you are or what?

Dsus2 Asus2 Bsus2
What I am is what I am. Are you what you are or what you are?

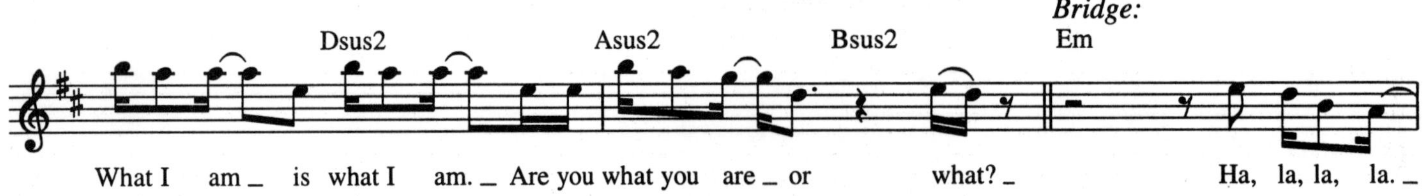
Bridge:
Dsus2 Asus2 Bsus2 Em
What I am is what I am. Are you what you are or what? Ha, la, la, la.

D
Em
D
I say, I say, I say I do. Hey, hey, hey, hey, hey hey.
Guitar Solo:
w/Rhy. Fig. 1 (Elec. Gtr. 1) 8 times, simile
Elec. Gtr. 3
Bsus2
Dsus2
Asus2
Bsus2
f w/envelope filter

Dsus2
Asus2
Bsus2
Dsus2
Asus2
Bsus2
Dsus2
Asus2
Bsus2
Pre-chorus:
w/Riff A (Elec. Gtr. 2) 2 times
Em
D
Em
D
Choke me in the shal - low wa - ter be - fore I get too deep.
Em
D
Em
D
Choke me in the shal - low wa - ter be - fore I get too deep.
Outro: w/ad lib. vocal
w/Rhy. Fig. 1 (Elec. Gtr. 1) 2 times, simile
Bsus2
Dsus2
Asus2
Bsus2
Choke me in the shal-low wa - ter be - fore I get too deep.
Repeat and fade
Dsus2
Asus2
Bsus2
Choke me in the shal-low wa - ter be - fore I get too deep.

GUITAR TAB GLOSSARY **

TABLATURE EXPLANATION

READING TABLATURE: Tablature illustrates the six strings of the guitar. Notes and chords are indicated by the placement of fret numbers on a given string(s).

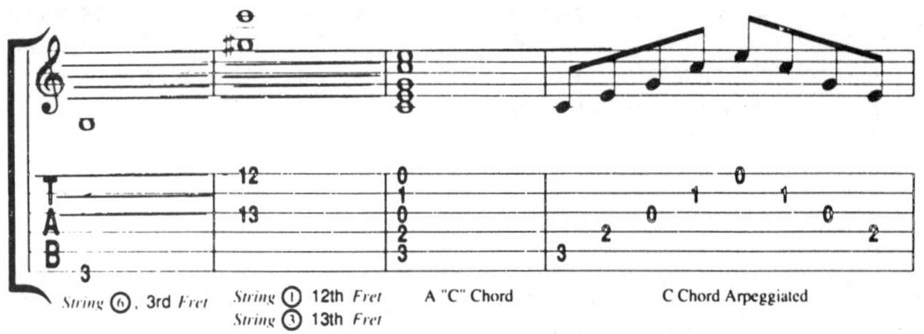

BENDING NOTES

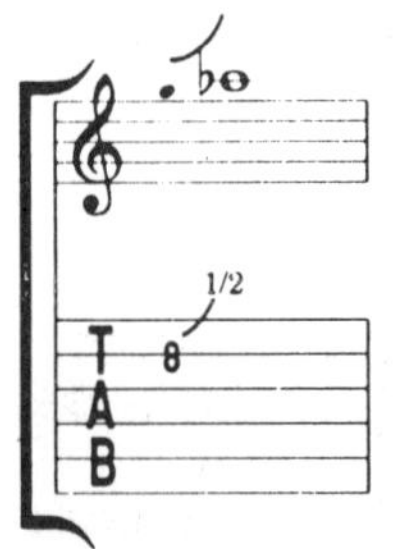

HALF STEP: Play the note and bend string one half step.*

WHOLE STEP: Play the note and bend string one whole step.

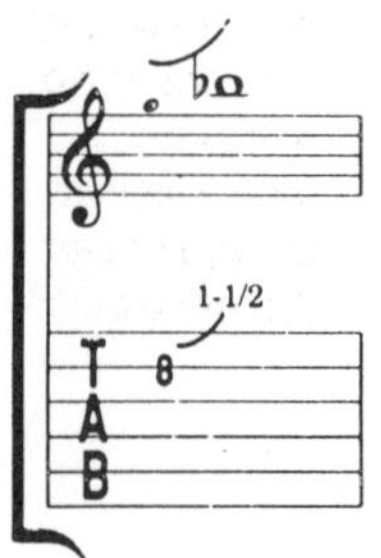

WHOLE STEP AND A HALF: Play the note and bend string a whole step and a half.

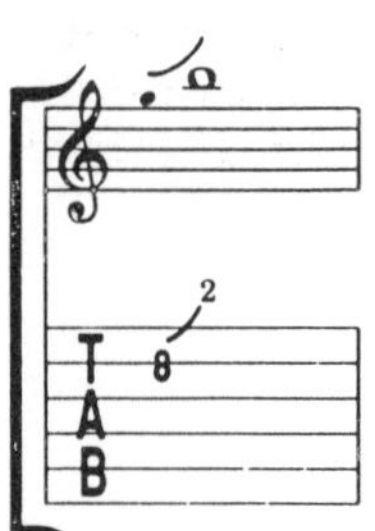

TWO STEPS: Play the note and bend string two whole steps.

SLIGHT BEND (Microtone): Play the note and bend string slightly to the equivalent of half a fret.

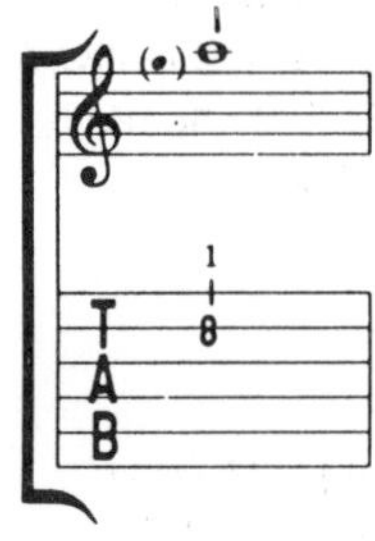

PREBEND (Ghost Bend): Bend to the specified note, before the string is picked.

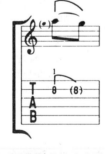

PREBEND AND RELEASE: Bend the string, play it, then release to the original note.

REVERSE BEND: Play the already-bent string, then immediately drop it down to the fretted note.

BEND AND RELEASE: Play the note and gradually bend to the next pitch, then release to the original note. Only the first note is attacked.

BENDS INVOLVING MORE THAN ONE STRING: Play the note and bend string while playing an additional note (or notes) on another string(s). Upon release, relieve pressure from additional note(s), causing original note to sound alone.

BENDS INVOLVING STATIONARY NOTES: Play notes and bend lower pitch, then hold until release begins (indicated at the point where line becomes solid).

UNISON BEND: Play both notes and immediately bend the lower note to the same pitch as the higher note.

DOUBLE NOTE BEND: Play both notes and immediately bend both strings simultaneously.

*A half step is the smallest interval in Western music; it is equal to one fret. A whole step equals two frets.

**By Kenn Chipkin and Aaron Stang

RHYTHM SLASHES

STRUM INDICATIONS: Strum with indicated rhythm.

The chord voicings are found on the first page of the transcription underneath the song title.

INDICATING SINGLE NOTES USING RHYTHM SLASHES: Very often single notes are incorporated into a rhythm part. The note name is indicated above the rhythm slash with a fret number and a string indication.

ARTICULATIONS

HAMMER ON: Play lower note, then "hammer on" to higher note with another finger. Only the first note is attacked.

LEFT HAND HAMMER: Hammer on the first note played on each string with the left hand.

PULL OFF: Play higher note, then "pull off" to lower note with another finger. Only the first note is attacked.

FRETBOARD TAPPING: "Tap" onto the note indicated by + with a finger of the pick hand, then pull off to the following note held by the fret hand.

TAP SLIDE: Same as fretboard tapping, but the tapped note is slid randomly up the fretboard, then pulled off to the following note.

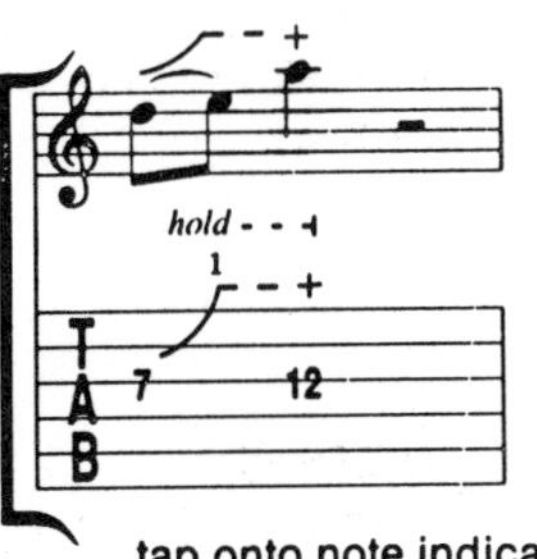

BEND AND TAP TECHNIQUE: Play note and bend to specified interval. While holding bend, tap onto note indicated.

LEGATO SLIDE: Play note and slide to the following note. (Only first note is attacked).

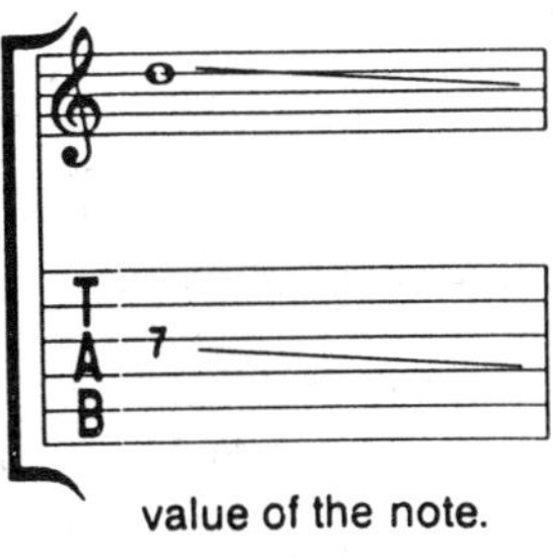

LONG GLISSANDO: Play note and slide in specified direction for the full value of the note.

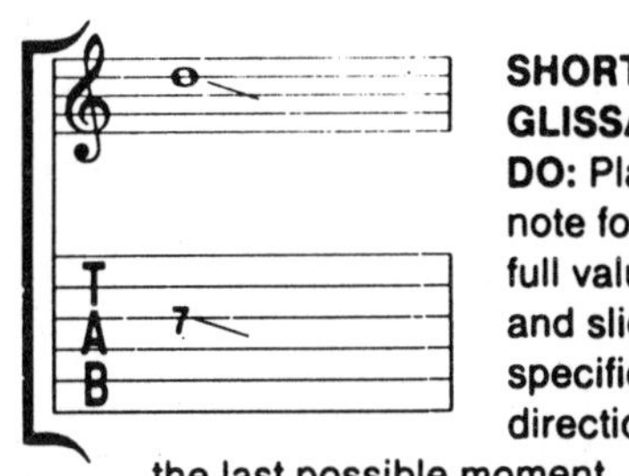

SHORT GLISSANDO: Play note for its full value and slide in specified direction at the last possible moment.

PICK SLIDE: Slide the edge of the pick in specified direction across the length of the string(s).

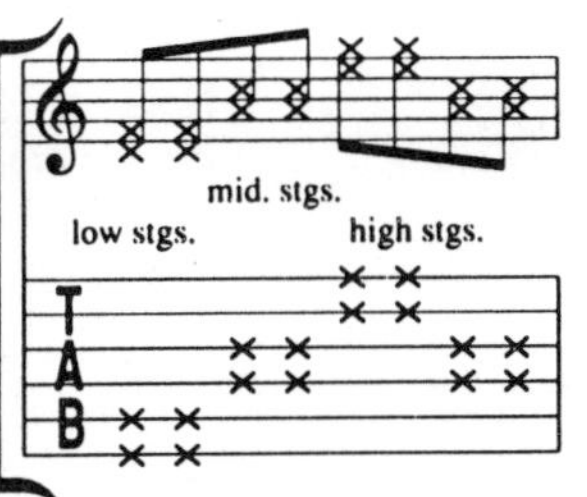

MUTED STRINGS: A percussive sound is made by laying the fret hand across all six strings while pick hand strikes specified area (low, mid, high strings).

PALM MUTE: The note or notes are muted by the palm of the pick hand by lightly touching the string(s) near the bridge.

TREMOLO PICKING: The note or notes are picked as fast as possible.

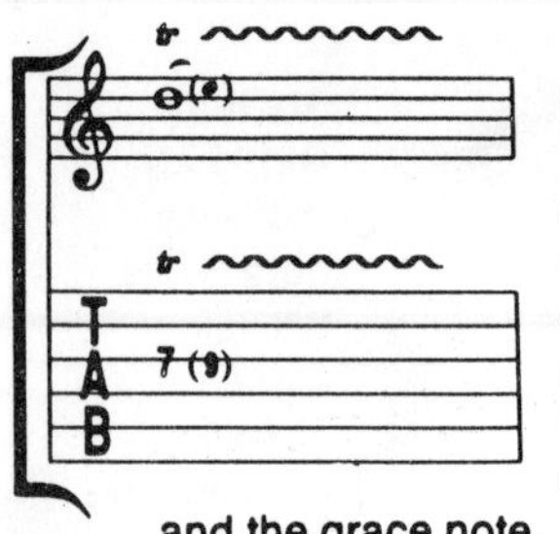

TRILL: Hammer on and pull off consecutively and as fast as possible between the original note and the grace note.

ACCENT: Notes or chords are to be played with added emphasis.

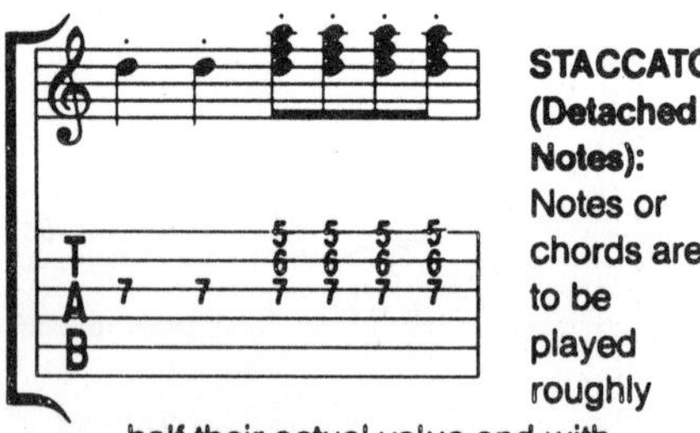

STACCATO (Detached Notes): Notes or chords are to be played roughly half their actual value and with separation.

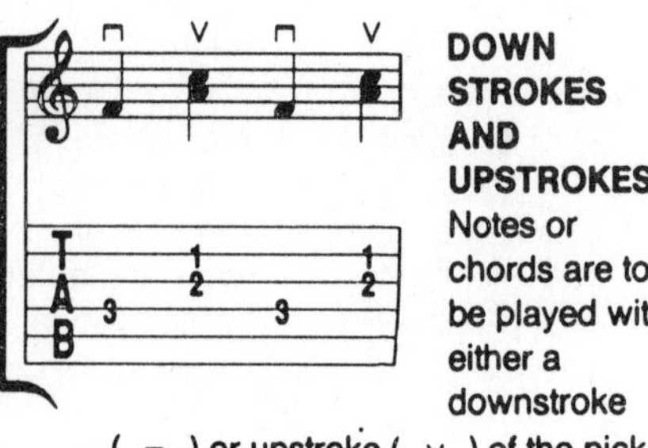

DOWN STROKES AND UPSTROKES: Notes or chords are to be played with either a downstroke (⊓) or upstroke (V) of the pick.

VIBRATO: The pitch of a note is varied by a rapid shaking of the fret hand finger, wrist, and forearm.

HARMONICS

NATURAL HARMONIC: A finger of the fret hand lightly touches the note or notes indicated in the tab and is played by the pick hand.

ARTIFICIAL HARMONIC: The first tab number is fretted, then the pick hand produces the harmonic by using a finger to lightly touch the same string at the second tab number (in parenthesis) and is then picked by another finger.

ARTIFICIAL "PINCH" HARMONIC: A note is fretted as indicated by the tab, then the pick hand produces the harmonic by squeezing the pick firmly while using the tip of the index finger in the pick attack. If parenthesis are found around the fretted note, it does not sound. No parenthesis means both the fretted note and A.H. are heard simultaneously.

TREMOLO BAR

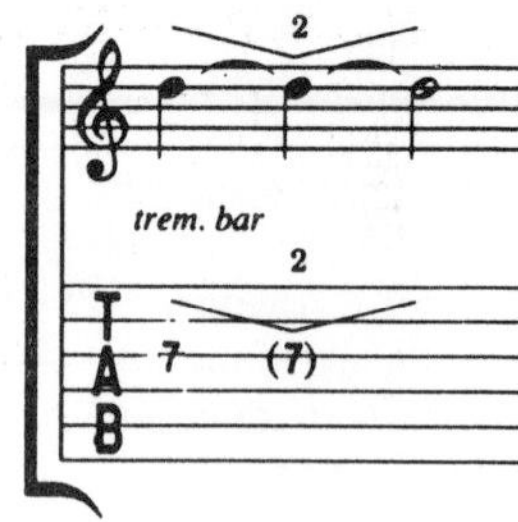

SPECIFIED INTERVAL: The pitch of a note or chord is lowered to a specified interval and then may or may not return to the original pitch. The activity of the tremolo bar is graphically represented by peaks and valleys.

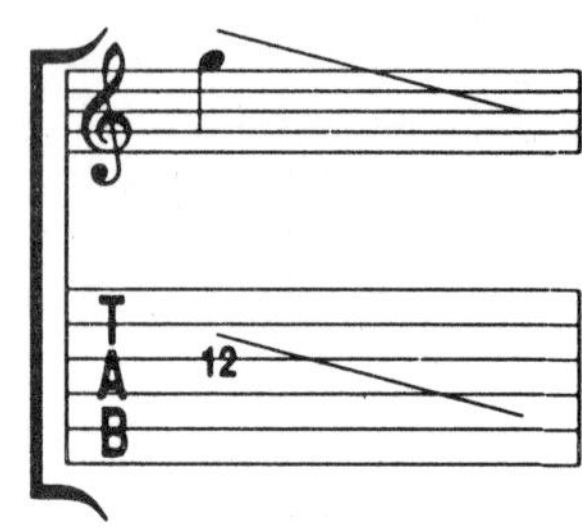

UN-SPECIFIED INTERVAL. The pitch of a note or a chord is lowered to an unspecified interval.